FANDOM:
CONFIDENTIAL

Warmest Regards,
Ron Frantz

FANDOM:
CONFIDENTIAL

by Ron Frantz

Introduction by
Robert Sampson

Cover illustration by
Peter Morisi

Illustration frame by
Richard Mosso

Midguard Publishing Company
Mena, Arkansas

FANDOM: Confidential
Copyright © 2000 by Ronald J. Frantz

Midguard Publishing Co. Cataloging-in-Publication Data
Frantz, Ron, 1953–
   FANDOM : Confidential / Ron Frantz ; Cover illustration by Peter Morisi and Richard Mosso ; Introduction by Robert Sampson. — Mena, Ark. : Midguard Publishing Company, 2000.
      p. ; cm.
Summary: Autobiographical memoir of nostalgia collecting and organized fandom.
   1. Frantz, Ron, 1953–   2. Hobbies—United States—Biography
   3. Comic Books—United States
   99-98011   AACR2
ISBN 0-9678273-0-2

Printed in the United States of America by Morgan Printing, Austin, Texas

First Edition

10 9 8 7 6 5 4 3 2 1

Edited & designed by Michael Ambrose

Midguard Publishing Co.
P.O. Box 1711
Mena, Arkansas 71953

This book is dedicated to the memory of

Norma Terrell
Manuel Seguin
Bob Sampson
Stan Blair

*They made a difference in the
lives they touched*

Contents

List of Illustrations

Introduction

by Robert Sampson

This book is about the Golden Age—the one that you lived through. It began in the sixties. It continued until now and, for some of us, may still be going on.

The Golden Age is a personal thing. History is studded with such ages. No eyes view them exactly alike. Some measure them by the 1938 appearance of *Action Comics*. Others by the first issue of *The Shadow, A Detective Magazine* in 1931. Still others, curiously biased, celebrate 1925 when Louis Armstrong and His Hot Five recorded the "Gut Bucket Blues." Pick any subject and reel time back. From someone's point of view, that's the Golden Age, when the hours dripped splendor and all things glistened.

This is a book about that most recent of Golden Ages. If you must pin it down, it includes from about the mid-1960s to the late 1970s, a time that hardly anyone remembers for placidity and fulfillment. For collectors, however, the time was unique. During those years collecting slowly transformed from a private hobby to a public business.

Were you collecting then? To our modern eyes, now barricaded in suspicion, the practices in the sixties seem intolerably casual. You traded with a few friends. You fingered over the stock in the local used magazine store. You cavalierly rejected today's rarities which were yesterday's glut. And usually you were satisfied with a ragged old tattered-cover thing, decorated with fingermarks and bottle stains, often enough, because no one had told you that a less-than-mint copy was valueless.

Value? You read for pleasure. What's value? I just want to complete the run. You bought sparingly through the mails. Few people sold magazines—or art—or books—for a profession; only a few amateur publications, filled with ads and artwork of grinding inadequacy, listed out-of-print titles. Marvel Comics had not yet eaten the world. Plastic bags were almost unknown. Original *Doc Savage* magazines sold for $1.00 each, all day long.

From that point, the golden spiral began. New comic book titles, like white flares, flashed over the sky. New ad publications appeared. They died.

Others reappeared, each fatter than the last.

At first, the ads said Trade.

Then, Buy!

Then: Hurry, Buy!

HURRY BUY FANTASTIC PRICES!

Dollars. Conventions. The Dealers' Room. Hamburgers and Coke among the stacked tables, bright covers scarlet blue yellow in violent action. The devoted collector squinting down his want list, balancing pocket money and trade items against asking price. Conventions bulged the calendars. Price Guides. The world filled with dealers.

Poster art. Star Trek. The hefty feel of that first black-and-white *Savage Tales*. H.P. Lovecraft. Carl Barks art. $1,800 for a #1 *Action*. Discount offered: *Shazam* #1 in batches of one hundred. DC *Tarzans*. Howard the what?

Incandescent carnival. Someplace along the line the hobby lost its modesty. From shabby books among friends, it burst into a White Hot, Gold-Dusted, Dazzling commercial exchange. With dealers and buyers, job lots, conventions, all the goads and pomps of business, unrestrained and unchecked. Let the buyer beware. Behind that ad, lushly promising, fangs are concealed. Send in a check and— Gotcha!

In the midst of the carnival, *"WE"* arrived. *WE* was a rough-looking mimeographed sheet that traded beauty for utility. It accepted your ad and got this into the buyers' hands within five days. *The Weekly Express,* it was called.

Stan Blair founded it. He was a powerhouse, full of high-potential energy. Since he was episodically retired, he could spend twenty-one hours a day on *WE*. To this modest little ad-sheet, he brought all the fervor of a missionary finding an unknown colony of aborigines.

Around the core of *WE* collected a variety of services. Under Stan's intense enthusiasm, advertisers and subscribers were urged to think of themselves as a club. *WE*—WE-uns. WE-uns banded together, striding forward, shoulder to shoulder. . . .

This theme tied together subsequent activities. Stan's idea was to energize a group whose members could be relied on. Their checks represented real money. Their trade items did not crumble brown at the edges.

It was a mixed group, these WE-uns. Part comics, some pulps, some boys' books. Plus cigarette cards, posters, movies, and bisque figures. The blood and spirit unifying the whole thing was trust. That WSA number after a name stood for honesty. In the carnival this meant something.

From these seeds, a flock of programs evolved. Of initialed names, like government programs, they were accompanied by a shower of bulletins, announcements, pronouncements, letters, reports, alerts—a boiling tide of zealous paper.

Eventually, Stan retired. To continue carrying the flag, Ron Frantz, gritting his cigar, stepped in.

What follows is Ron's story—and this book. Here is his story of life behind the scenes at the WE-works. He was Administrator of the WSA, meaning
that he straddled the prickly hedge of people and problems. He plunged into
battles that shocked through collecting. He had daily portions of the wild men
and wilder adventures in that hazy world where hobby collides head-on with
business.

In the following chapters, Ron sketches out some of these events. They
pour through the pages, the enthusiasts and fans, the dealers and ad-magazine
editors. The whole carnival shouts by—that fine gaudy time that still goes on.
It's all part of your times and personal story. It's in here: a record of our new
Golden Age, in which all things glisten.

—Bob Sampson
WSA 007

Bob Sampson, as drawn by his good friend Frank Hamilton.

Prologue

I began writing this book in 1978. The trek toward publication has been long and winding. There were times when I thought I would never get there. By my recollection, twenty-one years and nine months have gone by. Kind of makes a man wonder where the time went.

It began on one of those dreary days in February, when the mind has a tendency to wander when the body can't. I had just finished a two-and-a-half-year stint as Administrator of a nonprofit trade association known as WSA. As a student of history, it has often occurred to me how so much practical knowledge has been lost because people fail to document their experiences. For this reason, it seemed important that I begin to write while the memory was still fresh. In the back of my mind was a notion of posterity.

About a month later, I announced my intention to publish. That's when the fun started. The public reaction was not what I expected. Oddly, I found myself rebuffed by strangers, colleagues, saints, and, I daresay, one or two sinners. In the eyes of a few malcontents who feared the worst, I was committing an act of heresy. One would think I was calling for the abolition of the free press instead of writing a documentary.

I found these things curious. Then and now, I had no intention of producing an exposé. This is not to say, however, that there are not people of my acquaintance with skeletons hanging in their closets. There most certainly are, and they, no doubt, would loathe a telling of the truth. For example:

- A well known fan publisher is arrested for lewd behavior in a public restroom with a second consenting male. A short time later, he packs his bags and moves to a different state.

- A prominent attorney is disbarred from practicing law (and sent to prison) for malfeasance involving a union pension fund. You might say that he got caught with his fingers in the cookie jar.

- A comic book dealer with a national reputation is arrested for selling narcotics to an undercover police officer. The last I heard he was still serving time in a Florida prison.

I could go on, but I am sure you get the point. The bottom line is that these matters have little to do with the subject at hand. In behalf of those miscreants who have spent their days profaning the English of King James: Take comfort in the knowledge that you have misbehaved safely. There will be no reproach from me.

Because two decades have passed, many of the situations that once simmered like Pompeii in the wake of Vesuvius have gradually gone cold. It is now possible to reflect upon past events without being blinded by strong emotion or prejudice. That is the way it should be.

Perhaps you are curious why it has taken so many years to publish the book. It was common knowledge among various insiders that I had completed a preliminary manuscript by 1980. However, I was never satisfied with the result. In my opinion, the manuscript had all the charm of a ten-cent cigar. Feeling inadequate to tell where the smell was coming from, I dabbled with the text, writing a few words here or changing a few lines there. Nothing seemed to help. Finally, I decided that both the book and I needed a rest. From there, years came and went without fanfare on significant production.

In the meantime, a few acquaintances inquired if the book was ever published. Since I could not predict a publication date they often requested copies of the preliminary manuscript. I put most of them off. However, I did find their interest gratifying. It was nice to know that someone actually cared.

About five years ago, I took a hard-nosed look at the manuscript. Viewing it from a fresh perspective, it seemed to ramble on forever, not getting to the point. Making any sense out of it was like trying to extrude cement from a toothpaste tube. To say the least, extensive revisions were in order. Due to the considerable lapse in time, I found it necessary to check my memory against personal papers, notes, letters, and other related memoranda. This is the only way I could be certain of reasonable accuracy.

I would like to make a point about events I've elaborated upon in chapters three, four, and five. The perspective is, of course, mine. However, in a realistic sense, I was only one participant in a game with many players. Like a straight man in a Marx Brothers movie, I happened to be present when some of the events occurred. There is little significance in that and none should be implied by me or anyone else. It may be the American way to ballyhoo modest attainments to the skies, but that isn't my style.

Should you be a former WSA member, some of my recollections may hold special interest for you. In any event, I hope they prove helpful in informing some people and setting others straight on the facts. For those of you who may be unfamiliar with the subject, I hope you find this little journey down memory lane worthwhile. If so, I will have achieved my goal as an erstwhile author.

—RON FRANTZ
NOVEMBER 13, 1999

CHAPTER ONE

When All Things Glistened

Perpetual devotion to what a man calls his business is only to be sustained by perpetual neglect of many other things. And it is not by any means that a man's business is the most important thing that he has to do.

—Robert Louis Stevenson

The story you are about to read begins over a century ago. It is about the history of fandom. To try to condense the story into a few pages is a lot like trying to pack an elephant into a walnut. It takes a lot of squeezing.

By definition, fandom is a loosely knit following of fans, collectors, and dealers of any genre. The term was conceived in the early 1930s by science fiction fans, who invented a considerable amount of terminology to suit their own purposes. When comic book collectors began to organize thirty years later, they borrowed much of the language devised by their science fiction cousins. Later, other groups, lacking in imagination, made use of the same terminology.

At the core of fandom is a unique individual known as the collector. Collectors are endowed with a subliminal urge to collect things. There is no rational explanation for the behavior. The characteristic is probably not far removed from the primal instinct ingrained in squirrels for hoarding nuts. It is one of those divine mysteries that inclines one to believe that our Creator has a sense of humor.

It seems that every object produced by man or nature becomes the object of some collector's search. The love to acquire is a strong human urge. Men and women have collected artifacts since the dawn of time. A few centuries passed before man collected objects created by other men. By collecting military miniatures, the ancient Egyptian Pharaohs may have been the first.

In every field of collecting, the basic terminology is different. For example, coin collectors and model railroaders ordinarily do not share a common frame of reference. For this reason, the subject of this book requires qualification.

Specifically, the genre is known as nostalgia. It includes comic books, pulp magazines, Big Little Books, dime novels, radio premiums, toys, cinematic memorabilia, original cartoon art, animation cels, gum cards, cereal boxes, and other related paraphernalia.

Now as everyone knows, the average collector is reasonably sane. However, to those unable to understand their peculiar passions, collectors are often considered neurotic. Admittedly, there is a fair amount of truth to both conceptions.

From a psychological perspective, some collectors can be defined as obsessive personalities. In his book *Neuroses in Clinical Practice,* Dr. Henry W. Laughlin writes:

> The obsessive person is often an excellent hobbyist or collector. His interests in a hobby may overdevelop to the point of becoming inordinate or even fanatic. His hobby or collection may come to absorb a major proportion of his interest and energy.

Dr. Laughlin describes an obsessive as a person who exhibits traits that may cause interference with living or a limitation of social adjustment. In extreme cases the severe obsessive can merge into a psychotic state, such as paranoia or schizophrenia. This might explain why some collectors are prone to odd behavior.

Having been a member of the fraternity for over thirty years, I have known collectors of good character. By contemporary standards, their mere presence is a shock to the nervous system. On the flip side of the coin, some collectors are of such vile disposition that Hell probably won't have them. Most collectors, however, fall as a shapeless mass somewhere between the two. Unless one is a shrewd judge of character, it is often difficult to tell the difference.

About 1966, there was a book dealer in Oklahoma City who, for whatever reason, despised comic books, pulp magazines, and the novels of Edgar Rice Burroughs. He claimed the collectibles were less than gutter trash, more in need of incineration than preservation. His rationalization was that they were chemically unstable and might turn to dust at any given moment. In his infinite wisdom, he decreed that only an idiot would waste his time collecting them. By his reasoning, no one should collect anything except rare books or *National Geographic* magazine. He considered those respectable.

Director John Huston presented a different perspective of respect in the film *Chinatown* when he said, "Of course, I'm respectable . . . I'm old! Ugly buildings, crooked politicians, and whores all become respectable if they last long enough!"

It has been much the same with nostalgia collecting. The hobby became respectable with age. Much of this respect begins with certain artifacts selling for ludicrous prices. The average man on the street could care less that the first issue of *Captain America* has historical significance. He is more impressed that it is worth a lot of money. I'll not digress upon the point as it's a matter better left to sociologists or investment brokers.

For most of the twentieth century, the coin and stamp hobbies enjoyed the greatest respectability. The primary reason is they are promoted by the United States government. For the bureaucrats and politicians it became a matter of good business. Every stamp that goes into a collection represents pure profit for the government. A collected coin that the government does not have to redeem represents a similar profit.

The first American postage stamps were issued in 1840. They proved so popular for collecting purposes that thirty years later the government issued special printings and began staging philatelic (and numismatic) displays at trade fairs. The collecting of coins and stamps is socially acceptable because the objects are symbols of national identity. They are common to everyone.

Nostalgia, on the other hand, is collected for other reasons. It has taken several decades for the hobby to attain a moderate degree of public acceptance. How it evolved into a respectable hobby is a long story, with pathos comparable to a fable by Aesop.

Some call it a case of hero worship. Throughout the history of literature, heroes have stimulated the imagination. In the childhood of your grandfather (and perhaps yours, as well) the boyhood dream was to emulate the stirring adventures of the stalwarts of the printed page.

The literary concept of heroism has been around at least two thousand years. Contrary to popular opinion, it did not begin with Stan Lee and the Amazing Spider-Man. However, it might grieve modern comic book readers (and their publishers) to come to such a realization.

Written by an unknown author, *Gilgamesh* is the hero of an ancient Babylonian epic, searching for the secret of immortality. He fails in his quest, receiving at the end only some vague information about the abode of dead spirits. Then came *The Iliad*, by Homer, which is said to be the first story in which action is described in heroic proportion and style. By legend, Homer was an old, blind, wandering bard. In fact, he was the father of Western literature. Between Homer and Lee, thousands of other fiction writers made use of the same concept. If you want to be technical, even stories from the Biblical Old Testament brim with heroics. The human experience is timeless.

About 1860, a modern style of heroic literature appeared in the form of dime novels. For the next sixty years, dime novels precipitated story forms and character types that would later influence the development of pulp magazines, comic books, radio drama, television, motion pictures, and virtually

THE FIVE CENT
WIDE AWAKE LIBRARY

Entered at the Post Office at New York, N. Y., as Second Class Matter.

No. 1182. {COMPLETE} FRANK TOUSEY, Publisher, 34 & 36 North Moore St., N. Y., {PRICE 5 CENTS.} Vol. II.
New York, September 16, 1893. Issued Weekly.

Entered according to the Act of Congress, in the year 1903, by FRANK TOUSEY, in the office of the Librarian of Congress, at Washington, D. C.

SEA-DOG CHARLIE: or, The Adventures of a Boy Hero.

By W. I. JAMES, Jr.

He had managed to keep his right arm free, and now, reaching down into his pocket, he drew forth his heavy clasp-knife. Raising it to his mouth he opened it with his teeth. He knew he must free himself quickly if at all, for the terrible compression was fast depriving him of animation.

This September 1893 issue of *Wide Awake Library* was a turn-of-the-century equivalent of a comic book. Such magazines were called dime novels. The concept of a hero battling a fantastic foe was already old hat. Modern writers who think they are producing something new and marvelous need to wake up and smell the coffee.

every other form of popular entertainment.

The dime novels fused two lines of popular fiction, the frontier novels as popularized by James Fenimore Cooper (1820–1840) and the English Penny Books. *Maleska, the Indian Wife of the White Hunter* was the first dime novel. Its date of publication roughly coincides with the beginning of the Civil War. *Maleska* sold well enough to prompt publishers to produce more of the same. Within a decade, dozens of similar titles appeared, featuring tales of Indian fighters, frontier scouts, bank robbers, boy heroes, and various adventurers. Most of the characters are long forgotten. Only a few of the more prolific creations like Frank Merriwell, The Rover Boys, and Nick Carter are remembered by collectors or historians.

In terms of subject matter, dime novels consisted of sensationalist fiction. The covers depicted scenes of sizzling melodrama. Frequently, they had little to do with the inside story. Then and now, publishers know that the cover sells the product.

Some of the publishers grew fat and rich publishing these magazines. A good example was a former telegraph operator from Maine named Frank Munsey, who believed that the story was more important than the paper it was printed on. This doesn't say much since the paper was next to worthless. For Munsey, dime novels were the beginning of a publishing empire.

On January 16, 1920, Munsey bought the *New York Herald*, merging it with a smaller newspaper he already owned. As a matter of coincidence, this was the very same day the Volstead Act took effect, beginning Prohibition. One cannot help but wonder how many writers on that paper began their careers writing dime novels.

Children adored dime novels, especially young boys. They preferred the subject matter over schoolbooks and Sunday school lessons. This explains why dime novels incurred the wrath of teachers and ministers. Understandably, children were often discouraged from reading them. They did anyway, sneaking the magazines home, hiding them under the bed, peeking while no one looked. By some great miracle, these children managed to grow into adulthood without becoming sex fiends or violent criminals.

If you pay attention to the experts, the love of popular entertainment has produced multiple generations of demented children. In about twenty-year intervals, pulp magazines, comic books, Saturday morning cartoons, and video games were blamed for children disrespecting their elders or not eating vegetables. Zealots with notions of propriety instigated most of the rhubarb.

Some acted in the name of religion, while others nurtured political aspirations. Only in rare instances was the activity based on a genuine concern for the young. Since history has an uncanny tendency to repeat itself, look for it to happen again when a new form of entertainment appeals to the kids.

The dime novels ran their course about 1915. A few selected titles lingered through the late 1920s. Then the story lines assumed another guise and proceeded into the pulp magazines.

As it was with the dime novels, pulps were not revered by the literary establishment of the period. They too were condemned in classrooms and from the pulpit. Regardless, millions were sold, which meant that someone was reading them. This included such notables as Al Capone and Harry Truman. Curiously, Capone subscribed to a western magazine while Truman enjoyed the detective titles.

In 1977, Robert Brown offered a candid opinion about the pulps' literary merit:

ARE PULP MAGAZINES WORTH READING? DO THEY CAUSE BRAIN BURNS? The answer is a simple yes to both questions. Let's face it fans of the pulp, they are trash. Sorry, I don't care what half-baked intellectual rebuttal you have to present, the truth about these magazines is they were put out for the lowest I.Q. in the reading market and they show it.

The words may sound harsh, but in many respects Brown is correct in his evaluation. Upon even the most basic study, the average pulp appears to have been produced by a moron using a rubber stamp. In terms of redeeming social value, there was little to be found.

However, hidden away in that jungle of mediocrity are a few gems of imagination and literary achievement. A few pulp titles strived for and maintained a high degree of storytelling excellence. Such authors as Louis L'Amour, Ray Bradbury, Erle Stanley Gardner, Dashiell Hammett, Max Brand, Robert E. Howard, Johnston McCulley, Tennessee Williams, Raymond Chandler, Robert A. Heinlein, and Edgar Rice Burroughs began their careers writing pulp stories.

In recent years, much of this material has been reprinted or developed for television and motion pictures. Considering the writers were paid a only few cents per word, and usually less, to produce the work, their achievements are nothing less than remarkable. Even the worst pulp magazines have a charm that is unique to the genre. For such reasons they continue to be collected and studied.

The Argosy was the first recognized pulp magazine. It began in 1888, as an offshoot of the 1882 children's paper, *The Golden Argosy*. It propagated a market for inexpensive, contemporary literature for the entire family. Other titles soon followed: *Blue Book, All Story, Snappy Tales, Wild West Weekly, Cavalier, Detective Fiction Weekly,* etc. Most of them lasted for decades.

Serialization begins for *Tarzan the Invincible* in this March 1937 issue of *Argosy*. It's no coincidence that Tarzan looks a lot like actor Johnny Weissmuller. Cover is by veteran pulp illustrator Rudolph Belarski.
© 1937 by Edgar Rice Burroughs, Inc.

In 1931, a new direction for pulps began with the publication of *The Shadow, A Detective Magazine*. Based upon a character from a popular radio series, *The Shadow* was the first pulp focused on a solitary character. The idea had been common to dime novels a half-century earlier. For the pulps, it proved to be a startling innovation.

Within two years, many similar titles appeared: *Doc Savage, The Avenger, The Phantom Detective, The Spider*, and *Secret Agent "X"*. Once an idea achieves a marginal degree of commercial success, it breeds imitation. For, always, there is little originality in popular entertainment. Look to network television programming for a more contemporary example.

For a dozen years, the pulp heroes enjoyed vast popularity. Their appeal faded after the Second World War. Tastes in literature were changing, as they always do. One by one, the pulp heroes fell by the wayside. In 1950, Street & Smith (a major publisher of the genre) announced in *The New York Times* that the day of the pulps had ended. It was as if the president of the United States had issued an edict to this effect. From that point on, the entire pulp industry was on the brink of extinction. However, the pulps went down fighting. The publishers tried new ideas, new formats, but nothing worked. By 1955, the pulp field, like the kingdom of Thebes, had vanished.

There are several factors that can be attributed to the demise of the pulp magazines. The rise of television as an entertainment medium in the early 1950s was a factor. Television had an equally devastating effect on radio broadcasting and newspaper circulations. Then, the fledging paperback book industry (more or less) replaced the pulp magazines as a source of inexpensive reading material.

A few titles survived by changing formats. *Argosy, Blue Book,* and *Cavalier* switched to the slick magazine format. *Ellery Queen's Mystery Magazine* absorbed *Black Mask*. A few science fiction titles transformed into digests, where they continue to find an audience nearly half a century later.

Indirectly, the pulps led to the formation of science fiction fandom. Beginning in 1927, Hugo Gernsback added a letter department to *Amazing Stories* magazine. With Gernsback's encouragement, readers organized clubs. Some lasted for decades. From there, fans took matters into their own hands. They organized and bred like rabbits. Among the notables was Julius Schwartz, who published *The Time Traveler*, considered by some to be the first science fiction fanzine. Later, Schwartz became a prominent editor at DC Comics.

The history of fandom was defined by Donald Wollheim as the story of the struggle for organization. He writes:

Although there have been, and are, prominent personalities who claim no part in the fan clubs, it remains a fact that they owe their very claim of fame and identity to organization. For without some sort of organization, no fan would know another.

The fan clubs were only the first step toward organization. They led to later activities such as conventions and fanzines.

Before the pulps passed on, they helped shape a new publishing medium: comic books. Many of the earliest comics were produced by pulp magazine publishers. Artists and writers bore the pulps' influence like the mark of Cain. The first commercially produced comic book was *Famous Funnies #1*, July 1934. The issue paved the way for other titles. Henry Steeger, a pulp magazine editor (and later the publisher of Popular Publications), produced the issue. About six months later, the tabloid-sized *New Fun* appeared. *New Fun* was the first comic book containing all new material.

Most of the comics published before the 1938 appearance of Superman in *Action Comics* are so mundane they hardly rate discussion. Superman was the foundation upon which the industry was built. In all of literature, no character has been more imitated. Following Superman came an endless stream of long-underwear characters: Batman, Captain America, Wonder Woman, Plastic Man, Captain Marvel, and hundreds of others.

Superman first appeared in an obscure 1933 science fiction fanzine. His creators, Jerry Siegel and Joe Shuster, derived inspiration from Phillip Wylie's 1930 novel *Gladiator* and various other stories published in pulp magazines.

The influence of the pulps on the comic book industry was unmistakable. The business acumen was essentially the same. There was no bias on the part of the publishers, who printed titles on any subject that might catch a coin. By the early 1950s, comics were published on every imaginable subject: super-hero, funny animal, romance, war, western, teenage, mystery, horror, science fiction, radio, television, and motion picture adaptations.

In 1986, artist Frank Borth, a forty-year veteran of the business, reminisced:

> My biggest complaint about the New York comic book publishers in the 1940's was, they were all like a herd of circus elephants. They grabbed the tail of the one in front of them and followed each other around in a circle. They were not interested in quality, only what some accountant told them was selling.

The now defunct line of E.C. Comics developed a loyal fan following and stimulated the first move toward an organized comics fandom. It did not last long. In 1952, Bhob Stewart published the *EC Fan Bulletin,* the first of several fanzines devoted to the subject Despite the efforts of Stewart and other fans, the movement asphyxiated with the demise of the E.C. line in 1955. The *EC Fan Bulletin* remains little more than a footnote in the history of the genre.

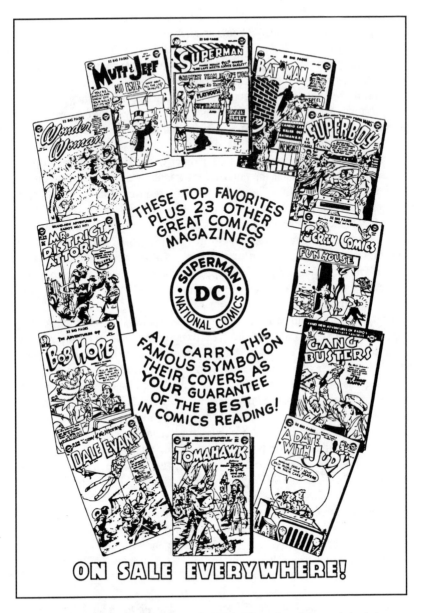

DC Comics house ad from April 1951. The advertisement depicts
an interesting variety of titles. It includes radio, film, movie, and
newspaper strip adaptations . . . plus original DC characters.
© 1951 by National Comics Publications, Inc.

A few years earlier, Dr. Fredric Wertham wrote a book entitled *Seduction of the Innocent*. As a psychiatrist associated with the New York Department of Hospitals, Wertham believed that comic books were not suitable reading material for children. In some instances, Wertham contended that comics were responsible for degrees of abnormality. In particular, the eminent doctor took umbrage over matters of violence and sexuality. He found the crime and horror comics of the period contemptible.

Some of Wertham's theories were, undoubtedly, a bit strange. Wertham saw elements of homosexuality in the relationship between Batman and Robin. Wonder Woman was a lesbian. Mickey Mouse and Donald Duck were horrible monsters that warped delicate, sensitive, juvenile minds. It's too bad Wertham is not alive to see some of the comics they are publishing today.

Wertham suggested that fantasy violence leads to overt violence. Such things as "funny animal" antics made children less reluctant to strike one another. He raised the question of whether there is any difference between Tom hitting Jerry with a frying pan and some construction worker hitting another with a pipe.

In basic psychology, students are taught that every living organism acts and lives appropriate to its environment. On this supposition, it is reasonable to conclude that if a child is exposed to excessive amounts of sex and violence, it will have a negative effect. In recent years, dozens of clinical studies indicate that Wertham was not too far off the beam.

For example, a 1960–81 study of 875 children in a semirural American county found that people were affected by the amount of television they watched. The results of the study established a direct correlation between childhood exposure to television and a proclivity for aggressiveness.

Any number of explanations might be given. One sensible conclusion is that young children are unable to distinguish fact from fiction. They regard television (or comic books) as a source of information about how the world works. For such reasons children crawl into storm drains looking for Teenage Mutant Ninja Turtles.

Seduction of the Innocent became a focal point for a movement instigated by parents and teachers. In 1946, the General Federation of Women's Clubs had exerted enough pressure on comic book publishers to force them to establish a regulatory code. A short time later, they considered the code inadequate and demanded government intervention. This was the beginning of a storm of public fury.

Continued public pressure forced several state legislatures to assign committees to look into the situation. In 1949, the state of New York turned the matter over to a special committee chaired by Joseph F. Carlino. On March 15, 1951, the committee delivered its report. It read:

The girls go at it on a typical *Crimes by Women* cover, Fox, #6, April 1949. Note the exposed brassiere on the blonde woman. This sort of thing annoyed Dr. Fredric Wertham, who had a peculiar notion that it was not suitable reading material for children. I can't imagine where he got an idea like that.

RESOLUTION CREATING COMMITTEE

Whereas, widespread public discussion has been occasioned on the subject of publications, commonly known and referred to as comic books.

FINDINGS

From its studies from the testimony of experts and from its painstaking examination of all the factors involved, the Committee finds:

1. A substantial majority of the publishers of comics are responsible, intelligent and right thinking citizens with a will to improve the industry.

2. A small, stubborn, willful, irresponsible minority of publishers of comics whose brazen disregard for anything but their profit, who recognize no duty to anyone and whose sole objective is financial gain without thought of the consequences of their depredations, are responsible for the bad reputation of the publishers of all comics.

3. The entire industry is remiss in its failure to institute effective measures to police and restrain the undesirable minority.

4. Comics are a most effective medium for the dissemination of ideas and when such a medium is used to disseminate bad ideas which may leave deep impressions on the keen, absorptive minds of children, the unrestricted publication and distribution of comics becomes a matter of grave public concern.

5. Comics which depict crime, brutality, horror, and which produce race hatred impair the ethical development of children, describe how to make weapons, and how to commit crimes, have a wide circulation among children.

6. The reading of crime comics stimulates sadistic and masochistic attitudes and interfere with the normal development of sexual habits in children and produces abnormal sexual tendencies in adolescents.

7. Crime comics are a leading factor to juvenile delinquency.

8. Instead of reforming their bad habits, the publishers of bad crime

comics have banded together, employed resourceful legal and public relations counsel, so-called educators, and experts in a deliberate effort to continue such harmful practices and to fight any and every effort to arrest or control such practices.

9. The Committee condemns the attempts by the representatives of crime comics, who hamper efforts by civic and religious groups to protect youths from the evil effects of crime comics.

10. The evidence adduced makes some action by the State imperative to protect its children.

When the comic book publishers showed no desire to begin serious reforms, the United States Senate took the matter into its own hands. A formal Senate investigation began in late 1953 at the United States Court House in New York City. Estes Kefauver, a senator from Tennessee, presided over the hearing.

The May 3, 1954, issue of *Newsweek* reported that within the first week, a Senate subcommittee had collected some frightening comic book literature, all having a heavy accent on sex and murder. The article said that hardened investigators were revolted by what they found. Considering some of the investigators participated in Kefauver's 1951 Senate investigation on organized crime in interstate commerce, it is probably safe to assume that the investigators were not squeamish.

Estes Kefauver was one of the most powerful members of the Senate. Kefauver had a long face, large jaw, peered at the world through thick glasses, and occasionally wore a coonskin hat. Kefauver wanted to be president of the United States. He came very close to it.

In any event, powerful forces had mobilized against the comic book industry. It was only a matter of time before the publishers would be forced to accept self-regulation. To avoid further governmental scrutiny, they banded together to form the Comics Code Authority. John Goldwater, the publisher of *Archie Comics,* was elected president. The publishers pooled an annual budget of $100,000 to police themselves, devising a regulatory code that forbade scenes of excessive gunplay, physical agony, gory or gruesome crimes, seduction, rape, or perversion.

A similar situation occurred in the 1920s when the motion picture industry went too far with sex and sensationalism. In particular, this outraged the Catholic Church, which decided to establish a censorship board. Greatly alarmed, the filmmakers decided to establish a decency code. With a show of moral indignation against the producers of naughty movies, the Hollywood moguls hired Will Hayes, the United States Postmaster General, to head their censorship board. In this manner, Hollywood narrowly circumvented a general censorship.

There was no sudden awakening of conscience by the motion picture industry. It was a matter of self-preservation. Following this example, the comic book publishers hired Charles F. Murphy, a federal judge, to control the Comics Code Authority.

Following the Senate investigation and the formation of the Comics Code Authority, the industry went through a period of change. Two of the more recalcitrant publishers, Victor Fox and William Gaines, were driven out of the business. For Gaines, it proved to be a blessing in disguise. To avoid the Code, Gaines transformed *MAD Comics* into a magazine and made a fortune in the process. One unfortunate aspect of the Comics Code is that many talented artists and writers left the industry, never to return.

Curiously, Dr. Wertham is often maligned by comic book collectors, who consider him responsible for the demise of the E.C. line. He was not. The truth is that E.C., and other comic book publishers, brought the situation upon themselves.

Richard Hughes was the editorial director of the American Comics Group. His flagship title, *Adventures into the Unknown,* was one of the first horror comics. Hughes survived the purging of the Comics Code by changing from blood and gore to lighthearted fantasy. Occasionally, Hughes printed letters from readers calling for a return to horror stories. Hughes, however, had a different opinion:

Ye editor happened to be around in those old days and failed to find them so glorious. Remember, comics were still in their infancy then. The standards weren't as high as they've become today. There is so much chance to do a better job today. [About] the zombie-vampire business—phooey! That's for amateurs. The stories you rave about were turned out by incompetents who couldn't hold a job today. With a few exceptions here and there, all they could do was shovel senseless horror at the reader. You should hear the trade talk among editors who were around back in the days you refer to, about writers bringing in the same old stereo-typed stories over and over again . . . about anything being used as long as it contained gobs of visual horror.

It was a boom market back in those days, with any writer, any artist at a premium, no matter how bad. But then the Comics Code Authority was created to eliminate the evils of this state of affairs. Morbid, senseless terror was ruled out, and elements of pictorial horror were eliminated. Without these easy short cuts to fall back on there was only one thing to do, and that was to concentrate on really good, imaginative stories. Only the better writers survived. Anybody who seriously calls for a return to the former days of screams, moans, and blood wouldn't know a good story if he tripped over it.

At the 1954 comic book Senate hearing, EC Comics publisher William Gaines stood at the podium and pronounced: "I'm proud of the comics I publish. Some may not like them. That's a matter of personal taste. My only limits are the bounds of good taste."

At that, Senator Kefauver held aloft a copy of *Crime Suspense #22*. The cover depicted a man holding a bloody ax in one hand and a dead woman's head in the other. "Is this good taste?" asked the Senator. "Yes, for the cover of a horror comic," replied Gaines. "I think it would be in bad taste if he were holding the head a little higher so the neck would show blood dripping from it."

Evidently, Gaines had peculiar notions of good taste. By contrast, Richard Hughes was a decent man who cared about the effects his comics might have on the reader. His stories were entertaining, yet they had a gentle, endearing quality that hardly anyone would find offensive.

Hughes's sense of decency carried over into matters of business. The American Comics Group was a last port of call for artists who were down on their luck. Hughes felt great empathy for these broken men, giving them work whenever he could. He rescued more than one artist from the bowery. Despite their differences, Gaines and Hughes left their mark on the industry. Both had a hand in the metamorphosis leading to the formation of comics fandom.

The beginning of comics fandom (as we know it today) occurred in September 1960, with the publication of *Xero #1* by science fiction fan Dick Lupoff. The magazine contained a series of articles about comic books from the 1940s, entitled "All in Color for a Dime." This set the ball in motion.

The next step in the evolution came in March 1961, when Jerry Bails and Roy Thomas published the first true comics fanzine, *Alter Ego*. It was followed a short time later by *Comic Art*, published by Don Thompson and Margaret Curtis. Don and Maggie later married, making it easier to list their credits.

When *Alter Ego* first appeared hardly anyone believed that comics fandom would last long. One skeptical reviewer writing in one of the established science fiction fanzines forecast that a fanzine devoted to comic books would soon lose interest, and perish. He was not much of a prophet.

From that point on, the floodgates opened. Dozens of fanzines came and went. According to scholars, the fanzine is the only original literary device conceived in the twentieth century. Among its admirers was Dr. Fredric Wertham, who personally collected fanzines and wrote a book on the subject in the early 1970s.

The rebirth of superhero comics in the early 1960s spearheaded the formation of comics fandom. A focal point was the letters page of *Justice League* #8, 1961. Editor Julius Schwartz published a plug for *Alter Ego* #3 that attracted hundreds of new subscribers to the fanzine. In the 1930s, Schwartz had been an activist in the science fiction movement and understood the plight of a struggling fanzine searching for an audience. Richard Hughes was also sympathetic, providing occasional support in his letters pages.

In 1964, comic book dealers Robert Bell and Howard Rogofsky began advertising in the classified ad sections of Marvel Comics. Hundreds of new collectors ordered back issues. Business was so good that other dealers soon provided competition.

Marvel offered out-of-print issues (when available) at twenty cents for the twelve-cent editions and thirty-five cents for annuals. About the same time, Marvel organized one of the first comic book fan clubs, the Merry Marvel Marching Society.

With each passing year, comics fandom became larger and better established. Much of the stability was due to older collectors (then in their twenties and thirties) becoming involved in the hobby. Many had collected since the 1950s, not knowing other collectors shared their interest or how to contact them.

In 1964 fans in New York City staged one of the first comic book conventions. Several hundred fans attended. Artist Steve Ditko was the only professional who accepted an invitation to attend. Unfortunately, Ditko was so disenchanted by the experience that he has yet to attend another, or at least as an invited guest. To this day, Ditko avoids comic book fans as if they were lepers.

Another institution that came into vogue simultaneously with conventions were the fan clubs. Many of the first comic book conventions were staged by fan clubs, some of which had strong ties to science fiction fandom. Among the notables were the Southern Fantasy Fan Federation, the Pittsburgh Comics Club, the Oklahoma Alliance of Fans, the Fans of Central Jersey, the Mobile Panelology Association, and the Dallas Science Fiction Fan Association.

Nationwide, dozens of similar clubs continue to come and go. Collectors, however, always remain the same. The beat goes on. Regardless of the festivities that go with organized fandom, collecting is essentially a private ritual. The quiet moments that one spends alone, reflecting upon the artifacts, is where the true joy of collecting lies. It is a difficult sensation to describe. It transcends the mere pride of ownership. Value is of minor consequence. Collectors are like snowflakes; no two are identical. To try to regiment tastes in collectibles would be like trying to standardize taste in womanly beauty.

"Wooda" Nick Carr spent more than thirty years collecting old pulp magazines. He knew as much about the subject as anyone. Carr broached a unique sentiment in 1972 when he wrote, "To be a collector, one must be a combination chemist, weatherman, insectologist, and a great prognosticator who uses with infinitesimal care, the instruments at his fingertips."

If you have ever been a collector, you will appreciate the humor of those remarks. Collecting is a lot like preparing a gourmet meal. Considerable care goes into the preparation of the cuisine. Later, there are a lot of dirty dishes to be washed.

The problem begins with: What to do with a multitude of collectibles once acquired? The storage of artifacts manufactured decades earlier is a perpetual dilemma. Once upon a time, collectors stored their treasures in cardboard boxes hidden under the bed. Only in recent years have collectors been preoccupied with pH factors, temperature, humidity, and mylar storage capsules. A cheap plastic bag was considered adequate for preservation, if anything was used at all.

Restoration became a specialized art. Skilled technicians perform wonders and charge $50 per hour for professional services. It is quite a change from a few years ago, when collectors repaired torn pages with Scotch tape. Color restoration was attempted with felt-tipped pens. One could collect without paying insurance premiums. There was no worry of an audit by the Internal Revenue Service. It was all considerably more simple.

Today, many collectors conduct their activities the same way an entrepreneur handles an investment portfolio. There is no room for sentiment. This is business. Their decision to buy and sell is based on what they think the items will be valued tomorrow. In comic book shops, twelve-year-old kids gloat how prices have inflated from one price guide edition to the next. You would swear the little money-grubbers were dealing in stocks or bonds.

About twenty years ago, writer Robert Bloch expressed concern over children spending too much time and money collecting comic books. He considered it sad and wasteful. Bloch was not implying that kids shouldn't collect things, as he considered the activity normal and healthy. However, Bloch felt that serious collecting should be left to adults.

This situation did not happen overnight. In fact, it took several decades. The hobby was considerably smaller in the 1960s. In those days, there was innocence among collectors that is difficult to imagine now. Almost everyone subscribed to the same collectors' journals. Collectors made up 99 percent of the fraternity. Most preferred to trade than buy.

Cases of skullduggery were no problem. Most collectors were familiar with one another, at least by reputation. In a rare instance when dishonesty was about to rear its ugly head, the mere threat of calling someone a chiseler in one of the fanzines was usually enough to persuade the other guy to keep his end of the bargain. If he didn't, other collectors avoided him like the plague.

You could almost count the professional dealers in the land on one hand.

WELCOME TO THE ANCIENT AND HONORABLE ORDER OF

Congratulations, favored one!

...For having the wisdom and wit to become a Merry Marvel Marcher!

Your name has been ceremoniously entered in our log book, and your dollar has been avariciously deposited in our treasury!

From this day forth, you will stand a little straighter, speak a little wiser, and walk a little prouder. You've made the scene! You're in! You've joined the winning team!

But, with such triumph comes responsibility. You must use your valued membership privileges judiciously. You must be true to the Marvel Code of Ethics: Be not arrogant towards those who have shunned our ranks, for they know not what they're missing. Be not hostile towards unbelievers who march with others, for they're more to be pitied than scorned. Be not intolerant of Marvel-defamers, for they too shall someday see the light. And, above all, be not forgetful that you have become our bullpen buddy. Henceforth, you shall never march alone!

Thus, we welcome you to the fold with this sagacious admonition—FACE FRONT! You're one of us now!

'Nuff said!

The Bullpen Gang

Only Stan Lee could make joining a comic book club sound like an award for lifetime achievement. Among the thousands of MMMS members was Mrs. King's little boy, Stephen. Maybe Dr. Wertham was right in thinking that comic books warped delicate, sensitive, juvenile minds.

The value of most collectibles was moderate. For example, in 1964 Richard Burgess sold a near perfect copy of *Shield-Wizard* #1 for the staggering sum of $2.50! In 1996, the same item was valued at $2,700. There are several reasons for such an astronomical rate of inflation. First, there was an influx of investors and speculators into the hobby. Second, the number of collectors increased by astronomical proportions. In 1962 there were perhaps three hundred organized comic book collectors on the North American continent. By 1990, the number had grown to an estimated 100,000. Since the value of collectibles is determined by supply and demand, prices go up as more dollars chase a dwindling supply of items.

By the late 1960s, prices began to climb. More collectors entered the hobby, slowly at first, then with increasing speed. Newspaper articles snickering about *Superman* #1 selling for one hundred dollars were routine. Collectors reacted differently. Some enjoyed their newfound prestige while others gritted their teeth. However, few took the hundred-dollar business seriously. That soon changed.

In 1970, Robert Overstreet published the first issue of the *Official Comic Book Price Guide* (commonly known as the *Overstreet Guide*). From that point on, things would never be the same for comic book collectors.

Before 1970, no price guides existed for comic books. There were several dealers who offered back issues for about the same price. This gave collectors a fair idea of what something was worth. This information was useful in trading. Usually, collectors bought from dealers as a last resort.

Of course, dealers ordinarily sell at higher prices. This is what they do for a living. Dealers have expenses that collectors do not, such as store rent, taxes, insurance, telephone, salaries, licenses. Their cash is often invested in inventories paid for years ago, still waiting for a buyer. Most collectors understand the predicament and do not hold a grudge. It is a matter of fact that dealers locate most of the collectibles produced before 1970. Without them, there would be far fewer collectibles available.

The Overstreet Guide had a modest beginning. Initially it was a research project started by Overstreet. He received help from various collectors who provided much of the data. A comic book price guide was welcomed by many collectors. When Overstreet advertised the forthcoming first edition, he projected a release date of October 15. The first edition ran to more than two hundred pages and contained over three hundred cover reproductions. Printed photo offset, it had a selling price of $3.50. For 1970, it was a quite elaborate (and expensive) publication.

Overstreet met his deadline. On November 25, 1970, one fanzine publisher announced receiving the first edition. He praised it to high heaven, calling it a major contribution to the hobby.

The Overstreet Guide has grown since that modest beginning. Each new edition is fatter, higher priced than the last. It has brought lasting change to the hobby.

One problem that emanates from any price guide is that it creates instant experts. Every collector meets one sooner or later. It is remarkable how these experts are inflicted with tunnel vision. They only see one price listed: MINT. It does not matter how horrible the condition of an item may be. It can be soiled, water-stained, or in complete fragments. Yet they still offer it at mint price, knowing that sooner or later some idiot will come along willing to pay it.

Beginning in 1970, the world filled with comic book experts. As prices continued to spiral upwards, the experts were joined by a swarm of investors and speculators. Among the notables was an attorney from Houston. This fellow traveled the convention circuit with a pocketful of money, buying every mint-condition Golden Age comic book he could lay his hands on. He rarely quibbled on price, paying top dollar. A lot of collectors thought he was crazy. However, when comic book values inflated several thousand percent in a few years, he made out like a bandit.

The fun really started in 1973 when Mitchell Mehdy paid $1,800 for a copy of *Action #1*. What made the transaction odd was that other copies were readily available for $300-$500. Then Mehdy had the audacity to announce his foolishness to the news media, who milked the story for all it was worth.

While appearing on Tom Snyder's late night talk show, Mehdy proclaimed that he had purchased the rarest comic book in the world. By his modest claim, it was the finest of a half-dozen copies known to exist. To say the least, it was an absurd notion. However, in almost no time, anyone owning a copy of *Action #1* advanced his selling price to an equal amount. Most Golden Age comics of equal rarity increased accordingly. From there, the inflation spread like wildfire.

About a year later, the Xerox Corporation paid $10,000 for a copy of *Action #1*. Xerox reportedly set aside a half-million to buy Golden Age comics for preservation. As a result of this manipulation, comic book values escalated by astronomical proportions. Indirectly, the Overstreet guide was the catalyst.

This was all well and fine for investors and speculators, but most collectors were left standing in the cold. Inflation did not end with comic books. Selling prices for pulps, movie posters, and similar items rapidly escalated. The following dialogue written in 1975 by Nils Hardin presented an interesting perspective of the problem:

> To be a collector is a privilege. I am here to give you that privilege. In order to obtain the status of a collector, one must be willing to pay the price. I know you, in your infinite wisdom—are willing to

do just that. You know that prices are going up all the time. I, therefore, am willing to sell to you now, before the prices go any higher. Kiss me!

Obviously, this sort of a person is a vampire, but a realistic one, and collectors are not often known to embrace reality. This is true not only of those who have been collecting for a short period of time, but also of veteran collectors. The disease is acute within the bloodstream of most collectors and is generally terminal. The disease takes the form of compelling the person to obtain (at whatever cost) some desired item—even though once obtained, it reposes on the shelf with all the items obtained the same way.

The odd thing is that many collectors are doing nothing more than sublimating the horrors that abound in the real world. They would be the first to change the course of events if they could, but they feel ineffectual in stemming the tide. Sublimation is the most desirable answer to that reality.

On the other hand, the vampire is a realist. He senses the unique susceptibility of the collector that he needs to sublimate to survive. The vampire survives because he is not only insensitive to what is taking place, but he has been instrumental in creating it. But what, you ask, of the collectors who collect for other reasons, the ones who may, after all, be in touch with reality? This kind of collector might say: "What the hell! If I want to pay $100 for an item (that is worth less) that's my business! It's my money and I'll pay anything I damned well choose!"

Fine, but there is one serious flaw in that logic. Most collectors enjoy collecting but they also have families to support, or have other financial obligations. They can't afford to plunge $100 into a magazine that will just sit on the shelf. A few do, but more don't. This is the sort of thing that has driven hundreds of collectors out of the field and will drive out hundreds more in the future.

Of course, price guides are not unique to comic book collecting. For example, they have been a facet of the coin hobby for almost a century. Price guides are published on baseball cards, records, stamps, antiques, pocket watches, knives, guns, plastic models, and God only knows what else. An unfortunate aspect of price guides is they destroy the normal supply-and-demand patterns that ordinarily would exist.

In most collecting fields, price guides are published by dealers. Leaving a dealer in charge of a price guide is tantamount to leaving Saddam Hussein in charge of the Middle East. These dealers have prior knowledge of which items are going up in price. It provides an opportunity for a few opportunists to

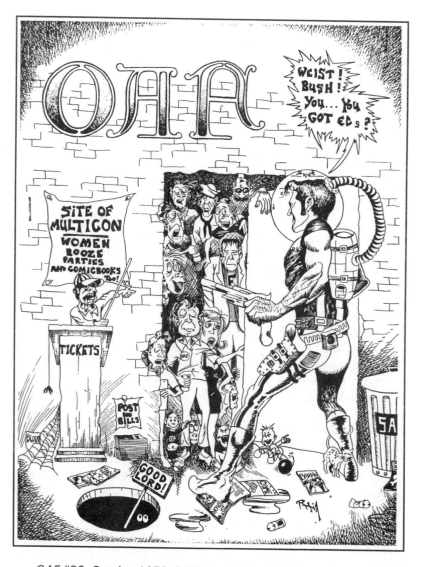

OAF #36, October 1970. Published by the Oklahoma Alliance of Fans. The EC Comics inspiration for the cover art is apparent. If there is any similarity to any living person, it's not only a coincidence . . . it's a dirty shame!

corner the market.

Now, if this sort of chicanery were to occur on the stock exchange, the government would consider it insider trading. Bureaucrats take a dim view of the practice. However, in the field of collecting, the practice is considered perfectly legitimate. It is not. Collectors should question the ethics involved, but rarely do.

The simple truth of the matter is there is no established price for anything. Values are subject to supply and demand. They are determined when buyer and seller agree in the marketplace. The value of gold is a good example. This is far removed from the economics of collecting, where prices are routinely adjusted upward from one price guide edition to the next. Only in rare instances are prices rolled back. This constant inflation benefits dealers, who are provided with an excuse to sell their merchandise at ever higher prices.

Price guides were never intended to be a bible. Their contents are not etched in stone. The values are subject to interpretation. In fact, any knowledgeable collector knows that collectibles have three different values:

1. What you can get for an item in cold, hard cash.
2. What you can get for an item in trade.
3. What an item is valued at in some price guide.

The three values are almost never the same.

No one knows to what extent prices in the comic book price guide have been manipulated. In all probability, more has occurred than the publisher would care to admit. The bottom line is that the values reflected in the guide are not always accurate.

In the 1950s, a pricing scandal almost destroyed the coin hobby. A handful of insurance companies manipulated market values by buying thousands of rare coins for speculation. Prices inflated when the coins gradually disappeared from circulation. Because there was no genuine shortage of rare coins, there came a day of reckoning. There was a crash in the market. Several insurance companies were wiped out along with hundreds of collectors. It took many years for the hobby to recover.

To date, comic book collectors have been spared such a tragedy. Although in recent years the market has shown signs of great instability. The comic book and baseball card hobbies have been ravaged by speculation. Many rare collectibles are now owned by noncollectors, purchased for investment purposes. The only time they change hands is when one speculator sells to another. As a result prices have gone through the roof. *Action* #1 is a splendid example. In 1984, it was valued at $14,000. By 1988, it had increased to $28,650. Then, in 1996, the price had inflated to $145,000.

In 1978, a dealer named Tanner Miles served as adviser to Overstreet. In this capacity, Miles provided supplemental information and pricing data. At the time, Miles experienced price resistance while attempting to sell his comics at prices listed in the guide. Naturally, Miles did what any sensible businessman would do: He lowered his selling prices.

This action brought a response from Overstreet, who inquired why Miles sold his comics for less than what the price guide stipulated. Miles simply told Overstreet it was necessary to sell at lower prices to stay in business. Of course, the implication was that Overstreet's prices were too high.

Overstreet did not like the answer. He told Miles that if he wished to remain as an adviser to the guide, he had to raise his selling prices. Miles told Overstreet to go to hell. The two parted ways, on something less than amicable terms. Miles was dropped as an adviser in the 1979 edition.

In 1974, Gordon B. Love published the *S.F.C.A. Comic Book Price Guide*. Feeling a sense of righteous indignation, Overstreet filed suit for copyright infringement. On this premise, the court granted Overstreet a temporary injunction, stopping the sale and distribution of the *S.F.C.A. Guide*.

It is difficult to understand the court's rationale. It ignored the fact that a copyright enables an author to control the reproduction of his work. It prevents others from copying his individual expression without permission. However, anyone is free to create his own expression (based on the same information) without permission of the author.

For example, most writers obtain at least a portion of their facts from other works published on the same subject. The practice is known as fair use. It has caused some squabbling among authors and publishers who disagree as to its definition. Fair use is commonly regarded as the use of copyrighted material to such a minor degree that it causes no injustice to the original author.

Overstreet thought no one else had the right to publish a comic book price guide. For whatever reason, Love chose to settle the matter out of court. The details are not a matter of public record. The final resolution prohibited Love from publishing a comic book price guide.

Call it poetic justice, but a few years later Overstreet faced a similar predicament. It began with his publication of the *Paperback Book Price Guide,* edited by Kevin Hancer. Hancer obtained a substantial portion of his information from another writer's research. The original author sued Overstreet for copyright infringement. In 1982, a prominent Oklahoma City attorney advised Overstreet to settle out of court. One can only surmise that Overstreet did. After a second edition, the *Paperback Book Price Guide* ceased publication.

Now, in the overall scheme of things, the price a collector pays for an item is a moot point. The act is a reflection of how badly a person wants an item. The desire of the individual to own something (and the methods he uses to get it) is the central issue.

As with most things, it is reasonably difficult to build a good collection. It

If a person paused long enough to blink, he might have missed this 1974 edition of the *S.F.C.A. Price Guide.* The cover art is by the late Don Newton, who had not yet made the transition from fan artist to professional.

requires time, patience, and an expenditure of energy. A little cash works wonders, also.

The majority of collectors are decent people. One does not mind being seen in their company. They usually make for suitable house guests. Most are old-fashioned enough to deal fairly with fellow collectors. They do not expect to get something for nothing. Should they find some treasure for less than its market value, they realize that lady luck has smiled upon them.

There is, however, another variety of collector. This sort has little use for conventional methods. He finds it preferable to lie, cheat, and steal to obtain those items dearest to his black little heart. Such a cad might be aware of the intrinsic value of an item, but he is more prone to know its monetary worth. To get what he wants, he will gladly cut your throat, then smile and drink your blood. He does not have an ounce of shame. However, contrary to popular opinion, his reflection still appears in the mirror, proving with reasonable certainty that he is only a vampire in spirit.

A good example is a well-known collector of Edgar Rice Burroughs memorabilia. I'll call him Fred. This fellow endeared himself to his colleagues by committing every sin short of murder. In the process, he acquired a remarkable collection, said to have been one of the best in the world.

Fred was about as friendly as a rattlesnake. At conventions, he often displayed a sign on his dealer's table that read: COMIC SICK KIDS KEEP AWAY! At one convention in the early 1970s Fred was confined to a wheelchair due to a broken leg. He was accompanied by his wife, who waited on him hand and foot. Considering his other charming qualities, it came as no surprise to see Fred verbally abuse the lady. It is certainly difficult to warm up to a fellow like that.

About 1975, Fred tracked down a popular pulp magazine illustrator who owned a dozen or so original oil paintings from the 1930s. Fred managed to buy the paintings at a fraction of their value, based on a promise that the paintings would be displayed in an art museum.

You can guess how much Fred's word was worth. A short time later, those paintings hit the market like a bombshell, at prices only slightly less than the national debt. Somehow, word of the treachery got back to the pulp illustrator. As you might imagine, he was quite upset. For years afterward, he refused to have anything to do with pulp collectors.

Finally, Fred got a taste of his own medicine. It began when his wife sued for divorce. The lady was represented by a shrewd attorney, who insisted that she receive half of their joint assets. Of course this included the Burroughs collection. A fair-minded judge decreed that the only way to determine the market value of the collection was to sell it.

When it was all over, the lady took her share of the cash and moved into a commune. Poor Fred was heartbroken. He wailed and moaned about the injustice of it all. Fred was probably surprised to discover that most of his colleagues shed few tears over his plight. Many, in fact, snickered up their sleeve. It was one of those rare situations that makes one believe that some justice still exists in the world.

Thirty years ago, comic book collectors occasionally brought portions of their collections to conventions for show-and-tell purposes. At a 1970 con in Oklahoma City, Charles Rice brought a suitcase containing a complete collection of the Golden Age *Captain America*. He had recently completed the collection. Then, it was an accomplishment to be admired. Today, it would be next to impossible unless a person had Ted Turner's bankroll, or a gift for grand larceny.

Rice was congenial enough to show the collection to anyone who wanted a look. Almost everyone was impressed. That evening, Rice and a few friends went out for a hamburger. After all, a person works up a big appetite trading comic books. The suitcase containing the collection was stashed behind a table for safekeeping. It proved to be a terrible mistake.

When Rice returned, he discovered the suitcase was gone. News of the theft echoed through the dealers' room like a crash on Wall Street. An immediate search was instigated. Surprisingly, no one saw the suitcase taken. The police were called to investigate. A short time later, the suitcase was found outside in a trash can. The comics were gone. There was little the police could do, not that they were particularly interested in apprehending a "funny book" thief. Questions were asked, but the thief could have been anyone.

Charles Rice was devastated. His prized collection vanished like a puff of smoke. Understandably, Rice was so embittered by the incident that he stopped collecting. The thief took more than his material possessions; he robbed Rice of his faith in his fellow man. The joy Rice had derived from the hobby was no longer there. It was a damned shame.

Another incident worth relating involved a dealer who was a familiar face at comic book conventions in the early 1970s. For the sake of anonymity, I'll call him Mike. He was a grim-looking, bearded Italian in his thirties. During his youth, Mike was said to have been a member of a Philadelphia street gang. Despite his somewhat sinister appearance, Mike was an affable person, well thought of by most of his colleagues.

About 1975, at a convention on the East coast, Mike detected a would-be thief stealing a comic book from his table. He immediately gave chase, catching the culprit just outside the dealers' room. At first the thief denied any guilt. He confessed only after Mike wrested the item from him. Then the thief turned belligerent, mouthing off something to the effect of: "So, you caught me, man! Biiiig deal! What are you gonna do about it (snicker), call the cops? Why don't you take your comic and go screw yourself!"

That was probably the worst thing he could have done. Mike had his own way of dealing with thieves. A heartbeat later, he delivered a well-placed knee to the rascal's groin, doubling him over in agony. Looking around at several witnesses, Mike said: "This man is sick. I'm going to help him outside." Then Mike escorted him to the alley where he proceeded to teach that misguided wretch a lesson in social responsibility. Putting it bluntly, he beat the proverbial stuffing out of the him! Afterwards, Mike dusted his clothing, collected his property, and strolled back to resume business.

Fortunately, most collectors have little skill in the art of pugilism. They tend to be somewhat less demonstrative. However, another occasion comes to mind where dishonesty resulted in physical violence. At another convention, a local radio disk jockey was caught stealing and narrowly avoided being thrown down a flight of stairs by the angry victim and a mob of bystanders.

Worse still, Howard Rogofsky was chased out of a New York convention by a dissatisfied customer brandishing a knife. According to one eyewitness, Rogofsky barely got away with skin intact. After that, Rogofsky no longer attended conventions. No doubt, it is safer to charge exorbitant prices by mail.

However, the most disgusting incident happened at a 1975 Dallas convention. Believe it or not, an unsuspecting teenager was a victim of armed robbery. I'll call him Archie, as he bore more than a passing resemblance to the comic book character.

It began when a dealer from Arizona took a fancy to Archie's mint-condition copy of *Human Torch* #1 and offered a trade. Foolishly, Archie agreed to meet him in his hotel room, alone. Behind closed doors, the dealer carefully examined the Golden Age comic. In return, he handed Archie a box of comics for his consideration. To Archie's surprise, the box contained nothing of value.

At first, Archie thought the offer was in jest. It was not. As any sane person would, Archie declined. He may have been young, but he was not stupid. At that point, Archie tried to take his property and leave. Instead of returning the book, the dealer snarled, "The trade is over! Take your comics and get out!"

When Archie refused, the dealer pulled out a handgun and ordered him from the room at gunpoint. Archie had no choice but to obey. You know how ugly those bullet holes can be.

The moment he was out of the room, the teenager scurried to find help. In a matter of minutes, Archie located the convention chairman and excitedly explained what had happened. On his way out of the hotel the robber was met by his victim, the convention chairman, and several witnesses.

When questioned about the incident, the dealer claimed he paid cash for the book and defied anyone to prove otherwise. Then he threatened everyone with lawsuits if they prevented him from leaving. Sadly, no one had the gumption to call his bluff. Instead of holding him until the police or the hotel security could be called to investigate, they let him go. With a haughty sneer on his face, he left the hotel with his ill-gotten gains. Contrary to popular opinion, crime does pay, or at least on occasion.

Years later, there was a rumor circulating around that this particular dealer had been gunned down in Mexico, over a drug deal that went sour. I have no idea if the rumor is true or not. If so, there is a certain degree of poetic justice involved. Stranger things have happened.

In the summer of 1978, the pulp collectors held their annual convention at St. Louis. It was a small gathering as conventions go. No more than thirty or forty people were present in the dealers' room at any time. The event was casual, more like a family reunion than a trade show. Few dealers sat behind their own tables. They were busy socializing. You were encouraged to rummage through stacks of pulps at leisure. "Just help yourself," they would say. "If you find something you want, let me know. I will be across the room trading. . . ."

The operative word was trust. Harmony permeated the gathering like a fragrance. It was a pleasant change from the hostile atmosphere one ordinarily finds at comic book conventions. There, almost everyone is suspicious of everyone else. Dealers dislike one another and engage in cutthroat competition. They bicker like children. Tables are covered with sheets of clear plastic to discourage sticky fingers. Standing behind their tables, dealers scrutinize legitimate customers with an eagle eye. Despite their best security measures, they still get ripped off. Thieves are everywhere. It's almost as bad as a street market in Algiers.

Years ago, Emerson pointed out that such people think they are born booted and spurred, to ride mankind. Such arrogant presumptions abound among nostalgia collectors. In a few short years the hobby evolved from a fraternity into a smarmy, greed-stained business. The majority found robbery at conventions far too risky. It was easier (and a lot safer) to cheat and steal by mail. The chicanery that often goes hand in hand with making money had only begun. . . .

CHAPTER TWO

The Incandescent Carnival

We all cross the line into cult behavior, conforming our view to those of others, keeping silent when we should speak up, anointing those who exert power or charm with a degree of defecation.

—Arthur Deikman, *The Wrong Way Home*

Many years ago, *Reader's Digest* published a delightful series of articles entitled "The Most Unforgettable Character I Ever Met." No doubt the subject of this story would qualify for such a distinction.

It is a story about a retired grandfather. By accident, he founded fandom's first weekly advertising journal. Later, he organized its first trade association. As fandom evolved from hobby to business, he became a self-styled champion of the little guy. His name was Stanley Blair.

Even among fans who knew him well, little is known about Blair. He was not a collector. Prior to his involvement with fandom, Blair claimed to have been a certified public accountant, serving as a trustee for corporations undergoing reorganization bankruptcy. In this capacity he restored a firm to solvency by managing its assets. By his own admission, several national corporations exist today due to his efforts.

Blair was an orphan. During the 1940s he was involved in hotel management. Blair married the former Elaine McGinnis sometime during the early 1950s. At one point in time, Blair owned and managed the Stag Employment Agency of Houston, Texas.

Blair's brother-in-law, Don McGinnis, described him as a highly secretive man, who rarely spoke about his past. Blair legally changed his name prior to marriage. McGinnis did not know Blair's former name, nor the reason for the name change. As a man of peculiar personal habit, Blair took care to sign his name in a precise manner, endeavoring to have each signature look as identical as possible.

In 1959, Blair suffered a near-fatal heart attack. He was hospitalized for a year, sustaining medical expenses of more than $100,000. His personal finances were obliterated. While recovering, Blair busied himself raising pedigree dogs. His personal favorite was the Great Dane. Blair kept eighty to one hundred of the animals on his premises, an idea that might have adapted nicely into a technicolor cartoon for Warner Bros. In addition, Blair dabbled in horticulture, developing a type of African violet.

In 1968, Blair and his wife moved from their home in Houston to Dayton, Ohio. They were needed to care for his terminally ill mother-in-law. While living in Dayton, Blair helped his brother-in-law with his business. McGinnis was the proprietor of Red's Book Store, a firm specializing in mail-order auctions of comic books, pulps, and other collectibles. Blair's participation in these auctions introduced him to fandom and several hundred collectors.

Blair frequently came into contact with collectors who had a few items they wanted to sell, or needed only a few items to complete collections. Their only option was to advertise in one of the irregularly published fanzines. It might be months before the advertisement generated a response. Blair conducted a survey to find out if an inexpensive, regularly published journal would benefit these collectors. An overwhelming majority felt it would.

Thus, on Sunday, September 14, 1969, the first issue of *Stan's Weekly Express (WE)* was mailed to one hundred fifty collectors. Before the first year ended, circulation increased to over two thousand paid subscribers. Although it seemed insignificant at the time, *WE* was a giant leap forward in the evolution of fandom.

Future historians might be interested to know that Blair patterned *WE* after *Joe's Bulletin,* an obscure journal for horticulture enthusiasts. Blair had been a subscriber during the 1950s. A decade later, he adapted much of its layout and philosophy for his own publication.

During his first year of publishing, Blair compiled a mailing list of 19,000 nostalgia collectors. Each week, he mailed one thousand complimentary copies. This relatively inexpensive advertising continued to build his circulation. Blair found names by trading advertising to dealers and fan clubs in exchange for mailing lists.

WE reflected Blair's personality. He was always doing something to stimulate interest. Contests, special issues, prizes became ordinary events. Blair established a rapport with his readers by encouraging them to participate.

Looking through back issues that have long since grown yellow and brittle with age, it is interesting to note certain subscribers and advertisers. Among the notables were Bjo Trimble, Russell Myers, Walter Koenig, and Forrest J. Ackerman. You found them rubbing elbows with such fine people as "Uncle" Gene Kousek, Jim Ivey, Joe Stoner, Manuel Seguin, Richard Garrison, Bob Beerbohm, Jerry Bails, George Schwartz, and Donald Puff. They were like

It has been said by more than one eyewitness that Stanley Blair bore a striking resemblance to actor W.C. Fields. Considering these reports came from two writers and a police officer, I can assume the descriptions were reasonably accurate. Blair never published a picture of himself. Since he passed away a few years ago, this picture of Fields is probably as close to the real thing as we are likely to find. It isn't much of a tribute, but it is the best I can do under the circumstances. It's the way I like to remember him.

old friends whom you welcomed into your home every week when the new issue of *WE* arrived. Some of them are still active today.

Blair was instrumental in organizing the pulp collectors. *WE* #40, June 14, 1970, was the first of several special issues devoted to the pulps. The idea was suggested by Richard Minter, who had collected pulps since the early 1940s. In 1962, Minter became one of the first dealers to specialize in the field. His reputation was impeccable. When Minter spoke, Blair listened. The advice was good.

The special pulp issue generated special orders of 1,750 copies, forcing Blair to reprint the issue. Due to its unprecedented success, a second pulp issue followed a few months later. It did equally well. A third pulp issue was published in June 1971. The issue featured an announcement by Ed Kessel for the first national Pulp Convention, held on November 27, 1971, in St. Louis. This convention (later dubbed Pulpcon) became an institution, continuing on a yearly basis for three decades.

The three special pulp issues brought the pulp collectors together for the first time. Later, they served as a blueprint for the much admired *Xenophile,* the first regularly published periodical devoted to the pulps.

Not many people remember that Blair was an adviser to Robert Overstreet, who published the first edition of *The Comic Book Price Guide* in 1970. Blair personally endorsed the guide and highly recommended that his thousands of readers purchase the first edition. This endorsement was a factor in the success of the project. Curiously, Overstreet has never seen fit to acknowledge Blair's contribution.

Two unrelated events occurred in the first year of publication that altered *WE*'s destiny. The first was a feud with the post office in Dayton, Ohio. It began when the post office started taking liberties processing the weekly bulk mailing of *WE.*

The established advertising deadline was Friday of each week. Blair printed the new issue Sunday, then mailed on Monday morning. Ordinarily, subscribers received the new issue by Friday. Blair began to receive complaints that issues were arriving as much as ten days late. Since customer satisfaction was important to Blair, he acted quickly to resolve the problem.

However, his complaints to the Dayton post office fell on deaf ears. Apparently the postmaster was unconcerned. This forced Blair to direct his complaints to higher authorities, including the United States Postmaster General. The problem got worse. The post office disposed of a large portion of one issue, forcing Blair to reprint.

Blair's problem with the post office continued for several months. Finally, with a bellyful of aggravation, Blair took his complaint to Charles W. Whalen, Jr., an Ohio U.S. representative. Whalen brought pressure upon the U.S. Postal Inspection Service, who began a belated investigation. Before the

JOE'S BULLETIN
Joe Smith, Publisher
Dorothea Smith Buick, Editor

209 Basswood Ave.   Dayton 5, Ohio

RETURN POSTAGE GUARANTEED

Everything offered for sale in This Bulletin carries a Moneyback
Guarantee. If not satisfied, return the merchandise
and ask for a return of the money.

A Periodical With A Mission

Joe's Bulletin is a periodical with a mission. It strives to tell its readers
where they can buy flowering and ornamental plants and bulbs at the most
reasonable prices, while making it possible for growers to market them at
prices which afford a satisfactory return.

Efficient Advertising
This is accomplished by supplying advertising upon the most reasonable
terms. The high cost of advertising is the biggest obstacle in the successful
conduct of the mail order business. It often eats up half of the returns the
advertiser gets. So he is constantly tempted either to boost his prices, or to
supply his customers with inferior stock. This destroys the confidence of the
customer in all advertising.

A Long Felt Want
The Bulletin seeks to fill the long felt want, an advertising medium which
sells the goods without demanding an unreasonable price for its services.
It accomplishes this by seeking its circulation among persons who are chiefly
interested in the attractive bargains offered by its advertisers, and finding
for its advertisers, persons who can supply them at the most reasonable prices.
It avoids expensive, exaggerated and flamboyant advertising, and encourages
simple and exact description of what is offered. In this way it saves money
for the customer, and makes money for the advertiser, by saving both from
the burden of expensive advertising.

Guaranteed Advertising
The Bulletin accepts advertising only from responsible advertisers, and
every advertisement is accepted on condition that the advertiser guarantees
that his merchandise will satisfy the customer. If he fails to live up to this
guarantee he is kicked out of the Bulletin. Fakers and chiselers, so prominent
in other advertising mediums, are scrupulously eliminated, and in flagrant
cases exposed.

Reasonable Rates
Advertising rates in the Bulletin are very reasonable. But in order to
make them so the advertiser must make his prices accordingly reasonable.
By doing this advertiser finds that his returns are so generous that the cost
of the advertising is almost inconsequential.

It might amuse the modern readership of *The Comics Buyer's
Guide* (which was influenced by *Stan's Weekly Express*) to know
that the genealogical ancestry of the publication dates to this
obscure 1950s journal of flower advertising.

smoke cleared, several postal employees were fired, including the postmaster.

Afterwards, there were no more delays in processing *WE*. The second situation, although no less serious, had deeper implications. An unbargained-for problem presented itself when an advertiser calling himself Ian Derek Dryden submitted a false advertisement. It was published in *WE* #39, June 7, 1970. Over one hundred subscribers responded to the ad. A short time later, Blair started to receive complaints. Blair investigated and immediately discovered a mail fraud in progress.

Blair was infuriated that anyone would use his publication to perpetrate such a scandal. He acted quickly to stop the culprit. The cover of *WE* #41, June 21, 1970, had the notice "WARNING ALERT!!" imprinted over the usual layout. An editorial informed subscribers of the situation and requested documentation of all transactions with Dryden. An avalanche of letters, phone calls, and telegrams followed.

After collecting enough evidence, Blair called the Dubuque, Iowa, police department. Upon hearing the story, the chief of detectives ordered the immediate arrest of Dryden. In a few hours the arrest was made.

Ian Derek Dryden proved to be not one but two people: Daniel Randal Kelch and Edward Joseph Herbert. The details involved in the arrest, calls by Blair to various civil authorities, and affidavits provided by the victims led to the speedy indictment, trial, and conviction of Kelch and Herbert. Due to Blair's quick action, restitution was made to the victims, an amount totalling more than $5,000.

Blair's personal expenses in what became known as the infamous "Dryden Affair" were $208.53. Blair spent the money graciously, with no thought of reimbursement. The grateful victims took up a collection without his knowledge. The funds collected exceeded Blair's actual expenses. This money was placed in a special account for the investigation of future mail frauds. It was not long before the money was used.

Two innovations resulted from the Dryden Affair that altered the course of the *WE* enterprises. The first was the creation of the WE Reporting Bureau (WRB), an entity dedicated to the investigation, reporting, tabulation, and prosecution of all known mail fraud in fandom. The second was the WE Seal of Approval (WSA), which promoted fair play in the hobby and suggested professional methods of doing business by mail.

In a highly improbable scenario, Blair divided his time between publishing and managing his trade association. Such divided allegiance would be tantamount to keeping your first wife's picture in your second wife's bedroom. It is difficult to imagine how Blair made the distinction in his own mind.

Psychologists call such situations role conflict. An individual who occupies more than one status at a time and is unable to enact one role without

---

S T A N ' S   W E E K L Y   E X P R E S S

P. O. BOX 207 [Daytonview Station], DAYTON, 45406, OHIO

DEAR FELLOW FAN:

This copy of   STAN'S WEEKLY EXPRESS   [otherwise known as   "WE"] is composed
of pages from several issues. It is a sample of the contents found in   "WE"   regularly.

SOME of these pages are mimeo rejects [blurred, smeared, or misplaced on pages] ... so in
this way are NOT representative of the subscribers copies. However, many of the ads are
current ... scan top margins for the LATEST issue number ... these will be pages from the
CURRENT ISSUE. These ads are up for buys.

"WE" has a program which encompasses ALL of Fandom. Each week extra [full] issues
of "WE" are sent as complimentaries to 1,000 fans. A different group is covered EACH
week. This program takes approximately NINETEEN WEEKS to circulate all those listed
in our files ... one complimentary copy to each fan every 19 weeks.

Between these full issues, "WE" sends [as postage costs permit] these PARTIAL copies
[such as YOU are now reading].

If YOU would enjoy receiving "WE" regularly -- please subscribe. "WE" welcome
YOU to become one of the WE-FAMILY and to benefit from the many facets of "WE" ...

    W. R. B. ... W. S. A. ... WE-WAY ... "wee" ...
    P. F. A. ... WE-CHEXS ... SUBSCRIBERS BONUS ...
    AND ALL OTHER SUBSCRIBER/ADVERTISER BENEFITS ...

WE-uns are a group of Fans who LIKE EACH OTHER. Each feels kindly toward his fellow-
WE-uns and is closely knit [through the pages of "WE"] into a FAN-ily, the
WE-FAMILY. Many deep friendships are formed and correspondence snowfalls over the
nation.

Do drop in visits are climaxed with drop everything parties. Cons become vacation trips spent
among the WE-FAMILY ... and "WE" is the travel folder.

"WE" is FANDOM'S   TELL-A-COMMUNICATION ... and your phone is
ringing II   HELLO -- HELLO -- are you there ?

                        Good Reading ......

                        Stan

                    Editor & Publisher - "WE"

P.S. Remember ... these are
ONLY "SAMPLE PAGES" of
"WE" ...   YA OUGHTA
SEE THE REAL THING ! ! !

        JOIN THE "WE-FAMILY" T O D A Y I I

PAID CIRCULATION ...   1,000 PLUS "WEEKLY" ISSUES .....

For many collectors, this page served as an introduction to *Stan's
Weekly Express*. Blair's casual approach to advertising warmed
the heart and often added another subscriber to the mailing list.
It is a shame that the personal touch has gone out of style in this
modern day of social enlightenment.

violating the other is encountering role conflict. In this instance, the strain was too much for Blair. In time his behavior became increasingly irrational. The dust had hardly settled on the Dryden Affair when Arnold Meyrowitz made his presence felt upon fandom. Blair often referred to Meyrowitz as fandom's most unique thief. It was a distinction well deserved. Over a period of five years, Meyrowitz bilked collectors out of money and merchandise totaling more than $50,000. Meyrowitz used several aliases: Neil Scharaff, Alan Scharaff, Harold Meyrow, Arnold Meyrow, and Robert Woods.

As a former employee of the U.S. Postal Service, Meyrowitz knew how the system worked. He exploited it to his advantage. His "hit-and-run" technique was a textbook study. It worked like this: First, Meyrowitz opened a post office box under an assumed name. Then a bank account. Next, he placed an ad in one of the fanzines, offering collectibles at very reasonable prices. Buyers sent checks to buy the nonexistent goodies. Then the villain cashed the checks and vanished. After a reasonable time, he moved to a different area to repeat the scam.

Meyrowitz had no prejudice about where he practiced his black art. Among his victims were collectors of comic books, pulps, films, books, stamps, and coins. His operations extended throughout the North American continent, eventually spreading to Europe, Asia, and Australia.

Blair received dozens of complaints about Meyrowitz. The investigation proved to be time-consuming. After spending hundreds of hours looking into Meyrowitz's shenanigans, Blair's interest evolved into an obsession.

In 1973, Meyrowitz was indicted for stealing mail while working for the post office. Before the trial, Blair provided dozens of documented mail-fraud cases to the U.S. Attorney representing eastern New York who, for whatever reason, declined to prosecute. As a result, Meyrowitz was convicted only of mail theft. He was slapped on the wrist and placed on probation. In no time Meyrowitz was back on the street engaged in his profitable mail-fraud business. A determined Stan Blair remained in hot pursuit.

A major change in Blair's life came on June 18, 1971. His mother-in-law passed away. With his family obligation discharged, he and his wife made immediate plans to return to Houston. There, Blair continued to publish *WE* and to operate his antifraud organizations. Plans were made for expansion.

Shortly after returning to Houston, Blair began publication of *WE-uns*, edited by his wife, Elaine, known in fan circles as "Mrs. Stan." The first issue was dated July 1971. The issue had sparse circulation, consisting of advance orders. It contained a variety of articles, featuring a tribute to Representative Whalen, followed by a thirteen-page documentary outlining the infamous Dryden Affair in boring detail. It also included articles by Nick Carr, Joe Stoner, Art Miller, and a delightful recollection by Bob Beerbohm about the disasters he encountered while traveling from Nebraska to California for a 1971 convention at Disneyland.

A second issue was planned for the following month. It never appeared. Publication was suspended when Blair suffered a stroke. It impaired his speech and vision, leaving one side of his body partially paralyzed. The *WE* enterprises came to an abrupt halt. For a time Blair's condition was critical.

Blair was absent from fandom for a year while he slowly recovered. While he was incapacitated, fandom experienced major changes. *The Comic Book Price Guide* attracted hundreds of speculators and investors to the hobby. As prices increased, new dealers appeared by the dozen. The personal exchanges that had been so common between buyer and seller all but disappeared.

The most significant development was the appearance of a new advertising journal called *The Buyer's Guide for Comic Fandom*. The publisher was a nineteen-year-old upstart named Alan Light. While Blair was absent, *TBG* assumed *WE*'s place in the market. Light patterned his publication after *WE*, adapting it to the tabloid newspaper format. *TBG* was enormously successful. This success led to the ultimate demise of *WE*.

Then, in October 1972, *WE* resumed publication without notice. However, much had happened while Blair was gone. Many older collectors who supported *WE* from the beginning had dropped out. They were no longer collecting. With these changes, *WE* suffered for lack of advertising. Circulation slowly dwindled. Blair held on grimly for another six months, hoping to turn things around. Several friends and supporters pitched in, trying to save it. Russell Myers contributed a drawing of Broom Hilda that Blair used for a cover. Several friends offered money or placed additional ads. Others, like Bob Sampson, produced special articles for publication.

The final months of publication were quiet. However, two unrelated incidents made them interesting. The first was a debacle over underground comics. These comic book–style magazines produced by semiprofessional publishing houses often contained adult subject matter.

Blair ran several advertisements for undergrounds, not knowing what they were. Several readers complained. One sent samples. After examining the magazines, Blair was appalled. In particular, Robert Crumb's work turned his stomach. Considering undergrounds a form of pornography, Blair excluded such advertising from *WE*.

This decision did not sit well with a few zealots who protested about censorship and a violation of constitutional rights. A minor rhubarb began, which invariably was carried to the pages of other publications. One idiot went as far as to compare Blair with Adolph Hitler. However, this caterwauling did not change Blair's mind. Considering that Blair needed all the advertising he could muster, this was an act of conviction. He stuck by the decision to the end.

The second incident involved a head-on collision between dealers Howard Rogofsky and Bruce Hamilton. It began when one of Hamilton's friends purchased a rare Golden Age comic book from Rogofsky for several hundred dollars. It had a false back cover, which Rogofsky had failed to mention in his advertising. This, of course, greatly decreased its value. The buyer tried to return it for a refund. Rogofsky refused.

Next, Hamilton tried to persuade Rogofsky, to no avail. Finally, Hamilton lodged a mail-fraud complaint with Blair. Upon a careful examination of the facts and the book in question, Blair jumped all over Rogofsky. At Blair's insistence, Rogofsky grudgingly agreed to make a refund.

Rogofsky wrote an open letter to Blair, in which he complained of the tribulations he experienced with collectors—some of which were very legitimate. Rogofsky reiterated his policy of not issuing refunds unless an item was defective. After all, he was not running a library. Rogofsky's advertising of the period included a disclaimer that said that tape on an item (for repair) was not considered a defect. Obviously he did not consider false back covers a defect, either.

Rogofsky ended the letter by stating, "If fans can use WRB to force dealers into running a library or reading service, then dealers might as well go out of business and fans can find their own supply of comic books."

Howard Rogofsky has never been a popular dealer. No doubt he often cried about it all the way to the bank. His selling prices (going back as far as 1964) were often ludicrous. As one might readily surmise, there is nothing like selling something for $50 that is readily available for $10 that breeds a certain degree of contempt. However, as Rogofsky said in his own words, he did not force anyone to buy from him.

Rogofsky's letter prompted a reply from Hamilton. It was not particularly sympathetic. Among other matters, Hamilton argued that Rogofsky should not be in the business if he were not prepared to write off some profit. He proceeded to chastise Rogofsky over unfairly grading his merchandise, charging fantastic prices, and profiteering. Considering that Hamilton has never been known for his lavish generosity, it was not unlike a pot calling the kettle black.

Evidently Rogofsky did not care for the insult. To avoid more embarrassment, he informed Blair that he no longer wished to receive WE. He would take his advertising elsewhere. Curiously, Hamilton also turned on Blair a short time later.

With the appearance of WE #100-101-102, March 1973, Blair suspended publication. It was not without coincidence that he announced the creation of the National Central Bureau (NCB). The new entity expanded the scope and coverage of WSA and WRB. With his publishing chores gone, Blair concentrated on the problem of mail fraud in fandom.

It was about this time that I became personally acquainted with Blair. In the summer of 1973, I was recovering from surgery to repair a hernia sus-

WE #80, June 1971. Undoubtedly, this is one of the most unusual fanzine covers ever published. The African looming over the exhausted mimeograph machine is symbolic of the publication making the transition to photo-offset reproduction. It was a big deal at the time.

tained on a construction job. During this time I was forced to sit at home for several months and do nothing.

About the middle of August, I received the final issue of *WE* in the mail. As it was, I had been out of collecting for about two years. I had not ordered the issue. With plenty of spare time on my hands, I read the issue from cover to cover.

A few weeks later, I wrote to Blair requesting advertising and subscription information. I did not know that publication had been suspended. A short time later, I received a two-page reply from Blair, bringing me up to date about the new National Central Bureau. He enclosed membership application forms. Obviously, Blair was looking for recruits.

I completed the forms and returned them to Blair. He rapidly processed my application. In no time at all, I became WSA #334. Initially, I didn't understand all the particulars. About October 1, 1973, I placed a call to Blair to discuss these matters. Being an overly curious young man, I had a dozen questions, which Blair answered with the patience of Job.

During 1974, Blair and I talked on the phone at least once a month. The conversations often lasted for more than an hour.

Through these conversations, correspondence, and a few exchanges of recorded messages on cassette tape, we became friends. In some respects, I probably knew him better than anyone in fandom.

I was often privy to his innermost thoughts. I am sad to say that only one of his cassette messages has endured the passing of time. The rest are long since lost. Now and then I listen to it. It never fails to rekindle memories of pleasant times. The following is an abridged transcript of that recording, dated May 25, 1974:

Hello, Ron . . .

It seems one of the mistakes I make on my tapes is to begin too soon, so part of my beginning discussion is cut off. I hope this is not so with this particular tape. Thursday evening is an excellent evening for me to tape, since the family is usually away. And, as you said in your tape that I should receive it today, I did. This is the one hundred and twenty-second day of 1974 and I have just finished filing the one hundred thirty-fourth mail-fraud complaint, by issuance of notice to the postal inspection service and the parties involved. So, you see by the end of the year, I anticipate some five hundred cases for this year alone.

Yes, two grandchildren are expected in the due course of time and a few months apart. My daughter in Kentucky will give birth first. My daughter in West Virginia will follow by a few months. We're hopeful that everything goes well with both of them. In fact, we would like to visit them. I might just do that about the time that Houstoncon is in process. That would be a good time to be out of town, don't you think. I'm not too popular with those people!

No, I am not mechanically inclined. I am mechanical in no way whatsoever, and probably can't screw a bracket on the wall. I simply don't have that ability. It's out of my category.

Now, you were talking about your 1967 Mercury, on April the 6th at a shopping center near us, Mrs. Stan was in the curb lane among three lanes of traffic, when some goofball woman shot across all three lanes and Mrs. Stan hit her broadside. It totaled our 1966 Rambler, four on the floor.

So, the insurance company hurried out here to deposit a check in my hand for the damage. Unfortunately, the damage was greater than the value of the car, so they paid me the full value of the car. Then, I went out and got myself a 1964 Chrysler 300. Chrysler has always been my favorite car. Since I did not want to spend a lot of money on a car, I got this at a bargain.

I bought it from a young fellow from Indiana who had come down here. The job he had been promised didn't turn out to be what he was told. He hung on and tried to change jobs. But the fact that he was new in the territory kind of did him in. After all, it's that way everywhere. Finally, as things got tighter and tighter, he couldn't do anything about his circumstances except keep plugging away trying to get a job. The brakes got bad on the car. He finally decided to park the car because he didn't have any money to fix it.

He finally decided to sell the car and I bought it for a little of nothing. I put the new brakes on it. It cost me fifty-eight dollars for turning one drum and replacing one drum. So, I'm very pleased with it. The car runs smooth as can be and has power to spare. It's as good as the Rambler was, and those are pretty speedy.

Now, about Oklahoma City and Tulsa: I have been through, around, and in and out of those cities many times. I am very familiar with them. Of course, each time I go through there, there are more freeways, changes of freeways, and so on. The places keep changing all the time. Hold on . . . that's my telephone! You can hear it ringing. Let me answer it. . . .

Okay, here I am again. That was a call from New York dealing with Arnold Meyrowitz. Now, I wonder who that is?! Boy, I tell you, there are more cases on Arnold Meyrowitz. Good old Arnie! One of these days we will hang him from the nearest telephone pole, if the government doesn't do something with him. It's like Howard Siegel said in his "Comic Collector's Corner" column in *RBCC*. He said the government is too damned stupid to lock Meyrowitz up and throw away the key. I'm inclined to agree with Howard. It really is bad!

Incidentally, a good friend of mine lives there in Oklahoma City. He's a member of the bureau also. He's one of your local attorneys. His name is Eric Jonathan Groves. I mention that because he and I have conversations from time to time about certain things. Now, the area you live in is very beautiful. I have always liked Oklahoma City and have considered moving there at one time or another.

Your five-dollar dog sounds very interesting . . . a combination German shepherd and Irish setter. That's really something. Now, let me tell you something about dogs in this respect: I don't know if I've ever told you or not, but I have a hundred-and-eighty-pound blue Great Dane. He's now almost ten years old. I've been out of the dog business at least that long.

Let me tell you about an old-fashioned house-breaking procedure. You might consider this and try it out on your dog. I have never found that it failed to be successful when you use it correctly. This is the process: First, put newspapers down on the linoleum, which in most instances will be the kitchen floor. Then you keep running the dog to the papers. Each time he wets or dirties on it, you take up the top layer of paper and dispose of it. Leave the next layer or two there because it retains the smell. You put fresh papers under it so it doesn't soak through on the floor.

Then, after what you consider a reasonable period of time, which might be a few days, a week, or whatever, you keep moving the papers further out; like from the kitchen to the porch, from the porch into the yard. Eventually, you eliminate the papers and the dog still goes out in the yard. Simple thought, isn't it? I've found it very successful over a period of years. Try it!

I'm glad that you are going to attend Houstoncon, although Houstoncon is probably my main reason for being absent from Houston at that time. As you know, I avoid personal contact with members of fandom. As I explained in my letter to members of the Bureau, the fact is, I'm technically in the mail-order business and would like to keep it that way. This is because of my interest in my family and the various other things that I'm involved in. Perhaps, someday I'll make an exception. But I really am tied up with so many things that, except for a phone call here and there, I don't have time to entertain.

I'll be perfectly frank about it, it was just like the time that Bruce Hamilton flew into Dayton and spent the evening with us. Yes, it's true: I enjoyed Bruce's company and the fact that he was there, but it sure wrecked my schedule for the rest of the week. After all, I have all this work to do. There is nobody else to do it. I really don't like to take the time to do other things because of the amount of work I have to handle. Now, I handle three times as much as I ever did. So, you can see my point.

Referring to your statement regarding *Ecclesiastes,* the third chapter, I agree with you. It's very interesting. Perhaps in the next tape or the one after that, I will take up some biblical references which might be of interest to you.

Concerning *One Stormy Night* by the Mystic Moods Orchestra, I certainly appreciate your sending it to me. In the future, if you are able to send me a couple more, I certainly won't object. The type and style of music is of interest to me. Like you, I enjoy it. So, it looks like we have a number of things in common.

I had numerous record albums but most of them were destroyed in the fire on January 14th. The heat just melted them and that was it. But there were a couple of bundles that I had packed when moving from Dayton to Houston that I never did unpack. They were sitting off in a corner. That's all that I have left.

Isn't it funny how things are coincidental? It makes one wonder. For example, you and Steve Barrington were talking about the cassette adapter to record telephone conversations. I bought one, yesterday. The only difference was, I only paid a dollar nineteen for mine at Radio Shack. I also bought one of those telephone amplifying cradles that you set your instrument in, that has a speaker you talk in and out of. I need this because my hearing is not as good as it used to be.

Boy, one thing happened today; I've sworn off all long-distance phone calls. I got my bill for last month. As I've mentioned before, my phone bill arbitrarily averages about two hundred dollars, but this one was for three hundred! That did it! I sent in the check this afternoon and said at that same time, that's it: no more phone calls. This has to be. The bureau is a nonprofit thing and that one phone bill put us in the red . . . deep! So, I'm going to have to skip the phone calls and fall back to cassette tapes which are much cheaper. Even if I send them air special (which costs about a dollar), I'm still ahead.

Your idea of taking your cassettes and rerecording them reel-to-reel is a very good idea. But you could say you're doing this for posterity, rather than such things as a Watergate scandal. After all, there is nothing political here. This is not an ex parte situation in fandom.

I'm glad that you talked to Paul Kowtuik who publishes *The Journal.* Strangely enough, I just got a card from him saying that he had talked to you. But he didn't say what about, and you didn't either, but so much for that. I'm glad you like *The Journal* and you feel that it is well done.

About Paul's problems with the mail strike in Canada: It was over two days ago in all provinces except Quebec. In Quebec, it ended yesterday. All mail is moving again both to and from Canada. So, the worst of it is over.

About *Inside Comics* #1, you said you caroused that little fine print and found me mentioned on pages 4, 9, 14, 33, 34. There isn't any doubt about it, the publisher is a publicity hound as far as I'm concerned.

On the Marvel comics original art rip-off, I think his interests are strictly to gain publicity and increase his circulation. I don't believe that justice enters the picture with him at all. There is nothing in his makeup, or anything he has written or said that has anything to do with justice being done.

However, there is one point that I must disagree with you on. Isn't this strange, I'm going to disagree with you. And that is, quote, the guy who signs the checks owns the artwork. That's the legal aspect of the matter. If you are employed by Bill to do artwork, and Bill pays you per hour, per day, per week, or per diem, the artwork is the property of Bill as your employer.

It is only right that the comics industry own the original art these artists are paid to do. That's their job. But the effort that results from it belongs to the publishers unless, and this is the exception, that they are paid on a commission basis. I doubt that very much. I doubt they are paid on the basis of how many of their strips, cartoons, are sold. Then, the dollars and cents revenues would have to be broken down like shares of stock. It would have dividends on it. Hold on just a minute, I have another interruption. . . .

Now, today is Friday. The interruption was due to the family arriving home. I hadn't seen or heard them until they walked in on me. So, I stopped recording at that point. In order to get this out to you, I had better finish the mail. It is now one-thirty, so I had better wind things up to get the mail over to the post office by three o'clock.

So, I'm going to let the rest of this ride and pick up on the next tape where I left off here. I will send this airmail, in hopes that you get it on Saturday. . . .

You probably noticed from the informality of the discussion that Blair and I talked about many things far removed from the problems of fandom. I often found these discussions more interesting than avocational matters. Blair was a

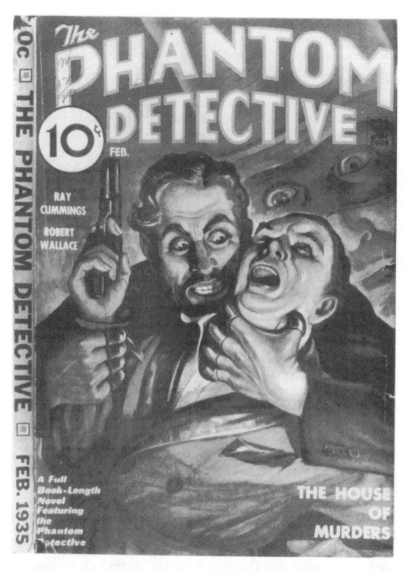

Stanley Blair would never admit it, but I suspect he had been a pulp reader during his youth. It might explain his affinity for the pulp collectors. This cover of *WE* #85 was a particular favorite of his.

man well versed in the vicissitudes of life and I learned a great deal from him. Blair and I never met face to face. What I remember most about him was his distinctive voice. He spoke clearly, using precise vowels and consonants. I suspect he had considerable experience in public speaking. His laugh was hearty.

To the best of my knowledge, only three members of fandom (Bruce Hamilton, Bob Sampson, and Manuel Seguin) ever laid eyes on Blair. The meetings occurred in the early 1970s. Each described Blair as being in his late fifties, short, stocky, balding, and resembling actor W.C. Fields. Hamilton went so far as to insinuate the physical similarity included a bulbous red nose.

I observed the evolution of the National Central Bureau almost from its beginning. The need for such an institution was valid. In a very short time, Blair had the new organization running like a Swiss watch. Blair had a gift for public relations. Soon, dozens of articles by Blair appeared in fanzines and it became fashionable to be a WSA member.

On November 20, 1973, Blair began to publish official reports. Today they make for dull reading, as much of the content is little more than a dry recitation of information. These reports were sold to members, at a cost of $1 each. The reports contained a National Warning Alert Advisory, a Consult the Bureau First listing, and a compilation of Complaints Filed and Disposition. These matters related to people who were in the process of being naughty. It all boiled down to an official "blacklist" of people suspected of mail fraud.

Each report also contained a listing of new members, plus articles about the official business of the Bureau or other matters of topical interest.

Blair was not a gifted writer. His penchant for indulging in the use of paralegal terminology often made for difficult reading. Because most of his readers had not been to law school, they had trouble understanding the legal terms. This included me. The best that can be said about Blair's writing is that it sounded very official.

The first report told of the suspension of a WSA member. It seemed this fellow had swindled another member, thereby trading in his white hat for something in a darker variety. It was the first time a member had been booted out of the fraternity. It was a dark day that left one feeling that nothing is sacred.

Then, on January 14, 1974, tragedy struck when Blair's home was devastated by fire. Fortunately no one was injured but the holocaust destroyed his clothing, furniture, and personal possessions. The National Central Bureau office was situated in a spare bedroom, and the fire destroyed most of the office equipment, fixtures, documents, and files of the Bureau.

Had Blair been a superstitious man, he might have wondered which of the thousand Hindu deities he had offended. Instead, he was remarkably philosophical about the ordeal. The thing that bothered Blair most was the loss of his houseplants, especially the African violets. Blair picked up the pieces and went on. It was not the end of the world.

NCB Report #3, January 20, 1974, contained a comprehensive article by Blair entitled "IF YOU HAVE A FIRE . . . WHAT TO DO . . . HOW TO PREVENT A FINANCIAL LOSS . . . KNOW YOUR RIGHTS." The title was a trifle unwieldy, but the article contained much useful information. It dealt with reconstructing your life in the aftermath of a fire, along with sound advice on dealing with the insurance company, restoration contractors, and insurance adjusters. One WSA member, an attorney, was so impressed with the article that he kept a copy in his safe-deposit box for future reference.

NCB Report #5, March 20, 1974, dealt with the formation of the National Central Bureau Publishers Alliance (NCBPA). The first members were:

Alan Light, *The Buyer's Guide for Comics Fandom*
Paul Kowtuik, *The Journal*
Gordon B. Love, *Rocket's Blast–Comicollector*
Nils Hardin, *Xenophile*

The formation of this alliance was a tribute to Blair's diplomatic skill. There was little love between three of the members, and the fourth had as much in common with the other three as an ostrich would have with a flock of penguins. As a group, they had difficulty agreeing on the time of day. However, they might have made an interesting barbershop quartet.

The Publishers Alliance was significant because it gave Blair an instrument to stop future mail fraud. After a person had been sufficiently naughty, Blair issued a "request for stop advertising" to the NCBPA. The culprit then found himself in the position of not being able to advertise in the major collectors' journals. It instantly curtailed his mischief.

During this time, Blair and *TBG* publisher Alan Light became personal friends. Blair received unlimited space in *TBG* for his various articles and columns. In return, Light frequently called upon Blair for advice in matters of business.

A short time later, Blair designated *TBG* as the "Official Organ of NCB." This meant that Light had almost exclusive use of Blair's articles. This had a positive effect on *TBG*'s circulation as many WSA members subscribed to follow their leader.

An unusual situation developed before the publication of *NCB Report #6*, April 1974. It would seem that WSA had a traitor in its midst. This unspeakable cad divulged confidential information to someone outside the Bureau.

If such an act appears insignificant, it was. To try to explain such a trifle is not unlike shooting at mosquitoes with a shotgun. It doesn't make a lot of sense. However, much of NCB's official business was conducted under a veil of secrecy. In theory, the Bureau's reports were for the eyes of members only.

BEST WISHES
TO STAN
AND WE
FROM
RUSSELL
MYERS
1972

Acting like a true gentleman (and a good friend), cartoonist Russell
Myers contributed this special cover for *WE* #89, December 1972.
© 1972 by the Chicago Tribune

We were supposed to keep it to ourselves. To further augment the plot, a clause in the consent agreement (signed by every member) specified the point in black and white.

Well, for whatever reason, some member squealed. The word was out that Blair wrote nasty things about people in his reports. Then, one of the subjects threatened Blair with a lawsuit. Blair was not concerned. A complete record of that person's misbehavior was on file. It could stand examination under scrutiny if it came to that. It was all true. However, it broke Blair's heart to discover one of his chosen flock was a blabbermouth.

Sadly, Blair was never quite the same. His behavior began to change. A sense of creeping paranoia clouded his judgment. Much of it was due to Blair working himself into a state of exhaustion. It made little sense to me at the time. I realize now that Blair probably suffered from a martyr complex. The harder he worked, the sicker he became. With illness, his thinking became increasingly irrational.

In our telephone conversations, Blair frequently spoke of how tired he was. Blair needed a rest. His wife and family pleaded with him to slack up, or quit altogether. He refused to listen to them, or me. Occasionally, he spoke of chest pains. Sometimes he had difficulty breathing. Obviously, Blair had heart problems. I earnestly feared for his life. It was as if he were trying to commit suicide by working himself to death.

Unfortunately, there is little that can be done to counteract the martyr complex. These individuals are compelled to sacrifice themselves for what they perceive as a noble cause. Trying to talk them out of it is an exercise in futility. Blair was no exception.

In this period, Blair and Alan Light began a nasty squabble with another fan publisher, setting off a chain reaction of controversy that lasted for years. Before it ended, Blair alienated many of his avid supporters.

Dr. Karl A. Menninger had some interesting comments on the subject of martyrs in his book, *Man Against Himself*:

> The behavior of many martyrs is essentially self-destructive, whether the victim is regarded as a saint, a hero, a psychiatric patient, or a foolish friend.
>
> Psychiatry is interested in examining the personality makeup and psychological mechanisms whereby the chief satisfaction in life is derived from suffering or deprivation. The paradox of joy out of pain is one of the crucial enigmas of psychology.
>
> Repeated opportunities occur for the study of clinical examples of martyrdom, characterized by an incapacity to accept or enjoy the pleasures of life and a compulsion to get into pitiable situations and derive comfort from the sympathy aroused by this plight.

It has been remarked that unnatural curbing of instinctual impulses tends to shrivel the personality and weaken the capacity for social adaptation. It is generally believed that severe restriction of normal physical pleasures leads to impairment of the qualities of good humor, generosity, frankness, and energy. To a certain extent this is true.

In martyrdom the individual thinks himself, portrays himself, or actually causes himself to be the victim of cruelty at the hands or circumstances of another person. This accounts for an element of guilt and self-punishment which seems to be one of the motives in martyrdom.

How much this applied to Blair's situation is a matter of speculation. However, the similarity of circumstances appears too great to have been a mere coincidence.

The fourteenth report, dated December 20, 1974, contained a brief financial statement. NCB's finances were in sad shape. The bottom line was that NCB sustained a loss of $420.95 for the year. Much of it was due to Blair's handling mail-fraud complaints from nonmembers. Many of those pikers neglected to reimburse Blair for the actual expenses incurred in their behalf.

Oddly, he didn't seem to care. Blair did not like to bother with administrative matters, billing in particular. It was not good business by any stretch of the imagination, but it was the way Blair did things.

Few people realized that Blair had little money of his own. Various family members saw to it that he had a roof over his head. Blair used the money he made from publishing WE (thousands of dollars) and applied it to NCB's financial losses. It was true. Blair was generous to a fault.

On December 12, 1974, Blair offered an interesting proposal to me:

I am setting up a new letterhead with new departments and divisions. How would you like to be Assistant to the Director, NCB Convention Alliance Division?

Of course, I was flattered. I accepted without a moment's hesitation. The initial plan called for the new division to be implemented in the spring of 1975. However, it did not work out that way.

The fifteenth (and final) NCB Report was published on January 20, 1975. They were discontinued due to Blair's deteriorating health. The timing coincided with the conclusion of the Arnold Meyrowitz case. On June 11, 1974, Meyrowitz was arrested in Boston while trying to withdraw funds from a bank account. Using the name Robert Woods, he had busied himself defrauding coin collectors.

Meyrowitz was arraigned in federal court on December 23, 1974, before Judge Caffrey. Meyrowitz pleaded guilty to charges of mail fraud. He was sentenced to two years in prison. With Meyrowitz safely behind bars, Blair felt his job was done.

There were still loose ends that Blair wanted to finish before settling back in a rocking chair. He planned to retire at the end of the year. Blair informed me of his decision in a telephone conversation on February 7, 1975. Then he dropped a real bombshell in my lap. He asked: "How would you like to be my successor as NCB Director?"

I had never conceived of such of thing. My first thought was that Blair had totally lost his mind. I had no qualifications for the job. At the age of twenty-one, I barely had sense enough to come in out of the rain. Most WSA members did not know me from Adam. In collecting circles, I was as obscure as a person could be and still cast a shadow.

My first answer was no. I suggested that he find someone more qualified. A few evenings later, we talked about it again. If nothing else, Blair was persistent. He seemed to think I would make a fine replacement. He claimed experience wasn't necessary. That was true. A more experienced person would not have touched the job with a ten-foot pole.

When Blair wanted to, he could charm a snake. He really poured on the peanut oil, telling me what a remarkable young man I was. All I needed to be a leader was a little instruction. He would teach me all I needed to know.

Ordinarily, when a person gives you that kind of spiel he is trying to sell you the Brooklyn Bridge. Unfortunately, I bought it. To make a long story short, I agreed to take the job. It was a decision I would later regret. For better or for worse, it changed my life.

Blair and I began to make plans. He planned to spend six months tutoring me about NCB's policies and procedures. Later, I would work with him in Houston for a few weeks to gain some personal experience. As it is with the best-laid plans of mice and men, none of these things came to pass.

In early April, Blair suffered a minor stroke. He did not require hospitalization. However, his doctor strongly suggested that Blair retire, as another stroke might be fatal. Finally Blair decided to listen. From my point of view, the timing was terrible. Lacking the good sense to turn and walk away, I agreed to take over on July 1, ready or not.

Blair had several other friends who offered to help. Under the circumstances, we agreed that it would be best to include several of them and divide the heavy workload.

Blair seemed to sense my reservations about running the organization by myself. Therefore, he persuaded Avery B. Klein to assume ownership of the Bureau through a lifetime grant-in-trust. As an attorney and certified public account, Klein was vastly more experienced with administrative matters than

I. Of course, that says very little as I knew next to nothing.

Blair announced his retirement in the July 1, 1975, issue of *TBG*. His own words tell the story:

A SPECIAL MESSAGE TO THE MEMBERS OF
FANDOM: MEMBERS OF N C B **

THE BUREAU HAS JUST FINISHED ITS FIFTH AND FINAL
YEAR OF OPERATION
THIS IS MY REPORT TO YOU

Due to my age, condition of health, an impossible workload (that of four people), and the continuous financial losses year after year, it is no longer possible to continue this bureau's operation.

TO REVIEW THE RECORD . . . In five years of operation, this bureau has handled some 3,000 complaints from both fans and members totaling some $75,000.00—of which some $40,000.00 has been recovered and returned to the complainants. In the same period, the bureau has handled over 30,000 pieces of correspondence . . . all as a one man operation.

Service has been provided to all—without thought to either my time or my expense. Not only have I provided 100% of my time and energies FREE but I have contributed the limited personal funds available. In spite of this, I have originated and devised programs and procedures that have provided (and will continue to provide) you protection from those who would engage in "sharp practices and fraudulent schemes" in order to obtain either your money or merchandise.

BUT NOW THE TIME HAS COME for me to consider my own personal aspect—of the demands made upon my time and energy. To continue would seriously jeopardize my own health. Therefore, common sense and good thinking establish the fact that I must appear to be selfish and halt the operation of this bureau for my own sake. Working seven days a week on the average of 15 to 18 hours cannot be continued.

Although this bureau (NCB) has ceased to exist right now, I have nevertheless provided that my ORIGINAL programs as devised for your protection and benefit (WSA and WRB) will continue so that you may know what you can count on in the future. The following individuals have already worked in some capacity in various assignments for the bureau and have chosen accordingly to carry out the remaining programs:

Fan cartoonist David Heath, Jr., produced this one and only installment of "The Man From NCB," published in *NCB Report* #6, April 20, 1974.

IN CONCLUSION . . . I have enjoyed working with the majority of fandom; and it is gratifying that I have been able to play in some small part in the betterment of fandom, as well as in the accomplishment of deterring numerous individuals who would take either your money or your merchandise. I strongly urge all WSA members to maintain their membership in the program—become active participants and show fandom that my five years of work have not been for nothing. You owe it to your fellow collectors to do so. Non-members of the WSA Program look to you as the criterion in business dealings. Don't let them down. Hold fast to the code of ethics—it is a life line in the increasing activities perpetuated upon fandom by the rip off artists.

So, without further ado, Stanley R. Blair, champion of the little guy, kissed his horse and rode off into the sunset. It is easy to imagine Randolph Scott and Hopalong Cassidy waiting on the far side of the horizon. The pathos of the scenario was considerable, but the story was not over. . . .

In the early 1970s, it seemed like half the people attending comic book conventions had hair down to their shoulders. Some of them still do. It was a sign of the times, along with love beads, peace signs, and psychedelic images. Here, WSA member Steve Lewis could have passed for a rock-and-roll musician. It's kind of funny how most hippies have grown gray-haired and quaint . . . that is if they still have their hair. I wish I did.

—from the collection of Richard Garrison

CHAPTER THREE

Of People and Problems

*A man is likely to mind his own business when it is worth minding.
When it is not, he takes his mind off his own meangingless affairs by
minding other people's business.*

—Eric Hoffer, *The True Believers*

Although I knew nothing of such matters at the time, I came to realize that the WSA Program is a study in the theory of social value. It holds that all values are psychological. Everything in the individual mind has been influenced by processes in the minds of others. The machinery of thought is a social attribute.

It begins with a realization that all of us are social beings. Through our interactions with other people, we develop primary relationships. These are usually members of our family or close friends. We also develop secondary relationships with those we know less well. The relationships combine to form a socialization process that shapes us into the people we are.

As members of society, we often become members of specific subcultures. Every social group has a culture of its own. To function, it must have goals and values. A central issue that every group faces is a struggle to maintain identity. Ordinarily, this is accomplished by promoting values and beliefs called ideologies.

Ideologies are universal in that they are found in every culture. The power of an ideology to mold people's passions and behavior is well documented. History is filled with deeds performed in the name of some ideology, both good and bad.

In most cultures, values are established by tradition. The form is determined by the environment. In some instances, values are publicized to indicate virtue. This practice was evident among WSA members who displayed a membership logo in advertising.

Symbols (such as the WSA logo) give unity to a culture. As a public expression of values, they form the focal point around which action takes place. The essence of the matter is that societies do not run on their own accord. The activities of any group require direction. There must always be a degree of decision making. Decisions are allocated among the membership of the society. The allocation of decision making is called authority.

For two and a half years I served as Administrator of the WSA program, a position that carried a power of influence and a nominal degree of prestige. For the first time in my life, I was in a position to exercise authority. As a young man with no experience in such matters, it was often a trying ordeal. In some respects, I felt a little like the apostle Paul must have when he wrote to the Corinthians: "When I came to you brothers, I did not come with eloquence or superior wisdom."

About a year earlier, I had become interested in organized bartering. Bubbling with youthful enthusiasm and a misguided sense of direction, I founded the International Fandom Inflation Control Club. In the 1979 edition of the *Fandom Directory,* fan historian Chester Cox noted:

> The IFICC was the first reaction to the spiraling cost of back issue collecting. With a small number of members, it is remarkable that it brought the problem of inflation out into the open when the problem wasn't even being admitted, and forced it into fandom's collective mind.

Despite all its crowning glory, IFICC lasted only a few years. It remains a minor footnote in the history of fandom.

Following Stanley Blair's retirement, most WSA members wondered if the organization would survive under new management. The concern was legitimate. I had doubts of my own.

In the beginning, most of the staff members were strangers. Before we could begin the matter of reorganization, it was necessary to become acquainted. During the first week of July 1975, Bill Cole, Harry Hopkins, Avery Klein, and myself got to know each other in a series of telephone conversations. I still have painful memories of the telephone bill.

My first conversation was with the Trustee, Avery Klein. His professional credentials were quite impressive as Klein was both an attorney and a certified public accountant. His law practice specialized in income tax cases. As a sideline, Klein sold plastic bags to collectors for protecting collectibles.

For all practical purposes, Klein owned the WSA Program by means of a lifetime grant-in-trust from Blair. I'm sure Klein must have sensed that I was green as grass. Initially, I worried that Klein might want to exercise authority over me. That was probably the last thing on his mind. Klein was too busy taking care of his own business to be preoccupied with WSA. Despite my youth and inexperience, Klein seemed to have faith in my ability to run things. Klein and I reached an early understanding. We agreed that routine administrative matters would be left entirely to my discretion. In return, I promised to consult him before implementing new policy or changing personnel. It proved to be a satisfactory arrangement.

The next evening, I spoke with Harry Hopkins for the first time. Hopkins was a young Air Force officer stationed in South Carolina. As WSA Registrar, he was supposed to be my assistant. It never quite worked out that way. Hopkins became more partner than assistant and more friend than partner. A steady stream of communication soon flowed between us. Many times we discussed problems, starting with opposing viewpoints. Most of the time we reached an amiable agreement. Our working relationship was a good example of two heads being better than one.

We had our differences. At times, I drove Hopkins crazy because of my methodical approach to people and problems. I preferred to deal with one situation at a time and was not very good at delegating authority. On the other hand, Hopkins knew how to organize and delegate. Due to his military training, he was used to getting things done in a hurry. However, in spite of it all we somehow managed to work together well.

Finally, I met Bill Cole, the WSA Special Services Coordinator. Cole merchandised the WSA logo rubber stamps and a kit of form letters used by members. On occasion, Cole helped with investigation research, when asked by Klein or myself.

By profession, Cole was a safety engineer. He owned a fire and safety equipment company in Boston. Like Klein, Cole supplemented his income by selling plastic bags. Cole collected Walt Disney comics. I still remember his cute advertising slogan: "For the best deal on Ducks nobody is better than us."

In the beginning, Alan Light, Joe Stoner, and Art Miller were also members of the staff. Stoner and Miller had been personal friends of Stanley Blair. By virtue of friendship, Blair placed them in figurehead positions.

Alan Light, however, was a different matter. Despite his being Blair's handpicked choice to direct the WSA Publishers Alliance, it became apparent that Light was more concerned with running his publishing business than being an altruist. The truth of the matter is Light had good sense.

In the beginning, Light and I were separated by ideological differences. He was a businessman looking to make a profit where I was a crusader interested in saving the world. We did not particularly like one another.

It had been Light's custom to display his WSA membership and Publishers Alliance logos on the title page of *TBG*. About a month after Blair's retirement, he stopped. I knew something was up, so I called to ask what was going on.

Light gave me an earful. It seemed he had experienced a change of heart. Light pointed out in no uncertain terms that WSA was dead on its feet. He felt that, without Blair, WSA was nothing. Thus he had no further use for the Publishers Alliance or WSA. Light intended to mind his own business and suggested that I do likewise. In other words, he told me to buzz off.

I shouldn't have, but I took Light's rebuff personally. To say I was insulted would be putting it mildly. In my opinion, Light had a short memory. Regardless of what he thought about me, I felt that he owed Blair more fidelity.

This situation brought about my first official powwow with Avery Klein. I was so aggravated with Light that I could spit. Had the matter been left entirely to me, I would have done something foolish. Fortunately, Klein had a cooler head. He felt there was nothing to be gained by driving a permanent barrier between *TBG* and WSA. Klein convinced me that the matter needed to be handled diplomatically.

Diplomacy was a new experience for me. According to legend, the first diplomats were angels who carried messages between heaven and earth. However, my feelings were far from angelic. At Klein's suggestion, I wrote Light a polite letter, accepting his resignation as Administrator of the Publishers Alliance. Gritting my teeth, I told Light that I had no hard feelings. The truth of the matter is that I'd have taken great pleasure in giving Light a swift kick in the pants.

About a week later, I received a reply from Light. He said he was pleased there were no hard feelings and there were none on his part, either. Light invited me to contribute WSA columns for publication in *TBG* as Blair had done. I agreed to do so, with some gratitude.

There were deeper implications to this situation than appointing a new Administrator. Without *TBG*, the Publishers Alliance didn't amount to much. Of the four original members, only three remained. For example, *The Journal* was no longer published. *RBCC* had become a fanzine. *Xenophile* was 95 percent pulp-oriented and very few fraud cases involved the pulp collectors. The rest of the Publishers Alliance members were small fanzine publishers who could not have sold a page of advertising if their life depended on it.

Without *TBG*, the Publishers Alliance was little more than a club for fanzine publishers. I remember thinking that I had made a mess of the situation. As a replacement for Light, I appointed Mike Robertson, a former fan publisher, to the post. Such as it was, it was my first official act as Administrator.

Besides tangling with Light, my first month on the job didn't amount to much. I received my first article of WSA mail on July 28. The letter was forwarded from Blair. It was from a man named Channing Corbin, a member of the National Crime Writers Association. It read:

Fan cartoonist Matt Feazell contributed this nifty cover for the *International Fandom Inflation Control Club Newsletter* #2, April 1975. A decade later, Feazell became quite popular in fan circles, drawing curious "stick figure" cartoons that appeared in various small press publications.

Dear Mr. Blair:

Taking notice of your agency in the most recent issue of NWC, I thought I would query you on a matter of research.

I have been busily engaged in checking into a man's background and the following is a basic and brief synopsis: ALBERT HOWARD FISH, born 1870 in Washington, D.C. Relocated to NYC where he married in 1898. The man was a nonentity up until December, 1934, where he was arrested for the abduction and murder of ten year old GRACE BUDD. Fish was tried in Westchester County, N.Y. in 1935, found guilty and executed in Sing Sing Prison in January of 1936.

I have generated a mass of authentic information relating to the trial, the crime, the execution, etc. But I have really been stymied as far as dredging up anything about this man's early childhood. Unfounded rumor has it that he was placed in an orphanage in Washington, D.C.

I am going to persist until I hit pay dirt. Do you have any suggestions? I have the trial transcript, the NY Times clippings, etc. I can use anything available on the subject. I would appreciate hearing from you at your earliest convenience. Thank you.

After reading this letter, I wondered what I was getting myself into. I had no idea why Blair sent the letter to me. Needless to say, I was of no help to Mr. Corbin. I have often wondered if Corbin ever found what he was looking for.

Within a month, my post office box began to fill with mail. Most of it required a reply. Many of the letters were mail-fraud complaints. Since I did not have any of Blair's records, files, or forms, I was in no position to help anyone.

It took Blair two months to sort out the paperwork on his end before the records could be transferred to me. On the first weekend of September 1975, I traveled to Houston to pick up the records. The occasion gave me an opportunity to combine business with pleasure by attending a convention for film fans.

I had planned to pick up the materials from Blair and was looking forward to finally meeting him in person. However, at the last minute, Blair informed me that he would have the materials delivered to my hotel. To this very day, I have often wondered why Blair chose not to meet with me personally. It remains something of a mystery in my mind. Evidently, there was something he wished to keep secret. Late Saturday night, Blair's nephew showed up at the hotel driving a Toyota pickup. As I helped him unload the boxes out on the sidewalk I began to despair over how to stuff eleven large boxes into a 1967 Mercury.

It involved a bit of trial and error but I managed to make it all fit. About noon Sunday, I left Houston for the five-hundred-mile drive back to Oklahoma City. I wasn't sure the car would make it because the rear end was practically sitting on the axle. The worry was for nothing. The car held up fine. About nine o'clock that evening, I unloaded the boxes and moved them into my office.

The next morning, I started to open the boxes and examine the contents. Wondering where to begin, I stood back and puffed on a cigar in total bewilderment. With much trepidation, I opened the flaps of box after box. Some contained office forms. Others had samples of old National Central Bureau correspondence. One box contained the SASE file that WSA members provided for communication purposes. Two boxes contained copies of *NCB Official Reports*. While examining the boxes in this way, I noticed one inscribed "URGENT" with a red magic marker.

I opened the box and discovered a second box inside. It had a notation for me to open it first. The box contained a personal letter from Blair. It read:

MY LAST OFFICIAL ACT AS DIRECTOR OF NCB; WRB; WSA

A PERSONAL MESSAGE TO RON J. FRANTZ

Dear Ron:

I look forward to your developing further the scope and coverage of the WSA Program and its affiliates in the coming years.

I believe that you can do it without any real problem. I am counting on it. The importance of my programs (still operating on the basic principles that were established in 1970) cannot be easily comprehended by the average fan, dealer, or collector. But you seem to have both understanding and comprehension and this in itself leads me to believe it will be tremendously successful under your direction and authority.

There are few words that can be used to express my appreciation for your acceptance of the responsibilities that go with the Administrators job—a thankless one at best—but more than necessary for the betterment of fandom as well as their protection—from which there are many benefits to all.

There have been many times that I have become thoroughly discouraged by the lack of support—either financial or moral—for the time and energy extended to provide these benefits and services. You too will be faced with such feelings from time to time. In my case, I continued on in spite of such apathy on the part of the participants. I am hopeful that you will do so too.

As you know, if it were not for my general condition of health, I would have continued on disregarding all other factors. But as I told you previously, it is no longer possible for me to do so. Even the winding up of the general affairs of the bureau has been an exhausting matter to me.

The eleven boxes of material will provide you with basic information; precedents as established by the bureau; a sampling of matters dealing with complaints from members against fans; complaints from non-members against members; and matters in general between the bureau and its own members.

In conclusion . . .

I can only say that I am glad that you have accepted this responsibility and I am sure that you will do the program justice.

Perhaps it was a sentimental gesture, but I framed the letter and hung it above my desk. It remained there for the duration of my WSA administration. It remains a treasured memento.

By the first of October, I began to realize that I had bitten off more than I could chew. Five hundred pieces of mail were stacked on my desk. I was struggling not only to catch up with the backlog of mail from Blair but also to maintain the incoming flow of new correspondence.

For at least a dozen years, the WSA membership logo was a familiar sight in many nostalgia-oriented journals, from small fanzines to massive tabloid newspapers. Like the Lone Ranger's mask, it was a symbol for justice and fair play. Each member had an individually assigned number.

At the time, I was employed as a salesman for a bottled water company in Oklahoma City. I arrived home about four-thirty every afternoon, very tired. After resting for an hour, I went to work on WSA business. Often, I worked until midnight. Then I would rise at six-thirty the next morning to start again.

After several months of burning the candle at both ends, I started to look like something the cat dragged in. It was murder on my social life. The girl I was dating at the time thought that I had lost my sanity, which was probably the case. My friends and family could not understand why I was doing all the extra work, especially since I was not getting paid for it.

A few years later, I figured out that had I taken a second job working at minimum wage instead of working for free on WSA, I could have made about twelve thousand dollars. That may not sound like a significant amount of money now, but at the time it was a hefty sum. In those days you could buy decent real estate for that kind of money.

I will admit that there was no rational explanation for my behavior. All I can say is the spirit of altruism burned in my blood. In my mind, I was performing a public service that, at the time, was more important to me than pursuing a formal education or career.

Harry Hopkins and Avery Klein had pestered me for months to prepare a direct mailing to the WSA membership and write a column for *TBG*. I was so busy trying to get caught up on the mail that I kept putting them off. Hopkins was anxious to get started in his duties as Registrar. If I had had any sense, I would have boxed up half of that mail and sent it to Hopkins to process. However, for some neurotic reason I wanted to do it all myself. The best I can figure is that I must have been riding a king-sized ego trip.

The incoming mail was giving me no breathing room. I began to dread the daily trips to the post office. About the end of October, Klein got me off the high horse by sending a "do it or else" letter.

So, about the end of October, I wrote my first WSA News & Report column, published in *TBG* #103. By that time, it had been four months since Stanley Blair had retired. Rumors were circulating in fandom that WSA had gone the way of all flesh. I opened the column by announcing in bold letters:

THE WSA PROGRAM IS ALIVE AND WELL!! THE REPORTS
OF OUR DEATH HAVE BEEN GREATLY EXAGGERATED!!

That rumbling noise you just heard was Mark Twain turning over in his grave. I should have been ashamed for the plagiarism. Since I had no experience in writing editorials, the only way I knew to make a point was to shout the message with exclamation points. In fact, I had not written much of anything. My only published work consisted of a few articles for Paul Kowtuik's *Journal,* and the less said about those, the better.

Investors Corporation of America

AVERY B. KLEIN, PRESIDENT
3386 CHALFANT ROAD
SHAKER HEIGHTS, OHIO 44120
—
216 - 921-7678

October 1, 1975
To be published in The Buyer's Guide-
the Official Organ of the WSA PROGRAM

TO WSA PROGRAM MEMBERS AND ALL MEMBERS OF FANDOM:

First allow me to introduce myself to you. As with many of
you, Fandom is a hobby with me even though I am a dealer.
By profession, I am a practicing Attorney and a Certified
Public Accountant licensed for both in the State of Ohio.
I am married and have two sons, ages 3 and 6.

Before retiring effective June 30, 1975, Stanley R. Blair,
selected a very able and energetic crew to carry forward
the WSA PROGRAM and other allainces which he so ably initiated.

During the past several months, RON FRANTZ, the ACTING
ADMINISTRATOR-WSA PROGRAM and his assistants, and BILL
COLE, the ACTING ADMINISTRATOR-WSA PROGRAM-SPECIAL SERVICES
and I have been hard at work assuming the responsibilities
which we accepted from STAN.

Several changes which we have been forced to make because of
a lack of finances to carry on even the barest of programs
are an annual dues structure and initial membership fee for
new members.

Initial Membership Fee......................$5.00
Covers membership certificate, I.D. card, some
mailings to members

Annual Membership Fee......................$2.50
Covers I.D. card and some mailings to members

STAN issued WSA numbers through Number 1000. The initial
membership fee will be applied against all members of fandom
who join and are issued numbers beginning with 1001. In
addition, all WSA members, except first year members who have
paid the $5.00 initial membership fee, will be assessed the
$2.50 annual membership fee. Failure the pay the annual
dues will result in suspension of membership.

This notice regarding WSA membership dues was published in
an October 1975 issue of *TBG*. Strange as it may sound, it really
annoyed Stanley Blair. Years later, Blair testified to the FBI that
the notice never appeared in print. I beg to differ. Not that it
matters much now.

In that first column, I briefly explained what I had been doing, trying to justify the months of silence. The biggest problem facing WSA at the time was a lack of revenue. Quite frankly, the organization was broke. Up until that point, I personally paid the bills for printing, postage, office supplies, and telephone. By the first of November, I had shelled out more than $500. I knew this couldn't go on.

I discussed the matter of finances with Cole, Klein, and Hopkins. We agreed that the only way to make ends meet was to assess members for dues. We knew it might create a furor because the members had been getting a free ride for years. Stanley Blair gave his services away, paying the bills out of his own pocket when all else failed. Personally, I was not that generous. It was necessary for WSA to pay its own way. Dues seemed to be the logical solution.

Because we expected some resistance, Klein insisted on making the announcement in *TBG*. I estimated that about 50 percent of the WSA membership subscribed to *TBG*, meaning about 500 members should have seen the notice. Only twenty-six members responded, generating $65. It wasn't much but at least it was a step in the right direction. Klein and Cole each chipped in loans of $100, which took some of the financial burden off of me.

Actually, the dues program didn't create much of a stink. There were a few complaints but no one resigned their membership. Most members seemed to understand the predicament. Note the following letter from Frank Hamilton:

Registered letters addressed to me are a rarity, thus when one arrived from WSA my consternation was considerable. While I couldn't recall any nefarious dealings for which I could be prosecuted, my immediate concern was with probable ex-communication from WSA, at the very least due to non payment of membership dues. This is hereby rectified herewith by the enclosed money order, as you have scared the bloody hell out of me. So, until you fully re-instate me I shall wear my number upside down to indicate my fall from grace.

Strangely, the biggest uproar came from Stanley Blair. Following his retirement, Blair moved from Houston to Richwood, West Virginia. One of his daughters lived in the area. Blair suffered from hypertension and wanted to get away from the problems of city living. Blair did not want to be bothered with WSA business. We visited on the phone occasionally but we rarely discussed WSA. I remember one conversation devoted entirely to his new hobby of raising guinea pigs.

About the first of December, I received an unexpected call from Blair. To say the least, he was irate. He demanded to know who gave me the authority to start collecting dues. Blair wanted it stopped. Further, he demanded that we issue refunds and make a public retraction.

Of course, that would have been senseless and I had no intention of doing it. I probably wasn't very diplomatic, but I told Blair that Klein had authorized the dues program and if there was a problem, he needed to take it up with him.

Blair slammed the phone down in my ear. Afterwards, Blair called Klein and read him the riot act. Ever the diplomat, Klein said he would discuss the matter with me and get back to him. A few days later, Klein called to tell me that Blair was upset about the dues and "suggested" we find another way to pay the bills.

To be honest, I was a little pigheaded. My answer was not only no, but hell no! If push came to shove, I was ready to resign. Of course, Klein didn't want that and, I presume, neither did Blair. Klein said he would try to smooth things over with Blair. I guess he did. A short time later, I got a letter from Blair that said, "I don't like this dues business but I guess I can live with it." I've often thought that since I had been paying the bills, that was damned generous of him.

I'm sad to say that my relationship with Blair began to deteriorate. Afterwards, things were never the same between us.

By this time, I was beginning to make a dent in the backlog of mail and could actually begin to see the light of day. After weeks of trial and error, I developed a routine. Upon receipt, I divided all new mail into three piles:

1. Immediate.
2. As soon as possible.
3. At my convenience.

Everything else (including my personal correspondence) had to wait until I could get to it.

Despite what I thought to be a good system, I still managed to alienate a few people. Harry Truman once said, "No matter what you do, there is always going to be some son of a bitch that doesn't like it!" I learned the hard way that he was right. However, most people understood my plight. They realized I had lots of customers and patiently waited their turn.

In the meantime, I continued to plod away. Besides answering the mail, I had to file it for future reference. In the beginning I used cardboard boxes that looked a mess stacked in the corner. Then, I chanced upon a wooden filing cabinet at a garage sale. It stood six feet tall and was made out of redwood and cedar. At one time it had been the property of the U.S. Army. It must have been fifty years old. I bought it for the princely sum of $10.

Naturally, the cabinet had been painted G.I. green and was as ugly as homemade soap. For several weeks, I worked on it in odd moments, stripping off the lacquer-based paint. When it was finally finished, stained and varnished, the cabinet was quite handsome. For the duration of my WSA administration, it housed the records. In fact, I wish I still had it. Not long ago, I saw

For almost three quarters of a century, science fiction fans have busied themselves publishing fanzines. For many writers and artists, it served as a training ground for a future career as a professional. Hundreds have successfully made the transition, or so it would seem. This issue of the *WSFA Journal* from September 1968 featured a delightful cover by Vaughn Bodé.

one like it at an antique store with a price tag of $500.

By the first of the year, it finally penetrated my bullet-proof skull that I couldn't do all the work by myself. The novelty of being in charge had worn off. Spending all of my spare time on this activity had gotten old. It was time to go to the bullpen and bring in a relief pitcher named Harry Hopkins.

As WSA Registrar, Hopkins's primary duties were clerical. He had the dubious task of keeping track of the membership. Considering there were over a thousand members who were constantly on the move, Hopkins had a fine time keeping track of them.

Hopkins had a big advantage over most of us because he had access to a U.S. Air Force computer. Almost no one had personal computers in those days. The PC revolution was still a decade away. None of us dreamed of such marvels as the Internet, which many of us take for granted today.

The WSA membership records we inherited from Blair were as much as two years out of date. It took Hopkins a while to locate everyone. In the process, he fed all the information into a computer. Then, one day, Hopkins sent a computerized list of WSA members in alphabetical, numeric, and zip code order. I don't mind saying that at the time it impressed the hell out of me.

However, Hopkins was a glutton for punishment. He wanted more to do. It became necessary for us to monitor WSA members for compliance in displaying their WSA logo in advertising. It was not my idea. It was a rule Blair conceived while he was running the store. Section one, article eleven, of the WSA membership agreement specified:

> In consideration for the granting of a WSA and assigned number, I will hold forth in all correspondence, advertising (regardless of media), buying, selling and trading, freely and without reservation in all transactions with other fans, such membership in the WSA Program, by display of the program's official logo containing my WSA and assigned number—so that all have recourse when deemed necessary by other parties to my transactions.

I began to derive inspiration from other sources. For example, I became an admirer of William Bennett Monroe, a former professor of municipal government at Harvard University. Monroe wrote:

> Administration is the art of adapting regulations to the foibles of mankind. It is the art of managing cantankerous, obstinate, fickle, and emotional people. Independence in a leader is a virtue, but it must be qualified by a sense of responsibility. Otherwise, it is not leadership but dictation. A successful leader must appeal to the reason of people without forgetting they have emotions. When he appeals to their emo-

tions, he must not lose sight that reason is what gives stability to opinion.

It seemed like good advice and I put it into practice. I began to think before acting. I had no interest in compelling WSA members to display membership logos on advertising. To my way of thinking, it was none of my business whether they displayed a logo or not. Then came that faraway voice in West Virginia insisting that it be done. In what was becoming a habit, Blair complained to Klein. Undoubtedly, Klein knew the world might come to an end if another WSA member failed to display his logo on an advertisement. As a dutiful servant, Klein brought the matter to my attention. I told him that I had no intention of doing it. Subsequently, Klein talked to Harry Hopkins, who volunteered to perform the task.

Hopkins began to monitor all the major ad publications for compliance, along with a lot of little ones. He was more proficient at it than I would have been. Hopkins sent violators a polite "request" to use their WSA logo on all future advertising. Most of the crew clicked their heels together and acquiesced. Unfortunately, two well-known members, Bob Overstreet and Bud Plant, decided to jump ship.

After receiving their letters of resignation, I wrote each a personal letter, asking them to reconsider their decision. It was a futile effort. Both felt that it was time to part ways. Under the circumstances, I couldn't blame them.

On Thanksgiving Day, 1975, I wrote my second WSA News & Report column. It provides some curious insight as to what was going through my mind:

> At this writing, I have now served as Administrator of the WSA Program for nineteen weeks. It has now been eleven weeks since my trip to Houston to retrieve (from Blair) the records and materials pertaining to the program. During this time, I have put in some 600 hours of service to the program.
>
> Without a doubt, this has been the most exasperating period of my life. It is hard to explain the sensations I have felt carrying out the Administrator's job. It is a difficult thing to assume another man's obligations, dedication, and sense of duty. It has been a learning experience. Unlike Stan Blair, I have little experience that qualifies me for a job of this nature. All I have going for me is a high school diploma and a few college hours.
>
> Perhaps you can see what is involved here: not possessing the legal and working knowledge that Stan had, I have had to devise my own ways of doing things. I am still in the midst of reading, absorbing, and learning from the materials provided to me by Stan.

George Bernard Shaw once said, "A man learns to skate by staggering about making a fool of himself. Indeed, he progresses in all things by resolutely making a fool of himself." The following incident is ample proof. It began when I received the following letter:

Dear Ron:

John Doe wrote saying that he had several of the comics that I was looking for. He assured me that they were in good condition. I sent him a check and he sent me the books. They were JUNK! Pages were torn into shreds—big chunks out of the covers—warped—water stained. They were absolute junk. I sent them back several weeks ago, demanding that my money be returned. I have received no communication or refund. I need your help. If I ever run into this creep at a convention, I'll probably break his face! Then, I'll need more help than you can give me. I implore you . . . put this clown out of circulation.

Sincerely,
Richard Roe

Since both men were WSA members, I felt obligated to try to resolve the dispute. I sent John Doe a letter of inquiry. Two days after I sent the letter, I received a second communication from Richard:

Dear Ron:

Only days after I sent you a letter regarding the questionable conduct of John Doe, and asking you to invoke the powers of the WSA to get my money back, I received a letter of explanation and apology from John, along with a refund. You can call off the dogs.

In a matter of days, I received an angry reply from John. He wanted me to chastise Richard for filing a wrongful complaint against him. At the very least, John wanted Richard drummed out of the corps. Before it was all over, I wrote several letters to John and Richard, trying to play peacemaker. The situation went from bad to worse. Had this been the eighteenth century, it might have ended with pistols at dawn. I imagine John and Richard are sworn enemies to this very day.

There is no doubt in my mind that I had made a fool of myself. I learned a good lesson from the experience. In the future, I let all complaints sit on my desk for ten days before asking questions. It was surprising how many times this scenario repeated itself over the next two years.

Things really began to get interesting on December 5, 1975, when I received a phone call from Bill Cole. Cole claimed that WSA member Robert

Montgomery, a competitor in the plastic bag business, had misrepresented the thickness of his bags in advertising. It began an unusual chain of events involving Cole, Montgomery, Avery Klein, Alan Light, Bob Overstreet, and the Federal Trade Commission.

Cole alleged that Montgomery advertised plastic bags in excess of 4.0 mil thick. In fact, they were only 2.2 mil thick. The cutting edge was that Montgomery sold his bags at a lower cost than what Cole (and Klein) sold a 3.0 bag for. Montgomery was cutting into their business.

If true, it was a violation of the WSA Code of Ethics. Cole asked if I would investigate the matter. At my request, Cole sent samples of Montgomery's bags along with samples of his own product. In the meantime, I collected samples from Avery Klein, Robert Bell, the Canadian Comic Bag Company, and everyone else in the plastic bag business. Since the issue of thickness had been raised, it seemed a good opportunity to see if everyone's nose was clean. George Orwell would have adored me.

After collecting all the samples, I asked my father for help because I knew nothing about measuring the thickness of plastic. As a chemist, Dad knew how to do those things. Using a micrometer to measure the bags, he discovered that Cole was right. The thickness of Montgomery's bags had been misrepresented. He also found out that everyone else was accurate in their advertising, within a tenth of a mil or so.

Based on these findings, I issued a statement to Montgomery, requesting an immediate reply. About a week later, I received a letter from Montgomery stating that the bags Dad measured could not have been his. Montgomery promised to send additional samples, along with a statement from his manufacturer.

Two weeks came and went with no word from Montgomery or his manufacturer. Based on the evidence at hand, I instructed Montgomery to alter his advertising or face a suspension of WSA membership.

Meanwhile, Cole became impatient. In a subsequent conversation, I explained what was going on and asked him to bear with me a little longer.

While I was waiting on word from Montgomery, Cole and Klein took matters into their own hands. On January 16, 1976, they filed a joint complaint against Montgomery with the Federal Trade Commission office in Boston. Obviously, they were looking after their own interests. However, it put the WSA Program in an awkward predicament. Cole and I had some heated words about it.

Trying to head the problem off at the pass, I placed a phone call the following morning to Bill McDonough, the FTC representative in Boston. I explained to McDonough that Montgomery, Cole, and Klein were all WSA members and I suggested we try to resolve the situation among ourselves before involving the FTC. McDonough agreed. He explained that it was standard

FTC policy not to intervene in cases when a trade association governed. He agreed to sit on the case for thirty days. I was grateful for his courtesy and cooperation.

Naturally, Klein and Cole were not happy that I had tabled their motion with the FTC. Klein asked for my resignation. When I refused, he threatened to remove me. At that, I said, "Listen, Avery . . . I may not be an attorney, but I recognize a conflict of interest situation when I see one. Obviously, you and Cole have a financial stake in this case. That disqualifies you from personal involvement. As a matter of ethics, you can't represent both yourself and the WSA.

"I'm sorry you don't like the way I've been handling the case. I'm doing what I think is right. Fire me if you want. But if you do, I will raise such a stink to the FTC that you and Cole will be conducting your business wearing a gas mask!" I don't think Klein found my candor refreshing, but he knew I meant business.

In the meantime, I learned that Montgomery had placed an advertisement with Bob Overstreet for the 1976 edition of *The Comic Book Price Guide*. In a subsequent telephone conversation, I explained the case to Overstreet and requested he withhold Montgomery's advertising until a final determination could be reached. Overstreet agreed to cooperate.

I made a similar request of Alan Light, as Montgomery did most of his advertising in *TBG*. Light seemed indifferent. He said he would think it over. A few days later, Light informed me by mail that he would not suspend a firm's advertising rights on a mere charge or allegation. Since he knew nothing about the thickness of bags, or even if it was important, he would rely on the FTC to tell him one way or the other. In other words, Montgomery was a good paying customer and Light was not going to alienate him; or worse, take any money out of his own pocket.

This letter prompted another phone call to Light and we had another round of head-butting. Light refused to budge an inch. I did not care for his self-serving attitude and I warned him that he was liable to find himself up to his neck in trouble. All I could do under the circumstances was proceed without him.

On Saturday morning, February 10, 1976, I was awakened about 8:00 A.M. by the phone ringing. I had worked until past midnight the night before. I was still half asleep. As I tried to clear away the cobwebs, I heard a voice on the other end ranting that he was going to sue me. He must have realized that I wasn't awake when I angrily blurted, "Who the hell is this?"

The voice on the other end belonged to Robert Montgomery. After telling me a second time who he was, his angry tirade about lawsuits started again. Montgomery discovered that I tend to be grouchy first thing in the morning. After a moment or two, I yelled back at him: "Listen, you stupid sonofabitch!

Before you sue me, you had better be damned certain of the facts!" This was followed by a pause on the other end of the line. In any event, it calmed Montgomery down long enough for us to discuss the matter a little more rationally.

Out of courtesy, I let him tell his side of the story first. Montgomery believed I was conspiring with Klein and Cole to drive him out of the plastic bag business. Of course, nothing was further from the truth. What really set him off was discovering that Overstreet had his advertising on hold until he got a green light from me. From his perspective, I was the villain of the drama. Montgomery said he had responded to my second notice and his manufacturer had supposedly sent a statement of guarantee.

Then it was my turn. I told Montgomery that WSA was not trying to force him out of the plastic bag business. I made it clear that I was impartial. I had already been to the mat with Klein and Cole and I would do it again if I had to. My only interest was the thickness of his bags. As the matter stood, my Dad had gauged three different batches obtained from three different sources. They all measured 2.2 mil thick. I told him that I didn't care what his manufacturer said because it wasn't true.

After Montgomery realized that I wasn't wearing a black hat, he took me into his confidence. Montgomery promised to pay a visit to his manufacturer to clear up the situation. He said that if I was right, he would alter his advertising. I couldn't ask for more than that.

About ten days later, I received a letter from Montgomery detailing his visit to the manufacturer. When he asked for a copy of the letter sent to me, he was told they were too busy. They refused to do anything else. From that, it became evident that a letter had never been sent. At Montgomery's insistence, a salesman measured one of the bags in his presence. Montgomery noticed that the bag was gauged in the middle instead of on the flap. Naturally it doubled the thickness. Since Montgomery was a newcomer to the business, he did not expect this kind of trickery. However, the salesman knew exactly what he was doing.

As a result, Montgomery returned all the bags he had purchased. In the future, he did business with a more reliable firm. Montgomery kept his promise and altered his advertising. Afterwards, I wrote letters to Overstreet and the Federal Trade Commission giving Montgomery a clean bill of health. In essence, the case was over.

As it all worked out, I came out of the debacle smelling like a rose. Klein and Cole apologized. In some ways, I had earned their respect. Personally, I developed some needed confidence. I realized that I lacked experience but I had learned to trust my instincts.

With this crisis resolved, it was time to move on to something else. Because relations between Light and myself had been stretched to the breaking point, I thought it might be necessary to find another place to publish my WSA

WE #104, March 1976. The art was submitted without a return address. It arrived one day out of the blue. The timing was impeccable: I was in dire need of a cover. For whatever reason, the artist wanted to remain anonymous. To this day, I have no idea who "Swenston" is. Maybe someday he will come out of the shadows and take a bow.

News & Report column. I expected to get the bum's rush from Light at any moment. Harry Hopkins and I discussed the possibility of starting our own periodical so we would not be at the mercy of any publisher.

Hopkins suggested we revive *WE* for the purpose. I thought it was a crackerjack notion. Then I discussed the idea with Stanley Blair, who liked the idea. His only stipulation for using the name was not to accept advertising for underground comics.

In the few odd moments of what I jokingly called spare time, I put the first issue together. For posterity, I picked up the old numbering. By circulating a flyer from Blair's old SASE file, I was able to drum up enough advertising to pay the printing bill. For economy, I changed the format to a digest size.

A complimentary copy of *WE* # 103 was mailed on February 20, 1976, to every WSA member. Hopkins provided the computerized mailing labels for the purpose.

Surprisingly, the revival of *WE* generated a lot of interest among WSA members. Cark Horak wrote, "It took the arrival of the current issue of *WE* to convince me that WSA had re-established solid footing. Enclosed is a check for a subscription and WSA dues."

Because Blair and I had not lately been on the best of terms, I was surprised to receive the following note from him:

I have received the new publication. I am very pleasantly surprised. You have done a fine job of putting it together and it is attractive as a publication. From experience, I know this involved a lot of work and you are to be commended for your efforts and the net result.

Sometimes Blair was a difficult man to understand. In the years since, I've often wondered if the flaw was in him, or me.

Suffice to say, my writing and editorial skills left much to be desired. Fortunately, a few friends came to the rescue. Nils Hardin, publisher of *Xenophile,* sent a delightful little book entitled *The Elements of Style* by William Strunk, Jr., and E.B. White, along with a brief note: "Ron . . . this is NOT a hint. I just happened to pick it up at a sale and thought you might like to have it. Or, you might prefer to throw it away."

If Hardin wasn't hinting, he should have. At that point I needed all the help I could get. Of course, I didn't throw it away. Over the years, I've worn the book out from constant reference. I learned more about English from that little book than I did in two semesters of study on the college level.

Not long afterwards, I received more help from an unexpected source. A new WSA member, Dr. A.D. Stewart, was an English professor at Midwestern State University. Stewart took one of my editorials and corrected the mistakes. The pages had almost as much red ink on them as black.

Stewart and I soon developed a kind of student-teacher relationship. For the next two years he continued to correct my editorials. In a very short time, there was a noticeable improvement. The pages kept coming back with less red ink on them. To this day, I am grateful for his patient tutelage.

A short time later I met Norma Terrell at a Tulsa convention. She knew a lot more about journalism than I did and offered her services as a proofreader. I was delighted to accept. In the process, we became friends. Sadly, Norma passed away in 1979, following a long and courageous battle with a brain tumor.

The WSA Program might have strangled financially that first year if not for *WE*. In the first issue I reprinted Klein's letter about dues. Unlike the notice in *TBG,* it prompted a good response. Funds for dues and subscriptions began to trickle in. By June 30, 1976, WSA had received $2,341. If not for these funds, WSA would have suffered a loss of $1,500, which undoubtedly would have put us out of business.

There is something about publishing that gets into your blood. Initially, I had planned to produce an issue or two and then turn it over to someone else. I changed my mind when I started having fun. It became a pleasant change of pace from the duties of administration that occupied most of my time. I found it interesting that some readers valued the periodical more than I did. In some strange way, *WE* became an important part of their lives. My work in this area was often more appreciated than the business of managing WSA.

Lacking any real sense of perspicacity, it was all beyond my comprehension. I think Jack Lemmon may have been right when he said, "If man understood the enigmas of life, there would be no need for the arts."

One thing I know for certain: If I had understood life, I would have been doing something else.

CHAPTER FOUR

Wild Men and Wilder Adventures

In tragic life, no villain need be! Passions spin the plot: We are betrayed by what is false within.

—George Meredith

In March of 1976, my personal life took a turn. Suddenly I found myself unemployed. While receiving unemployment benefits, I spent the next six months working sixty hours each week on WSA business. The timing for this sabbatical could not have been better. In no time at all, I found myself deluged with mail-fraud complaints.

Separating the cases into categories, about 65 percent involved people buying or selling comic books. Another 25 percent pertained to *Star Trek* fans. The remaining 10 percent were roughly divided among principals dealing in pulps, films, movie posters, and baseball cards.

One-third of the cases were simple disputes between buyer and seller, resulting from misunderstandings, personal problems, or postal delays. They were usually resolved without much trouble. The remaining cases involved situations where intent to defraud was clearly established. Many of the cases involved multiple complaints against the same defendant.

It was never my intention to become a full-fledged mail-fraud investigator. In April 1980, Mrs. Stanley Blair described the situation in a letter to the Federal Bureau of Investigation:

> Mr. Blair allowed Ron Frantz to take over the WSA division of the program and its affiliates. He had no intention for continuing the WRB (fraud) division since Frantz had neither training, experience, or tact for this part of the operation. It is a delicate operation and can cause trouble if not operated properly and within required guidelines.

That was true enough. But after serving six months as WSA Administrator, it slowly dawned on me that without the fraud bureau there was no reason to continue operations. It made little sense for WSA to exist as a paper institution, with eyes but no teeth. Blair and I had several discussions on the subject. Initially, he didn't like the idea. Later, he grudgingly approved.

In the beginning I imitated methods devised by Blair. For all intents and purposes, this consisted of sending letters of inquiry to defendant parties to determine the facts. In situations where intent to defraud was clearly established, it required working directly with the Postal Inspection Service. Later, I discovered that other federal agencies could be of help, in particular the Federal Trade Commission. In 1976, the FTC passed a series of regulations concerning the delivery of merchandise by mail. The major provisions are:

1. Should the seller be unable to ship the merchandise within the time stated in his advertising, he must notify the buyer of the delay and give him the option to cancel the order. If no time is specified, then the seller has thirty days to notify the buyer.

2. The buyer must be given a cost-free device for this purpose. This can be a postpaid envelope or a postcard. If the buyer requests, the order must be canceled and all money must be immediately refunded.

3. Should the buyer not respond to the non-delivery notice, it is presumed that consent for an additional thirty days has been granted to the seller. For delays longer than thirty days, the buyer must expressly consent to the delay or his money must be refunded.

4. Should the seller realize that the delay will be for an indefinite period of time, he may ask the buyer to agree to an indefinite delay. The buyer may still request a refund at any time.

5. Sellers of merchandise by mail must have a reasonable basis for any claims made in the delay of shipping.

The curious thing is that I never went looking for mail-fraud cases. They came searching for me. The first case involved a person in Austin, Texas, calling himself "Alex Martin." In April 1976, Martin placed an advertisement in *TBG* listing many collectors' comics at very inexpensive prices. At least two dozen *TBG* subscribers responded to the ad, half of them WSA members.

By May 15, 1976, I received a dozen complaints against Martin. They were all essentially the same. Each sent a check in payment for merchandise and received nothing in return. When writing to inquire about their orders, the buyers' letters were returned by the post office marked "Moved, Left No Forwarding Address." At that point, they realized they were a victim of mail fraud.

Because of the number of cases, I wasted no time contacting the Postal Inspection Service in Austin. The inspector in charge was a man named H.G. Croft. In our first conversation, I learned that Alex Martin had been apprehended. Croft suggested that I contact Robert Jones, an attorney representing the defendant.

Jones had quite a story to tell. "Alex Martin" was a sixteen-year-old with emotional problems. Evidently, he was from a wealthy family. When his parents discovered the mischief, they hired Jones to represent their son. Jones alerted Inspector Croft about the situation and arranged to make restitution to the victims.

Jones was very cooperative. He requested that I provide him with a list of the complaints I had received. He promised to make an immediate refund to each from his office. Of course, that was fine with me. To the best of my knowledge, Jones made a full refund to all of the complainants.

Under ordinary circumstances, this would have been the end of it. However, I learned that the street address used by Martin was a vacant house. A WSA member of the same age lived on the same street. It didn't take Sherlock Holmes to figure out Martin's true identity.

In a subsequent telephone conversation with Jones, I asked him to confirm the information. He declined on the basis that it would be a breach of the confidential relationship between lawyer and client. Jones suggested that I take up the matter with Inspector Croft. It became clear that Croft and Jones were in collusion when Croft refused to divulge the information.

In my ignorance of the law, I considered the possibility of trying to subpoena Jones's records. Before making a fool of myself, I discussed the matter with Avery Klein. He pitched a wet blanket on my simmering frustration by telling me that it couldn't be done.

Because the reputation of a WSA member was at stake, I was determined to resolve the question. I discussed the situation with a friend of mine who was a private investigator. He said that he could find out what I needed to know for $200. Somehow, I couldn't justify the expense, especially since it would have come out of my own pocket. I thanked him, anyway.

WSA member Manny Seguin was a sergeant on the San Antonio police force. Seguin offered to investigate the matter through police channels as he knew some people on the Austin police force. Before he went to all that time and trouble, I wanted to have another talk with Jones. During our conversation, I said something to the effect of: "I have good reason to suspect that your client and our WSA member are the same. The problem is that I don't want to suspend his WSA membership without proof. If you will tell me what I need to know, I promise not to make the information public." Before he could give me an answer, I quickly asked, "Is Alex Martin *****?"

Jones laughed, and said: I'm not supposed to answer that, but yes, he is. That was good enough. I thanked Jones for his time and deleted the name ***** from our membership records. Not long afterwards, I received the following message from Jones:

> I sincerely appreciate what you are doing for individuals that deal in comic books. I only wish there were additional organizations such as yours that could assist in policing our mail system. If I can be of further assistance, feel free to call.

Before the casebook had closed on Alex Martin, another case was already well in progress. In early June, I began to receive complaints against Carlos Johnson of Bronx, New York. The complaints originated from an ad in *TBG*. In less than a month I received thirty-three complaints against Johnson. Half of the complaints were forwarded by Alan Light's secretary, Jo Hansen. One of the worst-kept secrets in fandom was that Jo Hansen was Light's mother.

With little fanfare, I dropped the whole bundle in the lap of Postal Inspector N.H. Green. A month went by with no word from Green. Finally, I placed a phone call to his office. After spending half the afternoon tracking him down, Green and I had a talk.

I was appalled to learn that Green had done nothing, nor had he any intention to do so. In his opinion, intent to defraud had not been established. I could not believe it. The complaints against Johnson involved over $10,000. The evidence on hand was overwhelming. I could only surmise that Green didn't care.

It might be a good idea to interrupt my narrative to explain the function of the United States Postal Inspection Service. It is an investigative agency. Its function is to gather facts and evidence to determine if action is warranted under federal mail-fraud or false-representation statutes. Such action may consist of criminal proceedings by United States Attorneys, administrative proceedings by the Postal Service, or both. Contrary to popular opinion, the Postal Inspection Service has no authority to effect refunds or adjustments. If postal inspectors do not investigate, no action can begin against a perpetrator of mail fraud.

Immediately following my conversation with Green, I placed a call to the office of Louis Lefkowitz, Attorney General for the state of New York. I had a lengthy conversation with an official in the Consumer Fraud Division. I was informed that the agency had received complaints against Johnson. However, they were only interested in victims who lived in the state of New York. As it was explained to me, criminal statues in that state applied only when one resident defrauded another. On this basis, Lefkowitz declined to prosecute.

Two weeks later, I placed a second call to Inspector Green. By some great miracle, he had finally seen fit to perform some routine investigation. Green had learned that "Carlos Johnson" was an alias. It came as no great surprise that Green was unable to find him. I realize that the Postal Inspection Service isn't exactly Scotland Yard, but I don't think Green could have found the seat of his pants, using both hands and a compass. Green informed me that he needed additional information (more complaints) before he could justify transferring the case to the United States Attorneys.

To accommodate the Inspector, my next WSA News & Report column in *TBG* included a public notice, requesting that anyone who had done business with Johnson immediately contact Inspector Green.

When it came to my attention that Carlos Johnson was an alias (which I had suspected), I considered the possibility that he might be Arnold Meyrowitz. About this time I discussed the matter with Stanley Blair. His reaction was surprising. Blair's voice was tinted with excitement. He wanted to know all the details.

About a week later, Blair called to inform me that Johnson was not Meyrowitz. Through connections of his own, Blair learned Meyrowitz was still in prison. When Blair delivered his report he sounded disappointed. I suspect that had Johnson been Meyrowitz, Blair might have ended his retirement to take up the chase.

However, Blair and I discussed my problem of getting Inspector Green off of high center. Blair suggested that I contact my congressman. It seemed like a sensible suggestion. A short time later, I established communication with John Jarman, Fifth District, Oklahoma. In a personal letter to Jarman, I explained the situation and requested his help.

On August 18, 1976, I received a letter from Jarman, asking that I call. After calling his Oklahoma City office, a secretary asked me to hold on for a minute. She said Jarman wanted to speak to me personally. A moment later, she had him on the line. Jarman and I discussed the Carlos Johnson case for about twenty minutes.

I was impressed with Jarman's sense of civic responsibility. Jarman expressed genuine concern for the victims. He was dismayed by the lackadaisical attitude of the Postal Inspection Service. Jarman promised to check into the matter and promised every possible assistance.

I should point out that this was something Jarman did not have to do. In a few months Jarman would retire from Congress. It would have been easy for him to look the other way. Instead, he proved to be a genuine servant of the people. We could sure use a few good men like him in Congress today.

About two weeks later, I spoke with Jarman again. He assured me that

Green was working on the case. As a result of the notice in *TBG,* the number of complaints against Johnson now totaled over fifty. Green was obliged to transfer the case to the United States Attorney. Jarman also informed me that the Federal Bureau of Investigation was now involved in the case because Johnson had fled the state of New York. Evidently, the FBI knew who he was but they weren't talking.

Afterwards, I had several conversations with various officials in the office of the Assistant Attorney General in charge of criminal affairs and the United States Attorneys representing eastern New York. Initially, the outlook was promising. However, as time went by their interest died. The investigation was choked by bureaucratic red tape. It was as if everyone was in charge of the case, and no one.

On March 23, 1977, I spoke with Inspector Green by phone while vacationing in New York City. He had nothing new to report. According to Green, the FBI had not located Johnson. Evidently they were not trying very hard. For reasons beyond my comprehension, the FBI office in New York refused to discuss the matter.

After Jarman left office, his successor, Mickey Edwards, had no interest in the case. There was a very simple reason: None of the victims lived in his congressional district. Edwards saw me as some kind of a troublemaker. I think the fact that I had campaigned for his opponent in the Republican primary had a lot to do with it. Obviously, I was not one of his favorite constituents.

To the best of my knowledge, Carlos Johnson was never brought to justice. For me it was a keen disappointment. In behalf of the victims, I had spent more than two hundred hours working on the case. Apparently it was all for nothing.

In August 1976, I received the first of many complaints against Middle Earth. The firm was located in Denver, Colorado, and owned by two WSA members, Steven Allen and Dennis Wakabayshi. Middle Earth published limited edition art portfolios featuring such popular illustrators as Frank Frazetta, Jeff Jones, and John and Marie Severin. The firm had an impeccable reputation for quality and service.

Initially, I was not concerned about the complaints. I assumed they were caused by printing problems or postal delays. I sent a personal letter asking them to check the matter and let me know what was going on. Several weeks went by and I heard nothing. Then I started sending official letters of inquiry. These, too, were ignored. Finally, I tried to reach Allen or Wakabayshi by telephone, to discover that the number was no longer in service.

Shortly thereafter, I received a letter from Middle Earth (written by an employee) informing me of the recent death of Steven Allen. It seems that

UNITED STATES POSTAL SERVICE
Postal Inspector

OUR REF: AV:jcf

SUBJECT:

DATE: April 14, 1977

CASE NO. 242-50587-F

TO:

Mr. Ron J. Frantz
Chief of Operations
WSA Program
P. O. Box 95171
Oklahoma City, OK 73109

Dear Mr. Frantz:

Mr. Albert J. Manachino has referred to me a copy of a letter in which
you list a number of individuals who have made a complaint regarding
the transaction with Middle Earth, Denver, CO. This Service is currently
making inquiries into the firm and I will incorporate the names of those
persons from whom you have received complaints with other complaints
which I have on hand.

In your letter you request a reply from the firm by April 18, 1977. I
am interested in knowing whether or not you receive any response and
will appreciate your advising me as to this.

I am enclosing herewith a self-addressed envelope for your convenience in
making reply.

Sincerely,

Albert Velthoen
Postal Inspector

As a rule of thumb, I had to knock a postal inspector down and
sit on him to get any attention. Most of the time the process was
about as slow as pulling teeth through the ear. You can imagine
how delightful it was to have a postal inspector contact me first.
Albert J. Manachino later became a quite prolific (and popular)
author of science fiction stories.

Allen had been the senior partner of the firm, managing the business. This included negotiations with various artists. After Allen's death, the artists refused to honor their commitments because they were not being paid. Despite these technical problems, the employee promised me that Middle Earth would honor its debt to customers, providing product or refunds.

Over the next few months I received a dozen new complaints against the firm. Some dated back two years. Under the circumstances, I wanted to give Middle Earth ample opportunity to set matters straight and keep its WSA membership in good standing. The only problem was they were not making much of an effort.

Then Middle Earth vanished from the face of the earth. No one associated with the firm could be reached by phone. They did not reply to my letters. At that point, I had no choice but to issue a National Warning Alert Advisory to the WSA membership, suggesting they not do business with the firm. I asked Mike Robertson to send a "Request for Stop Advertising" to the members of the WSA Publishers Alliance.

These actions prompted a quick response from Middle Earth. I received a phone call from an employee named Polly. She informed me that one portfolio was at the printer while another was being finished by the artist. The proceeds from two portfolios would put the firm back in business. Polly promised the outstanding complaints would be taken care of within thirty days. Based on this promise, I agreed to hold the matter in abeyance for that length of time.

The time came and went with no word from Middle Earth. Then, on April 4, 1977, I wrote a letter to Wakabayshi informing him that his WSA membership had been suspended. I demanded that he make full restitution to the complainants no later than April 18, 1977. As I expected, Wakabayshi ignored the letter.

On May 1, 1977, I filed a formal complaint against Middle Earth with Paul C. Daw, the Regional Director of the Federal Trade Commission in Denver. In a subsequent telephone conversation with a subordinate, the FTC informed me that they intended to investigate the case.

In the meantime, I received a letter from Postal Inspector Albert Velthoen. Velthoen requested that I provide full documentation of all the cases on file against Middle Earth. This was a pleasant change of pace. Ordinarily, I had to scream bloody murder to get any attention from the Postal Inspection Service. Of course, I was delighted to cooperate.

Over the next few months I had several telephone conversations with Velthoen. Evidently he was comparing notes with the FTC. According to Velthoen, Wakabayshi had badly managed Middle Earth's finances following the death of Steven Allen. He did not have the recources to effect refunds and remain in business. Velthoen agreed to monitor Middle Earth's cash flow. He assured me that Wakabayshi would honor his debt. A year later he was still coughing up refunds. For all I know, he still may be.

In this same time frame, I began to receive an unusual number of complaints against *Star Trek* dealers. Much of this can be attributed to *Star Trek* fans joining the WSA Program in great numbers. Among them was a lady in Detroit named Mandi Schultz. After several letters and phone calls, I appointed Schultz to serve as the Official WSA Representative to *Star Trek* Fandom.

It seemed like a good idea at the time. Schultz personally knew most of the people dealing in *Star Trek* material. On the other hand, I knew very little about the hobby or the people in it.

To say the least, *Star Trek* is a commercial phenomenon. The original television series has been broadcast in over one hundred countries and translated into thirty languages. Currently, over one hundred companies produce *Star Trek* merchandise. *Star Trek* novels have sold more than thirty million copies. To date, seven major motion pictures have appeared along with four different television series.

Star Trek was the brainchild of writer-producer Gene Roddenberry. Roddenberry had an interesting background. He was a fighter pilot during the Second World War. Later he was a commercial aviator and Los Angeles police officer.

The first episode of *Star Trek* aired on September 8, 1966. Set two hundred years in the future, *Star Trek* followed the adventures of the starship *Enterprise*, whose mission was to explore unknown worlds. The stories were well written, dealing with current social issues set in extraterrestrial settings.

Star Trek was canceled by NBC in 1969. From the start the series suffered from poor ratings. The program was unattractive to network advertisers because the majority of viewers were teenagers and children.

A few years later, *Star Trek* enjoyed remarkable success in syndication, developing a cult following in the early 1970s. The cult organized itself and lobbied to get the series brought back to television.

In the beginning, the *Star Trek* fans did not have a home of their own. They gathered at science fiction conventions. Ordinarily, they were not appreciated by the often haughty science fiction fans.

Later, the trekkies (as they were often called) converged upon comic book conventions. Being a tad more pragmatic, these promoters adored the trekkies because they bought tickets. Before long, some comic book dealers began to peddle *Star Trek* merchandise. They were not proud. A person could make a tidy profit selling photographs of Captain Kirk or plastic Spock ears. Unfortunately, some of the merchandising got out of hand.

Schultz wasted little time making her presence felt. Her first target was two women named Basta who operated a nationwide fan club known as the Star Trek Association for Revival (STAR). During 1974 and 1975, STAR allegedly received $25,000 from fans for memberships. Members were supposed to receive a subscription to a newsletter, a photograph packet, and other materials. Many received nothing.

In 1976, STAR dissolved without notice. Funds in the club treasury mysteriously disappeared. The Bastas refused to answer letters or to make refunds for canceled memberships. As Schultz began to investigate, her efforts were hampered by members of the Star Trek Welcommittee.

Supposedly, the Welcommittee was a nonprofit service organization manned by volunteers who devoted spare time to answering fan questions about *Star Trek*. Some Welcommittee officers operated individual chapters of STAR. Naturally, they feared a backlash of bad publicity if the Bastas' activities became known. These people felt the publicity might have an adverse effect on *Star Trek* revival efforts if word reached Gene Roddenberry.

As Schultz continued her investigations, she incurred the wrath of various Welcommittee officials. They admonished her (publicly and in private), demanding that she stop the investigation. Obviously, they wanted the matter swept under the rug.

In this same time frame, WSA began to receive complaints about a *Star Trek* fan club for actress Nichelle Nichols. Unlike STAR, this club operated for several years without a hint of scandal. However, over a six-month period, the Nichols club began to experience trouble. The club newsletter ceased publication. New members did not receive materials due them. As the complaints trickled in, Schultz issued letters of inquiry to the club president. They went unanswered.

After Schultz completed her preliminary investigations, she transferred the cases to me for disposition. I gathered all the cases into a neat bundle and sent them directly to Virginia Walker, the club president, by certified mail. It included a demand for her to provide complainants with immediate refunds. I gave her ten days to reply. After that, I would file the complaints with the Postal Inspection Service.

This prompted an immediate response. Ms. Walker told me about a past disagreement between her and Mrs. Schultz. It became clear that the two ladies disliked one another because of some past personal confrontation. Walker refused to have anything to do with Schultz. However, she was willing to cooperate with me.

Walker had an interesting story to tell. She was experiencing financial hardship caused in part by the Star Trek Welcommittee. At one time Walker had been the publisher of the Welcommittee newsletter. Walker contracted the job to a local printer, who printed the monthly newsletter at reduced rates in exchange for a three-month notice of termination.

In February 1976, the chairperson of the Welcommittee transferred the printing to a friend in Denver. The chairperson ignored the contract with the first printer. Of course, this resulted in a breach of contract. Then, the printer billed Walker $10,000 for the unfilled part of the contract. To avoid being sued, Walker used most of the club treasury to make a partial payment to the printer. Then she agreed to pay the remaining debt with a percentage of her monthly salary. In the interim, Walker lived below poverty level, a situation I could well relate to. One of the problems with altruism is that it doesn't pay very well.

I had suggested to Walker that she might do well to consult an attorney regarding a possible breach of contract suit against the Star Trek Welcommittee. Walker seemed very uncomfortble with that prospect. By her way of thinking, it would have been like suing the church. Call it a case of misguided loyalty.

Walker did not have the funds to meet her obligations. Because of the unusual circumstances, we worked out an agreement for her to make the refunds as soon as possible. Most of complainants were agreeable. However, there was one jerk in Minnesota who didn't like it. He accused WSA (and me) of acting in collusion with the Nichols club to defraud him.

For some reason the accusation irritated me. To shut him up, I sent a refund out of my own pocket, along with a personal note telling him what he could do with the money. It involved sticking it into the part of his anatomy where the sun doesn't shine. Of course, it wasn't a very professional thing to do, but it sure made me feel better.

I had serious reservations about the integrity of the Welcommittee. The next case involving them removed all doubt. It did not involve mail fraud in the traditional sense, but it had other curious aspects.

In April 1976, a young lady named Cross began corresponding with a man named Hoover. Early in their correspondence, Hoover read several science fiction stories written by Cross. Then, Hoover asked if he could show the stories to some friends in the publishing business. Supposedly, one of them was writer Isaac Asimov. Hoover claimed to be a friend, business associate, and coauthor with Asimov on some television scripts.

Hoover told Cross he could get one of her stories in an anthology Asimov planned to publish in 1977. Cross had dreams of being a published writer and agreed to go along with Hoover's recommendations. In his letters to Cross, Hoover elaborated about Asimov, detailing bits of the writer's neurotic personality. He claimed that Asimov had peculiar working habits and a total irreverence toward formalities and proprieties.

During their correspondence, Cross began to notice inconsistencies in Hoover's letters about himself, the publishing business, and Isaac Asimov. Hoover made plans to meet with Cross at a convention, share a hotel room, and meet with Asimov. The convention was conveniently canceled. Other meetings, as well as promised phone calls from Asimov, never materialized.

Hoover blamed the delays on Asimov and his alleged idiosyncrasies. In the meantime, Hoover asked Cross to write some science fiction stories of a peculiar sexual nature, claiming Asimov wanted them for test stories. It took a while, but Cross finally began to smell a rat. Matters came to a head when she confronted Hoover. Cross wanted proof that one of her stories would appear in the Asimov anthology.

Hoover's reaction was typical. In a heart-wrenching sob letter, he claimed her doubts wounded him to the marrow. Hoover severely admonished her for having no faith, called her unreliable, and stated she would get nowhere as a writer without his connections. Clearly upset, Cross tried to contact Hoover by telephone. Hoover claimed (to his wife) not to know Cross and refused to speak with her over the phone.

After the call, strange things began to happen to Cross. She began to receive hate mail and obscene phone calls. Some of it was from people she knew. Others came from total strangers. The letters and phone calls accused her of taking advantage of Hoover, garnished with accusations of sexual impropriety.

Before long, Cross realized her reputation was being smeared. Not knowing where to turn, Cross asked for WSA assistance. About the middle of August, Mandi Schultz and I discussed the case by phone. I wasn't sure what we could do. It sounded to me like a case for a good lawyer. However, it seemed appropriate to help if we could.

Schultz examined all of Hoover's letters to Cross, an amazing amount of verbiage written to someone whom he claimed not to know. Obviously, there was only one way to get at the truth and that was to ask Asimov. Schultz sent Asimov a letter and enclosed copies of Hoover's letters mentioning him. Asimov responded with the following letter:

Dear Mrs. Schultz:

I am sorry the young lady has been so victimized. I don't know this man who pretends to know me. Nothing he describes as having taken place in connection with me ever took place. His description of my character and my idiosyncrasies are totally wrong.

I do not fly. I do not read stories. I do not hate autograph seekers. I do not visit people unexpectedly, typewriter in hand, and so on and so on. In short, this whole thing seems to be a fraud with myself one of the victims.

Asimov's letter cleared the air. There is no doubt that Hoover used the name of a prominent author to perpetrate a scheme that reeked of fraud and slander. Clearly, Hoover had other intentions.

After documenting the case, Schultz published her findings in several *Star Trek* fanzines, hoping to partially rectify the damage done to the name and reputation of Cross.

Here I am, threading a film on a 16 mm projector at Wintercon '76. I will be the first to admit that I didn't look much like an Administrator. I was twenty-three at the time. This same picture was published without my prior knowledge in *All About Star Trek Fan Clubs* magazine. It all sounds innocent enough, but I ended up catching hell from some of those *Star Trek* people.

Since Hoover was a member of the Welcommittee, various members of that group took issue with Schultz for trying to protect Cross. On November 27, 1976, I received the following letter from Schultz:

> Dear Ron:
> You really would not believe the comments I have received on this Hoover-Cross-Asimov business. My area captain for the Welcommittee wrote me a four page letter raking me over the coals. It ended with a suggestion that I get psychiatric help because I had to be mentally unbalanced to handle the affair as I did. After all, Hoover didn't do anything wrong—he just tried to ruin Ms. Cross' life, that's all.
> You would not believe how many of the Welcommittee defended Hoover. They thought my actions were just terrible. The Welcommittee does not want to help fandom, they just want to keep their own reputation clear. They don't care who gets hurt in the process. Cross is not one of them, Hoover is.
> They are standing behind his actions even though they admit that he was wrong. The Welcommittee refused to look at the evidence I presented. God forbid that we should confuse the issue with facts. Don't forget that Hoover tried to get Cross into a hotel room. But since he didn't do anything to her physically, the rest of Hoover's actions didn't matter. Thus, sweep it under the rug (along with the Basta mess) and don't tell anyone about it.

About a month later, Schultz wrote to inform me that due to pressing family matters, personal problems, and poor health, she was resigning as WSA *Star Trek* representative. The personal abuse she received from the Welcommittee, people in some instances she considered to be friends, was more than she could handle.

I picked up right where Schultz left off on the Basta case. After filing complaints with the Postal Inspection Service, I discussed the case with Bill McDonough of the Federal Trade Commission. Based on the information at hand, McDonough said charges of mail fraud and conspiracy to defraud could be filed if the Welcommittee was acting in collusion with STAR. He asked me to keep him informed.

During the next few months, I received several letters and phone calls from Welcommittee officials insisting that I stop investigating the Basta case. Obviously, they were running scared. Out of the blue I received a phone call from a so-called "attorney" in Chicago, warning me not to implicate the Welcommittee in any WSA investigation. I just laughed and suggested that he talk to the Federal Trade Commission and United States Postal Inspection

Service. I never heard from him again.

At this point, I decided that it was time to take the bull by the horns. I wrote a letter to the legal department of Paramount Pictures, suggesting they look into possible trademark and copyright infringements among principals involved in the Basta case. I guess they did. Not long after that, Paramount started cracking down on *Star Trek* dealers selling unlicensed merchandise.

In October 1976, I had a chance meeting with a prominent *Star Trek* dealer at a Dallas convention. I had driven down on Saturday to spend the day. About five o'clock that afternoon, WSA member John Harper asked if I would watch his table while he went to eat. Seems like I was always doing that for someone. While I was watching his table, a stranger walked up and started a sales pitch. I didn't care much for his manner. As politely as I could, I suggested that he come back later and talk to Harper.

Then the fellow turned abusive. He said, "Listen, jerk! I don't have time to come back!" He scowled, handed me a flyer, and said, "Be sure that Harper gets that!" While he was standing there, I glanced at the letterhead and recognized his name. I had been working on several mail-fraud cases against him. As a matter of coincidence, his live-in girlfriend was a former Welcommittee officer. The lady (and I use the term loosely) had recently abandoned her husband and small children to live with the *Star Trek* dealer.

For the first time, I came face to face with a subject of a WSA investigation. In a way, I found the situation amusing. I asked him, "You don't know who I am, do you?" He replied, "No, and I don't care."

Then, I said, "You should. I'm the guy who keeps receiving mail-fraud complaints against you." At first, he looked a little nervous. Then he said, "So . . . you're the WSA! You don't look like much to me." After that, he cast a few aspersions on my parenthood, coming darned close to getting a punch in the nose!

Keeping a grip on my temper, I said, "We could stand here all day insulting one another. But I think we would be better off to try and resolve the problem. Are you going to take care of these mail-fraud complaints or not?"

His candid reply was: "I don't have to tell you shit!" He made an obscene gesture, then turned and walked away. The guy was right. He had no legal obligation to give me the time of day if he didn't want to. However, I related the incident in a letter to the postal inspector in charge of the case. The inspector must have been more persuasive than I. Not long afterwards, the recalcitrant dealer made good on his debts.

My first wife, the former Maxine Broadwater, operated a fan club for actor William Shatner prior to our marriage. In the spring of 1977, *All About Star Trek Fan Clubs* magazine profiled her club. The article mentioned that Maxine and I were soon to be married and she would be moving the club to Oklahoma. Without telling me, Maxine sent my photo to the magazine, where it was published along with my mailing address. The article made me sound like a genuine, dyed-in-the-wool *Star Trek* fan. This was hardly the case.

Over the next few months, I received about two dozen letters from various *Star Trek* fans. Most were written by people who wanted information about Shatner. In one curious letter, the writer wanted to know what *Star Trek* episodes I had appeared in. Of course I was never in a *Star Trek* episode. (Not that the thought of seeing myself in one of those goofy alien costumes wasn't funny.) Several of the letters came from women. One proposed marriage. The fact that I was already engaged didn't seem to matter. Another offered to meet with me (any time or place) for recreational sex and enclosed a rather provocative photo of herself. One can only imagine the kind of fan mail that Shatner himself must have gotten.

Then I received the following letter:

Dear R:

The word is out! You can't get away with this! You are being watched. The next time you cross us will be your last. You will die a slow and painful death . . .

I had become accustomed to being insulted by strangers. It seemed to go with the territory. However, I had to draw the line at having my life threatened. Obviously I was dealing with a mental case. The letter was unsigned, with a Kansas City postmark.

Naturally I was a little concerned. The threat of physical violence could have been real. For this reason, I contacted the FBI office in Oklahoma City. A few days later, they sent an agent to my home who made a report of the incident. Because of the other problems I had experienced with Star Trek fandom, I suspected there might be a connection between the death threat and the sex offer.

The FBI agent considered it a possibility. He took the letters, envelopes, and photograph for evidence. I never heard anything else about it. I am pleased to say that no one (with the exception of a few fast-food restaurants) ever tried to kill me. However, for quite some time I made certain to keep my door locked. I got into the habit of looking behind me when I walked down the street.

Next on the agenda came a rare problem involving the pulp collectors. In the summer of 1976, Jim Steranko published an article in *Mediascene* entitled "The 100 Most Valuable Pulp Magazines," by Terry Stroud. In some respects it was a laughable situation as Stroud attempted to pass himself off as an expert on the subject. He was not. His pricing was nothing more than pure speculation, with little basis in fact. Stroud made a business of offering esoteric comics and paperback books at absurd prices.

When Stroud tried to play the same game with pulp magazines, he infuriated many of the old-time pulp collectors. This included Richard Minter, a
man who had collected pulp magazines before Stroud was born. As a spokesman for a group of pulp collectors, Minter asked Steranko for equal time. He
was turned down, cold.

One afternoon my phone rang. Minter called to ask if I could do anything
to help. Unfortunately, there was not much I could do. However, I agreed to
speak with Steranko in Minter's behalf. After failing to reach Steranko by
phone, I sent several letters, all of which were duly ignored.

A few months later I met Steranko at the 1976 Creationcon in New York.
Steranko was, without a doubt, one of the most obnoxious people I have ever
met. It took him less than a minute to insult me. I had hoped that Steranko
might be willing to listen to the concerns of the pulp collectors. I would have
been better off talking to a fire hydrant. Considering Stroud an expert, Steranko
said the subject had been covered to his satisfaction. He had no intention of
letting Minter voice a different point of view in his magazine.

Afterwards, I suggested that Minter tell his side of the story in *Xenophile*.
I knew that the publisher, Nils Hardin, would understand the concerns of the
pulp collectors. The best way to deal with Steranko was not to buy (or advertise in) his magazine. Some of the pulp collectors did just that.

I ran into Steranko again at a 1979 summer convention in Tulsa. The
promoter of the show, John Harper, asked if I would do him a favor by taking
Steranko on a tour of local used bookstores. It was kind of a curious situation.
After Steranko insulted almost everyone at the convention, none of the local
fans wanted to do it.

I didn't want to do it, either. But since I owed Harper a favor, I felt obligated to do him the service. The thought of spending an afternoon with Steranko
didn't thrill me. I would have felt more at ease dancing the fandango with
Carmen Miranda.

Before we started out, I suggested to Steranko that he keep a civil tongue.
It was a hot afternoon and the air conditioner in my car was on the blink. I was
in no mood to put up with any nonsense from him. After we were together for
a few minutes, a change came over Steranko. In pure Jekyll-and-Hyde fash-
ion, I watched him turn into a human being. After a while it occurred to me
that his rude behavior in public was an act. Steranko had a peculiar notion that
it was good for his image to make an ass out of himself in public.

When we arrived at the first bookstore, I got a kick out of watching him.
Steranko was like a kid in a candy store. At one point we were about ten feet
apart, scanning the shelves for lost treasures. Suddenly Steranko yelled, "I
can't believe it! I've been looking for this for twenty years!" He clutched the
book to his chest as if it were made out of pearl. As he explained it to me, the

book (on stage magic) was written by a disciple of Houdini. For Steranko, finding the book was a dream come true.

A few minutes later, I stumbled across an ancient-looking book with an occult symbol on the cover, displayed on a stand by itself. I picked it up out of curiosity. The book appeared to be written in gibberish. Noticing my puzzled expression, Steranko asked what was wrong.

I showed him the book. Steranko's eyes bulged when he saw what I had been reading. He snatched the book out of my hands and said, "Don't you know what this is?" I didn't have the foggiest idea. According to Steranko, it was a book of black magic published in England during the 1800s by a coven of witches. According to legend, the book was bound in human flesh.

It sounded to me like something out of a 1930s *Weird Tales* story by Seabury Quinn. At first I thought Steranko was pulling my leg. He was not. As I walked away, Steranko had a smile on his face as he thumbed through the pages. My thought was that maybe he understood some of that gibberish. I'm sure being a former stage magician must have helped.

There were times during my WSA administration when I could have used a little hocus-pocus. When I wasn't sticking my nose in somebody else's business, I spent time promoting WSA and expanding its services.

In some respects WSA had a problem because of its "secret society" image. Much of it can be attributed to Stanley Blair never appearing in public. Since Blair was not a collector, some members of fandom questioned his motives and looked at WSA with suspicion. I daresay that some of it was justified. For this reason, I tried to attend as many conventions as possible.

Since WSA was not the Mafia or the Internal Revenue Service, I wanted to make our services more accessible to members of fandom. The best way to improve our public image was to hold an open meeting at a major convention.

On Saturday, November 27, 1976, we held our first WSA Board of Directors meeting at the Creationcon in New York City. WSA staff members Avery Klein, Bill Cole, Harry Hopkins, and myself directed the meeting. It was an open forum. The following is an edited transcript of the meeting:

RON: First of all, I would like to thank all of you for coming. I see several members of the media, a lot of our members, and a few celebrities. We are glad to have you present. We have a number of things to discuss today, but one of our panel members has another appointment so we are going to give him the floor first. This is Bill Cole of WSA Special Services Division.

BILL: My name is Bill Cole and I have worked for the WSA Program for about two years. I am a firm believer in the program and the principles that were established by Stanley Blair. Stan brought comic book collecting into a more professional field. When I first got into WSA, Stan asked me to take care of the special services.

Ron is now about a month behind answering his mail. We all have a lot of mail that comes in every day. Don't forget, this is not our full-time job. I am a safety engineer and I run two corporations. It might take Ron or me a while to answer your letter, but we try to answer all our mail. If at any time you wish to call me, just leave your name and number with my answering service and I will get back to you.

If there are any questions, I will now accept them from the audience. But before I do that, I would like to comment on the outstanding job Ron has done. He took this program from nothing. He was not involved with the program as Stan Blair was. He took it, and pulled it together in a couple of months, along with help from Avery Klein and Harry Hopkins.

QUESTION: *Have you heard any new developments about the Carlos Johnson case?*

BILL: No, I myself have not, but Ron has. I don't want to get into that right now because that Ron's area. I'm going to let him handle it. Ron will write to a lot of people, including myself and the other board members, regarding cases like Johnson. Mainly, what the rest of us do when we receive a complaint is to forward it to Ron.

RON: Due to the fact that we have a lot of nonmembers here, it would be a good idea to go into the history of the WSA Program. I don't think there is anyone more qualified to tell you about it than the man sitting next to me, Mr. Avery Klein.

AVERY: I first got involved with Stan Blair and the WSA Program when the "Dryden Affair" came about. Since then, I have talked with Stan numerous times. Once he developed the WSA Program he began bouncing ideas off of me. When Stan decided to retire a year or so ago, he asked me if I would take over as Trustee of the Program.

As he explained it, the Trustee's function would be more or less limited as far as policy decisions and such. Ron Frantz would be handling the day-to-day operations and major policy decisions. I agreed to accept the responsibilities of being Trustee; watching over WSA and hopefully trying to develop new programs with Ron and whomever he selected to go along with. I am sort of sitting in a glorified position watching the day-to-day operations which are handled by Ron.

QUESTION: *I am a member of the program and I have been wondering what I can do in getting help from WSA if I'm ripped off by someone who is not a*

This picture of Adam Malin was taken about 1971. Malin (along with his partner Gary Berman) provided the facilities for the WSA Board of Directors Meeting at the '76 Creationcon. Malin went out of his way to be helpful. One could not have asked for a more gracious host.

—from the collection of Richard Garrison

WSA member?

RON: The WSA Program will investigate all mail-fraud cases; members against nonmembers, members against members, or nonmembers against members. It is a rare instance when we receive a complaint regarding a WSA member.

AVERY: Let me explain one thing. Stan worked about eighteen hours a day with the fraud division. He, more or less, took this phase with him when he retired. Actually, it was Stan's request that fraud division be completely terminated, but Ron has carried it on to a limited degree. Over the years, Stan made contacts with the federal government and the postal service. Therefore, he used his influence with congressmen and senators to get action on some of the difficult cases. Ron does not know the same people and can't do the same thing that Stan was able to do. He's doing his best with it but some of the cases are pretty difficult. It's a big country and some of these situations are ugly. Stan realized all that when he retired. That is why he terminated the cases he was handling.

QUESTION (Murray Bischoff, *TBG* columnist): *I sort of have the feeling that your organization puts down fans who are not a member. It's like you are saying that unless you are a WSA member, you have a bad reputation in fandom. Otherwise, I have no complaints about the program.*

HARRY: I think the question has merit, if I can stick two cents in here. As I see it, if you order from a WSA member you have a recourse through WSA if something goes wrong with the transaction. It could be that the guy is on vacation. I know one WSA member who was gone for three months on a cruise. He had complaints filed on him. When he got back, he discovered that WSA was holding the complaints. That saved his reputation.

BILL: I look at the WSA Program as something like the Chamber of Commerce. I belong to the COC in Boston and I will do business with other members quicker than I do with nonmembers, because I know that I have recourse, and they with me. It is sort of like the safety council that I belong to. People like that, because they know that I am a professional. I think we are doing the same thing with WSA, upgrading the role of fans and dealers as professionals.

QUESTION: What does the Registrar do?

HARRY: First of all, I am a Lieutenant in the United States Air Force. I really don't have much spare time. However, I do spend as much time as possible on WSA. I believe in the WSA Program. I believe in what Stan Blair did when he was around and I believe in this crazy, fuzzy-faced person (Ron) sitting over here.

The Registrar is the catchall for just about everything. Everything that Ron doesn't have time to do, the Registrar gets to do. I'm the first point of contact for all members as they enter the program. I send out the membership applications and general information booklet to applicants. I send out about ten a week and only get back about three. I think that people on the outside read the self-imposed requirements of membership and then decided they can't live up to it. The people that do want to live up to it become WSA members.

Also, I have the dubious duty of sending out those little letters that say "you didn't use your WSA logo in your advertisement." I want you to know that this is the very same letter that Stan Blair used. I've gotten some pretty heavy flack about it. I want to explain the reason why we want you to use your WSA logo. This is how WSA gets its advertising. We can't afford to buy advertising space on the $2.50 a year that everyone pays for membership dues. If we charged more, we could; but this is one of the ways that we keep down costs for our members. Also, it gives you reliability. To other people, it tells them that they have recourse through WSA if you don't honor your obligations.

I want you to know that if you receive one of those little letters in the mail reminding you to use your WSA logo, it isn't because we are mad at you. Rather, it is because it is you as fans and advertisers that keeps the program going. It is nothing more than a reminder for you to carry out what you promised to do when you joined the program.

QUESTION: *What can you tell us about the new* Star Trek *division?*

RON: Our new WSA *Star Trek* Division is headed by Mandi Schultz. Mandi is a longtime I fan. She is well known among the *Star Trek* people. The problem of mail fraud in *Star Trek* has become pertinent over the last few years. About a year ago, Mandi approached me with the idea of setting up a special *Star Trek* division. So, Mandi accepted my appointment to serve as the Official WSA Representative to *Star Trek* fandom. In this capacity, Mandi investigates all complaints pertaining to *Star Trek* under my direction and authority.

QUESTION: *Do you do what you do for your organization for money?*

AVERY: The answer is NO! We do not get paid for what we do. We just do it!

QUESTION: *What do you guys collect and what do you do for a living?*

AVERY: I am a CPA and tax attorney. I collect comic books as a hobby. I got into dealing as a collector back in 1967 or 1968. I am more of a collector at heart, than a dealer. I am trying to build three collections for my children.

RON: I began collecting comic books back in 1961. I first became aware of comics fandom in 1965 from *RBCC* ads being run in Marvel Comics. I have collected almost exclusively through the mails for the past ten years. I work part time as a bus driver for Oklahoma City Public Schools, which provides me with ample time to work on WSA matters.

HARRY: I didn't start collecting until 1963. I am one of those people referred to as a Marvel freak. My first real exposure to fandom came with *RBCC #32*, whenever that was. For a living, I run a computer for the Air Force.

QUESTION: *How many WSA members do we have now?*

HARRY: We currently have 1,104 numbers assigned. On the active list, we have 837 to date. Some of the members are now deceased, or did not renew their membership back in 1973. Also, a dozen or so WSA members have been suspended for violations of the Code of Ethics.

QUESTION: *I was just wondering about dues. When does the fiscal year end and the new one begin?*

AVERY: The fiscal year ends on June 30th. Stan Blair retired on June 30, 1975. The fiscal year runs from July to June.

QUESTION: *How is* WE *doing and what is its current circulation?*

RON: Currently, *WE* has a print run of 500. The current paid circulation is about 350. I am very optimistic about it. We are getting a lot of regular advertisers and the ads seem to be pulling well for them.

HARRY: It's going to go on, even if we have to pay for it ourselves.

QUESTION: *I have always wondered how you can tell for sure if a person is a WSA member or not.*

RON: To date, we have never had a problem with anyone falsely claiming to be a WSA member. If you ever run across anyone doing this, we would certainly like to know about it. In fact, should this situation ever arise, I will board a plane to where that person lives, swear out a warrant for their arrest, and stay there until the warrant is served.

Next year we are going to publish a WSA directory. When you pay your dues you will be asked to send information pertaining to your collecting interests and special wants. We will publish that information in a booklet that all dues-paying members will receive a copy of.

QUESTION: *What is the WSA Convention Alliance and what will it do?*

RON: The WSA Convention Alliance is for the purpose of stopping people who are ripping off fans and dealers and conventions. It will be a matter of the WSA working hand in hand with various conventions around the country. We

WE #113, October 1977. Frank Hamilton offers a touching tribute to pulp illustrator Walter M. Baumhofer. This was the final issue I published before stepping down as editor and publisher. I had hoped to go out with a bang. In some respects, I think I did.

will provide the conventions with personnel from our membership to help monitor the convention. It will not be a police organization, but a service. We will help watch a dealer's table if he closes down so that nothing will be stolen during his absence.

In closing, I would like to mention one additional thing for the benefit of Gary Groth and Mike Catron. In the past, *The Nostalgia Journal* was owned by an outfit in Texas called The Syndicate, Inc. A few years ago, an unpleasant conflict developed between the National Central Bureau and The Syndicate, Inc. I do not wish to go into all the gory details because I consider this matter long dead and gone. But at the time, Stan Blair issued a thing called NCB Directive #1 which prohibited the display of the WSA logo by members advertising in *The Nostalgia Journal*.

At this time, I would like to verbally rescind that directive. I will be officially rescinding it in print, shortly. I would like to go on record as saying that the WSA Program endorses the new *Nostalgia Journal*. I think everyone here will agree that Gary and his associates have run a clean and aboveboard operation. Their efforts in behalf of fandom should be encouraged.

The meeting concluded at that point. For me, the matter of endorsing *The Nostalgia Journal* was a classic example of opening the mouth and inserting the foot. I'll comment more about it in the next chapter.

However, our meeting was a success. I had a good time meeting WSA members who lived in the New York area. I met my first wife at the convention. In fact, we had our first date in the movie room, watching a *Red Ryder* western. Nine months later, we were married in New York. WSA member Kevin Pagan attended the wedding.

The WSA Convention Alliance never got off the ground. The same was true for an entity to be known as the WE Hall of Fame. The idea was to acknowledge people who had made outstanding contributions to fandom. No member of the WSA staff (past or present) would be eligible for the award. A committee would determine a yearly winner. Unfortunately, both ideas died for lack of participation. Perhaps it was just as well.

In May of 1977, I told Harry Hopkins and Avery Klein that I planned to resign as WSA Administrator at the end of the year. After almost two years of service, I was just plain wore out. I figured it was time to get on with my life and let someone else deal with the problems of fandom.

However, another matter influenced my decision. It began in February 1977, when a young WSA member sent a letter of resignation. He explained that his father had been blacklisted in the 1950s by Joseph McCarthy's House Un-American Activities Committee.

The young man felt that WSA was practicing a form of blacklisting by publishing the names of people suspected of mail fraud. The thought had never occurred to me. Now, I believe that everyone I ever accused of mail fraud was guilty. There was physical evidence to back up the allegation. Usually, there was lots of it. However, I began to wonder what might happen if an innocent person were falsely accused. The thought was very disturbing to me. I had no desire for anyone to associate what I did with the likes of Joseph McCarthy.

I discussed my feelings with Blair. He felt I was overreacting to the situation and suggested that I take a vacation. During the third week in March, I spent a week in New York. It didn't help.

After I was married in July of 1977, I began to wind down my WSA activities. I transferred most of the workload to Harry Hopkins, who would succeed me as Administrator. In October, I published my last issue of *WE*, which announced my forthcoming resignation as WSA Administrator.

Since it would be my last issue, I wanted to do something special.

It had been years since the last special "pulp" issue, so I figured it was time to do one. The issue featured a marvelous cover and article by Frank Hamilton about pulp illustrator Walter Baumhofer. The issue proved to be quite popular. Jerry De Fuccio, the former associate editor at *MAD* magazine, expressed his pleasure:

> That's a particularly delectable issue of *WE* as I am a very big Walter M. Baumhofer fan. I recall in 1956, I had been instrumental in getting artist Bob Powell a very lucrative account with Topps Gum Cards. Things had gone sour in the comic books for him, so it was a a timely rescue for him, I suppose.
>
> Powell wanted to give me something prized and unique. He had done comics for Street and Smith so he had acquired a *Doc Savage* original cover painting by W.M.B.
>
> It was a tantalizing choice between the *Doc Savage* cover and a lampshade on which Powell had painted his myriad comic book characters. Naturally, discretion and friendship meant I had to select the lampshade over the *Doc Savage* painting. And I'm not sorry.

Coming back down to earth, the announcement of my forthcoming resignation seemed to catch a lot of people by surprise. Afterwards, I received several letters from WSA members, asking me to reconsider my decision. The only person who really seemed to understand the situation was my friend Bob Sampson, who wrote:

> Dear Ron:
>   Sorry to hear that you are retiring. Or perhaps not. The load that you have been carrying is OK for a short while. But this being an ombudsman—and unpaid at that—gets too burdensome for a part-

time effort. It's difficult to earn a living and spend all your time on fan activity, too.

Congratulations, then, on a splendid job. You kept right in Stan's tradition, amplifying and expanding the effort, instead of merely imitating it. You have done a first class job and we're proud of you. Thanks.

In my last few weeks, I encountered a minor problem while attending a social function. In December of 1977, I had the pleasure of meeting artist Alex Toth at a convention in Oklahoma City.

Late one evening, about a dozen collectors met with Toth in his hotel room. It had been a pleasant evening. We listened while Toth regaled us with stories from his long career in comics and animation. Suddenly the phone rang. Toth stopped to answer it. The call was from his wife. While he talked, it became apparent that Toth had become irritated.

When he returned, one of the guys asked what was wrong. Toth shook his head, and told a story about trading pages of his original art for some 1930s Sunday newspaper comic pages. Evidently, after the trade had been made, Toth's trading partner had a change of mind and wanted to cancel the deal. He returned the original art and demanded that Toth return the Sunday pages.

After a few days had passed, he wrote Toth a nasty letter, telling him that he had five days to return the Sunday pages or "the WSA Program would hound him to the end of the Earth." With a pained expression on his face, Toth said, "I guess I will have to write WSA and try to straighten out this mess."

At that point, several people in the room started to chuckle. At first, Toth didn't understand what was funny. Then Robert Brown said, "I don't think you will have a problem with the WSA, Alex." When Toth inquired why not, Brown pointed at me and said, "That is the WSA sitting across from you."

Toth seemed a little puzzled at first. He looked at me and said, "YOU are the WSA?" Feeling a little embarrassed by the unexpected attention, I told Toth that I was the WSA Administrator . . . or at least I would be for the next few weeks.

I asked Toth who he had been trading with. Of course, I knew the person; too well, in fact. He had been a thorn in my side since almost the first day. This guy was constantly squabbling with someone. Seemed like I was forever trying to play peacemaker in his behalf. He really wasn't a bad person, just hot-tempered and a little childish.

I told Toth not to worry about a thing. I would take care of the problem. As the matter stood, Toth had no obligation to return the Sunday pages unless he wanted to. It was his choice and I encouraged Toth to do whatever he thought was best.

I called Toth's trading partner a couple of days later. Most of the time, I

After we met in 1977, Alex Toth and I corresponded for a time. It explains this cute little cartoon. Toth came very close to doing the cover illustration for this book. Unfortunately, he got bogged down with deadlines on animation work with Hanna-Barbera and had to beg off. Oh well. You can't win them all.

just wrote a letter. However, since the time was short, this situation called for a more direct approach. In a parental kind of way, I told our WSA member that he was acting like a jackass! It was time to grow up and play nice. I never did find out what Toth did with those Sunday pages.

My final task was to prepare the records for shipping. I had accumulated a ton of paper that had to be sorted. Some of it was of a personal nature, which I kept. Other portions had little importance and were disposed of.

In the meantime, Harry Hopkins busied himself reorganizing WSA. He appointed Scott Tillman director of the mail-fraud division. John Hemmings became the new editor of *WE*. Steve Barrington, Gregory Pipel, William Turner, Richard Fifeld, Chester Cox, and Mariane Soroka (who later became Mrs. Harry Hopkins) joined the staff in one capacity or another.

I had one telephone conversation with Tillman, briefing him on some of the fraud cases still in process. Tillman had no idea what he was letting himself in for. However, I didn't want to discourage him. Tillman would find out soon enough that he had opened a can of worms.

During the next few weeks, I shipped out a dozen boxes of material to Hopkins, Tillman, and Hemmings. Then my job was done. I was ready to be a full-time husband and father. A new career was waiting in the field of retail management. Once again, my life was my own. For a while I felt like a fish out of water.

Hopkins and his staff would soon face new problems. I was hardly out the door when the WSA staff began to quarrel among themselves.

As I look back on my WSA days from twenty mileposts down the road, the following lyric by the Grateful Dead holds a special sentiment:

Sometimes the light's all shining on me. Other times I can barely see.
Lately, it occurs to me what a long, strange trip it's been.

How true.

CHAPTER FIVE

Battles That Shocked Through Collecting

The greatest battle a person must constantly fight is to uphold proper principles, known truths against everyone he deals with. A truth cannot be defeated. But when a man refuses to know what is right or deliberately accepts, or does what he knows is wrong . . . he defeats himself. The truth remains unbeaten.

—Steve Ditko

Many years ago there was a professional wrestler named "Wild" Red Berry. On his way to the ring, Berry wore a faded old warm-up jacket. The words "I AM RIGHT" were sewn in bold letters on the back. It seemed like Berry had a perpetual feud going with someone. He was never at a loss for words.

In 1957, Berry appeared as a contestant on the *You Bet Your Life* radio show. The following is an abridged transcript of Berry's dialogue with Groucho Marx:

GROUCHO: How do you account for your success in the ring, Red? You don't seem to be particularly large and muscular. How can you beat all these gorillas? Are you better at memorizing the script?

BERRY: Because of my brilliant intellect. I cause my opponents to proceed into a state of bewilderment, genuine uncertainty, and a disturbing state of inferiority. On the horns of dilemma, I paralyze, pulverize, terrorize, demoralize, eradicate, destroy, demolish, ostracize, and drive them to the sudden depths of despair . . . and right through the mat!

GROUCHO: You just talk 'em to death, is that it? Red, you know, I'm astonished that a man of action can be so articulate. How do you account for this streak of Demosthenes here?

BERRY: Due to the fact, Groucho, the cause of so much trouble in this old world is that people are not able to express themselves adequately, accurately, convincingly, and expressively. I have made it a habit, and taken plenty of time so that people can understand what I have to say, so even the most stupid dolt among them may understand what I have to say!

GROUCHO: Well, why are you looking at ME that way?

Obviously, Berry lived in a world of make believe. However, he understood the difference between ideals and reality. This is more than can be said about some members of fandom. Behaving as if foolishness were a virtue, fans often achieve notoriety by feuding. These acts frequently produce behavior patterns that would have shamed the Hatfields and McCoys.

Sadly, this nonsense began in the 1930s among science fiction fans. It has continued in varying degrees to the present. Although disagreements between fans are routine occurrences, a fan feud is something more. In these confrontations combatants strive to eliminate one another from existence as a fan. A mere difference of opinion is usually all the justification required. The childish warfare is then bitterly carried on in fanzines, correspondence, and personal meetings. Lawsuits are contemplated over the drop of an insult.

In the early 1970s a more serious type of fan feud emerged. Unlike the tame ideological confrontations between fans, these feuds began with greed. Most of the feuding took place among fanzine publishers. In the beginning, these amateur fan publications served as a mode of communication between fans. Fans produced them as a labor of love as there was little profit to be made.

Initially, fanzines were something of a sociological phenomenon. Essentially uncensored, fanzine publishers rarely abused their freedom of speech, using the periodicals to foster a sense of camaraderie that crossed the lines of age, ethnic, and social backgrounds. It would be difficult for anyone to find fault with that. Fredric Wertham once commented that "fanzines show a combination of indepence and responsibility not easily found elsewhere in our culture."

By the late 1960s, fandom was experiencing growing pains. Fanzine circulations began to grow as more collectors entered the hobby. Fanzines slowly evolved from crude-looking mimeographed productions to professional looking, photo-offset magazines. Somewhere along the way they lost their sense of

Early fanzines are as scarce as the proverbial hen's teeth. Due to very limited circulations, few have survived the passing of time. The few remaining copies are usually buried in private collections and rarely see the light of day. This particular copy of the *Science Fiction Advertiser* from 1954 had once belonged to Joseph W. Miller, publisher of one of the first Edgar Rice Burroughs fanzines . . . *The Barsoomian*. The cover art is by fan favorite Morris Scott Dollens.

modesty. A few fanzines accepted advertising from collectors who desired to buy or sell collectibles. Before long, entrepreneurs took advantage of the profit-making potential. They were the founding fathers of the adzine.

The most successful of the adzine entrepreneurs was Alan Light, of East Moline, Illinois. In 1970, Light launched *The Buyer's Guide for Comic Fandom*. He was the first fan publisher to use the tabloid newspaper format. In the process, he made himself quite wealthy. By 1980, *TBG* was circulated weekly to over ten thousand subscribers. Naturally, this success inspired imitation.

At the time of *TBG*'s inception, two moderately successful adzines existed: *The Rocket's Blast-Comicollector* and *Stan's Weekly Express*. Both publications soon suffered a loss of advertising and circulation. Because comic book fans are not known for their fidelity, *WE* and *RBCC* passed away quietly. Their demise affected only a few fans.

Having introduced the tabloid format to fandom, Light resented other people imitating his product. Acting in his own best interests, Light entered into feuds with these upstarts.

The first *TBG* imitator to incur Light's displeasure was *The Mirkwood Times*. Despite a lackluster beginning, *TMT* showed a potential that was never fulfilled. The details of the conflict are now vague and known primarily only to the principals involved. *TMT* folded after the sixth issue.

In September 1973, the first issue of *The Journal* appeared. It was published out of Essex, Ontario, by a teenaged journalist named Paul Kowtuik. Beginning with the second issue. *TJ* merged with the defunct *Mirkwood Times,* boosting circulation to more than five thousand subscribers.

A short time later, Kowtuik experienced problems with Light. It began when Light submitted an advertisement for *TBG,* which Kowtuik published. In return for the courtesy, Kowtuik submitted a similar advertisement for publication in *TBG*. Light promptly rejected the ad on the basis that he would not allow a competitor to advertise in *TBG*.

Kowtuik was understandably miffed. It was the beginning of a bitter dispute between the publishers, which threatened to blow itself out of proportion to its real importance. Then, on October 14, 1974, National Central Bureau director Stanley Blair intervened. At the mutual request of Light and Kowtuik, Blair devised a formal agreement ending the open hostilities.

Demonstrating a keen sense of business acumen, Light immediately escalated *TBG*'s publishing deadlines from biweekly to weekly. Kowtuik lacked the necessary capital to keep up. He maintained his monthly schedule. Kowtuik's advertisers deserted him in droves, putting the kiss of death on *The Journal.* The final issue, #27, was published in December 1975. Alan Light had effectively dispatched another competitor. His next foe, however, would be more formidable.

The demise of *The Journal* was not particularly noticed. A new Texas-based periodical called *The Nostalgia Journal* assumed its place in the market. *TNJ*'s publishers were soon embroiled in a squabble with Light and Stanley Blair. The conflict received a lot of commentary within the fan press, most of which was inaccurate, incomplete, or badly distorted. Contrary to popular opinion, the heated dispute did not become a conflagration overnight. Rather, it was a situation where one incident led to another.

Four years earlier, a seemingly unrelated incident set the stage for the drama. In the spring of 1971, while Blair was busy publishing his *Weekly Express*, he received a request from Larry Herndon, the spokesman for a Dallas convention called D-Con. According to Herndon, an agreement existed between the Dallas, Houston, and Oklahoma City factions specifying that the annual Southwestern convention be rotated yearly between the three cities. It was known in fan circles as the Tri-Fan Alliance. Houston staged the 1970 convention and the 1971 event was scheduled for Dallas.

Herndon alleged that Earl Blair (no relation to Stan) violated this agreement by openly promoting a 1971 Houston convention. Herndon requested that Houstoncon's advertising be withheld from *WE* in light of Earl Blair's breach of promise. Herndon made similar requests of other publishers, but only Stan Blair honored it.

Naturally, this did not sit well with Earl Blair. Earl claimed that no formal agreement existed between the parties involved. Earl promised to provide Stan with documentation to substantiate his position. He failed to do so. Houstoncon '71 went on as scheduled. In the program booklet, Earl chastised Stan for withholding Houstoncon's advertising.

Stan defended his position by publishing an editorial entitled "Houstoncon vs. WE" in his own publication. It should have set the matter to rest. It did not. In particular, a permanent barrier was wedged between Houston and Dallas. Despite the open hostilities, both conventions did well. There is no visible evidence that Houston affected Dallas in terms of attendance. The two conventions were held one week apart. Many fans attended both.

There was more to the conflict. In truth, both groups were partially at fault. The following rhetoric published in the March 1971 issue of *OAF* points to some of the specific issues:

> How much bombastic baloney from south of the Red River are we [in Oklahoma] going to have to listen to? Isn't it about time that the fast-mouths of both cities laid it on the line, and stopped tap-dancing around the facts.
>
> HOUSTON!! How about knocking off the pious lip smacking and just come right out and say that you can't be trusted to keep your word! Why not admit your sense of honor is about as strong as your ability to withstand the urge to make a quick buck. You're holding a

convention in Houston for one reason . . . YOU WANT THE MONEY
IN YOUR POCKETS THAT A CON WILL BRING IN, AND YOU
DON'T WANT TO SHELL OUT FOR THE DRIVE TO DALLAS!
Only an idiot would believe that a city that gets the con the very next
year would jump the gun and break a promise out of a "concern for
comic fandom."

DALLAS!! You finally got caught, didn't you? You snickered at
comic book fans once too often. Do you really think that comic book
fans are as childish as you pictured in your D-Con editorials? Maybe
they are a bit on the cracked side, but even a four year old collector of
SUGAR & SPIKE could look at your convention plans and see you
did everything but confine comic book collectors to the Mens' room.
You did not offer a single comic book guest. You did not offer a
single movie guest, which most comics fans are. Your film line up
looked like the program for a girl's church group. Then, you topped
it off by telling everyone that: "This will give us a chance to show
SCIENCE FICTION FANS what kind of a con Dallas can put on!"

The Dallas and Houston factions were divided by ideological differences.
They had little in common. Historically, science fiction and comic book fans
have difficulty seeing eye to eye.

For whatever reason, Stan Blair sided with Dallas. Blair believed that he
was doing the right thing. Strangely, some of the Dallas fans, including Larry
Herndon, resented the way Stan Blair handled the situation. Blair did not understand why. Although these feelings were inconsequential at the time, lin-
gering resentments resulted in future conflict.

Three years later, Alan Light and Larry Herndon reached an agreement.
While Herndon promoted the 1974 D-Con, Light agreed to publish convention
advertising free in exchange for distribution of a *TBG* promotional flyer at the
convention. Somehow, a portion of Herndon's advertising reached Light too
late to be published before the convention. Angered at what was his own neg-
ligence, Herndon did not distribute Light's flyers.

In response, Light denied Herndon advertising privileges in *TBG* and canceled his subscription. Not to be outdone, Herndon joined with Joe Bob Williams, Gordon Bailey, Don Maris, Mark Lamberti, and a secret investor later
revealed to be Bob Overstreet to start *The Nostalgia Journal*.

Complimentary copies of the first issue, dated July 1974, were distributed at the 1974 Houstoncon. On a table display, fans were asked to provide
their names and addresses to receive a free six-issue subscription. While attending the convention, I filled out cards for myself and several friends not in
attendance. This included Stanley Blair.

The second issue of *TNJ* arrived a few weeks after the convention. Blair

Program book for the 1971 Dallas summer convention, featuring
a sketch by Richard Corben. Guests included Forrest J. Ackerman
and Robert "Psycho" Bloch. The only disappointment came when
Frank Frazetta canceled at the last minute. For some odd reason,
Frazetta preferred to meet an art deadline instead of spending a
weekend mingling with 500 comic book and science fiction fans.

also received the issue, which contained a news release he had written about mail-fraud artist Arnold Meyrowitz. The same release was published simultaneously in *TBG* and other publications.

Shortly thereafter, Blair received a bill for $9 from *TNJ* for publishing the text as a quarter-page advertisement. This action displeased Blair, who was unaccustomed to paying for the publication of his news releases. Nevertheless, he paid the bill.

About this same time, Blair received several mail-fraud complaints against Larry Herndon. The complaints alleged that Herndon had failed to ship prepaid merchandise ordered by mail. There was a good reason: Herndon had been ill. Blair was unaware of the situation. As a matter of protocol, he sent Herndon several letters of inquiry.

These letters angered Herndon, who felt that he was above that sort of thing. He answered Blair with a sharply worded reply. Considering that their relationship was already strained, Herndon's reply manifested growing feelings of hostility. Herndon's obligations were eventually fulfilled by Don Maris, who purchased the business.

The third issue of *TNJ* was published in August, followed by a fourth issue in September. In a very short time, *TNJ* generated considerable interest within fandom. This interest was reflected by the following review published in a 1974 issue of *Inside Comics*:

> Here's another contender for the adzine championship title. The champ is still THE BUYER'S GUIDE, but some say it may be weakened from all the challengers its been KO-ing lately. But TBG's ringwise slugger Alan Light is a tough defender of the crown. It remains to be seen if TNJ's Gordon Bailey can muster the Sunday punch needed to put Light on the canvas.
>
> TBG has it over TNJ in bulk and reach, hitting 6500 subscribers to TNJ's 6000 and easily tripling TNJ's handful of pages. But Bailey can slam a hard one-two under Light's defenses with lower ad rates and free subscriptions. They're both dancing in the early rounds, but Bailey is impressing them all the way to the back seats with his fancy foot work and battle savvy.
>
> He should, they're the same tactics Light used to pound his way to the top—the mailing lists gathered at conventions, from names gleaned in fan publications, and fan's submitting requests for freebies. Bailey has an entourage with his from many collecting bents: radio, films, premiums, comics, etc. due to these name gathering techniques. The question remains: can Bailey deck Light? Right now the smart money's on the champ. But the odds aren't as wide as they've been in other matches. The spunky challenger has a good organization behind him

and the ability to toss a mean haymaker. He's showing a lot of moxie in the front end of the bout. Up until now, Light's jaw hasn't stood still long enough for anyone to see if its made of glass. Bailey ought to be the guy to find this out. If he doesn't pull an upset, we can at least look for him to go the distance.

On October 1, 1974, Stan Blair wrote Gordon Bailey, informing him that he had not received issues three and four of *TNJ*. Blair requested the issues along with a letter of confirmation. Blair did not receive a reply. Blair wrote again several weeks later, repeating his request.

About the first of November, Blair received a hostile reply from "L.T. Dean" of the *TNJ* back-issue department. Dean informed Blair that *TNJ* had replied to both his letters, "even though he did not have the courtesy to enclose an SASE." He let Blair know that *TNJ* back issues were available for fifty cents each. He compounded the situation by asking if Blair wished to receive future issues. Of course, L.T. Dean was Larry Herndon. Perhaps he thought it comical, pretending to be someone else. Blair, however, was not amused.

On November 4, 1974, Blair replied that he had no intention of paying fifty cents each for issues he should have received as part of his subscription. Further, he asserted that his only need of *TNJ* was for monitoring purposes. If he could not receive issues, he would arrange for WSA members to withdraw their advertising from *TNJ*.

Shortly after this letter was written, Blair requested that I visit with Don Maris in his behalf. Maris owned a comic book store in Norman, Oklahoma, and we saw one another from time to time. About a year earlier, Blair had negotiated a settlement between Maris and Alan Light over a conflict in publishing comic book reprints. As a *TNJ* stockholder, Maris was not actively involved with its publication. However, Blair felt he could receive an honest evaluation of *TNJ*'s intentions from Maris. Upon reflection, this seems like something Blair could (or should) have done himself. Blair must have had some personal reason for asking me to do it.

According to Maris, several *TNJ* subscriptions had been discarded by an incompetent computer programmer. Blair just happened to be one of the losses. Maris could only assume that the "L.T. Dean" business was a misunderstanding. He did not believe that *TNJ* would deliberately prevent Blair from receiving issues.

The dispute between Blair and *TNJ* escalated following the publication of issue #6, November 1974. In the issue, a reader presented the following question to editor Joe Bob Williams: "Does *TNJ* support The National Central Bureau?"

Williams replied: "We do support NCB and other organizations concerned with expediting fair play in fandom. The Director of NCB (Blair) is a good friend of several of our associates and NCB has a good track record. So while we are not personally a member of NCB, we do support their principles of fair play and honesty."

This statement infuriated Blair. He did not consider himself friendly with *TNJ,* nor did he feel they supported him. Blair felt *TNJ* was trying to ride his coattails and he wanted no part of it. On November 9, 1974, Blair sent a registered letter to Williams demanding a retraction. He warned that if he did not receive notification within seven days, he would make the necessary retraction himself.

Williams did not take the threat seriously. He ignored Blair, which proved to be a mistake. True to his word, Blair issued his own retraction, published in *TBG, RBCC,* and *The Journal.* Next, he issued National Central Bureau Directive Number One, prohibiting WSA members from displaying membership logos while advertising in *TNJ.* The directive was mailed to approximately one hundred WSA members with SASE on file.

It came as no surprise when an unidentified WSA member provided *TNJ* with a copy of the directive. Upon receiving it, *TNJ* threatened to sue Blair.

At the 1974 Wintercon held December 1-3 in Oklahoma City, I had an opportunity to discuss these matters with Joe Bob Williams. I had hoped that some compromise could be reached to avoid unnecessary litigation. As unimportant as it seemed at the time, this incident set off a chain reaction that, over the next five years, would destroy the WSA Program.

I found Williams to be friendly and cooperative. He seemed genuine in his belief that all of *TNJ*'s problems with Blair were a misunderstanding. He hoped the matter could be resolved without going to court. Williams requested Blair's unlisted telephone number so he could discuss the matter with him personally. I gave Williams the number.

With Williams's consent, I provided Blair with a basic summary of our conversation in a letter. Upon receiving it, Blair passed the information along to Alan Light. I never understood why. Quite frankly, I considered my conversation with Williams a personal matter. There was no reason for Light to know what Williams and I had talked about. In my opinion, it was none of his business.

Nevertheless, Light used the information as the basis for an editorial in *TBG* entitled "A Cover-up In Fandom?" Light criticized *TNJ* for quarreling with Blair, questioning the integrity of Williams's comments. Light meant well. He felt Blair was getting a raw deal from *TNJ* and tried to defend him.

A few months later, I learned that the *TNJ* staff was very upset with me. They believed my conversation with Williams was a ploy to set them up. They accused me of being a stooge for Light. Nothing could have been further from the truth. I had never met the man. To this very day, we have never laid eyes on one another.

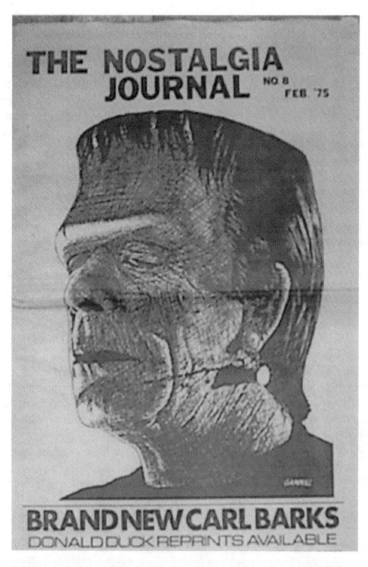

By this eighth issue, dated February 1975, things were really going well for *The Nostalgia Journal.* This particular issue totaled 52 tabloid-sized pages. Kerry Gammill (soon to be a popular artist at Marvel Comics) contributed the cover. Sadly, the publishers were unable to sustain the momentum. A year and a half later, the periodical was sold to Gary Groth and renamed *The Comics Journal.*

Williams did not call Blair, as he had promised to do. Instead, Light's editorial prompted *TNJ* to file a libel suit against Light and Blair. I understand that at one point *TNJ* considered naming me as a third defendant.

Immediately following Light's editorial, Williams countered the charges with an editorial of his own. It said very little. Williams promised to reveal *TNJ*'s version of the squabble in the next issue. For some reason, that bit of rhetoric did not see print. Meanwhile, Light tried to settle the case out of court, offering to buy 51 percent of *TNJ* for $10,000. The offer included several stipulations suggested by Blair:

1.   No *TNJ* staff member or stockholder would start another adzine for a period of three years.

2.   No *TNJ* staff member or stockholder would divulge any facts regarding the transaction without Light's permission.

3.   Light would immediately assume full editorial control of *TNJ*.

4.   Gordon Bailey would replace Joe Bob Williams as editor.

It was a reasonable offer. However, Williams considered it insulting. He refused to sell his shares of stock and convinced several other stockholders to do the same.

Blair walked away from the situation. He felt that his Directive had severed all ties between the National Central Bureau and *TNJ*. He had nothing more to say. In a personal letter to me of December 13, 1974, Blair wrote, "Frankly, I detest being involved in a row of my own. I really prefer to spend my time protecting the people who really need NCB."

Six months later, Blair retired. Being in ill health, he paid no attention to the outstanding litigation. Ironically, Blair lacked the necessary funds to hire an attorney. When Light learned of his predicament, he stuffed three $100 bills into an envelope and mailed it to Blair.

Following Blair's retirement, I became Administrator of the WSA Program. I made no effort to enforce Blair's edict prohibiting WSA members from advertising in *TNJ*. Frankly, I needed a lawsuit like I needed another nose.

In August 1975, the case of *The Nostalgia Journal* v. Alan L. Light and Stanley R. Blair had its day in court. Blair chose not to appear. As a result, the court enjoined Blair from publishing or communicating libelous statements against *TNJ*. The matter of *TNJ* v. Alan L. Light was rescheduled for a later hearing.

On October 22, 1975, Light distributed a flyer to everyone who placed an advertisement in *TNJ* #15. The flyer questioned *TNJ*'s circulation figures. Light alleged the figures were flagrantly overstated, basing his allegation on information obtained from the postmaster at Lewisville, Texas. Light claimed that only 2,101 copies were mailed instead of 7,000.

TNJ countered these allegations by distributing an undated flyer of its own. It stated that Light's flyer was full of inaccuracies, incorrect conclusions, and false information. *TNJ* defended its circulation figures by declaring that issue #15 was sent in three staggered mailings, with 4,730 copies mailed in total. Remaining copies were distributed at conventions.

In another undated flyer, Light alleged that the staggered mailings of *TNJ* #15 were completed a month and a half after the advertising deadline. He stated that only 2,101 copies were mailed as of October 16, 1975, accusing *TNJ* of rushing 3,000 additional copies into the mail. He called it a scandal. Then *TNJ* issued a second flyer to counter Light's. The entire situation reminded one of children pointing fingers and calling one another names.

While attending a Dallas convention in October 1975, I chanced upon Larry Herndon, Gordon Bailey, and Joe Bob Williams sitting together in the hotel coffee shop. I accepted an invitation to join them. The conversation was mostly casual. I guess it was inevitable that their feud with Light would pop up during the conversation. Williams was a little cold in the beginning, remembering our last conversation at Wintercon '74. Williams gradually warmed after he convinced himself that Light and I were not a pair of Siamese twins.

During our talk, the three men said they were weary of the feud. It had become time consuming and expensive. I offered a logical solution: Stop the name calling and suggest that Light do the same. In spirit, they were willing. They just didn't know how to go about it.

It so happened that I had been giving some thought to the subject, as most of the particulars involving the feud had crossed my desk. It's like Yogi Berra once said: "You can observe a lot by just watching." I had a few ideas, which I outlined to them. I was pleased they found them tentatively acceptable. They said, in their own words, "We're willing to quit if Light is."

The following Monday morning, I called Light to discuss the matter. During our conversation he expressed similar sentiments. He, too, was ready to quit. In principle, he agreed with my plan for an out-of-court settlement.

A few days later, I completed a rough draft of the agreement. I phoned both Light and Herndon, reading it aloud to both. Each approved. Herndon pointed out that it was necessary for each *TNJ* stockholder to approve, then sign, the agreement. We agreed that the document would first be sent to Light for his signature. Then he would send it to Herndon for all to sign. Briefly, the document read:

1.   Both parties agreed that I was to serve as witness to the agreement and mediator to both parties.

2.   Both parties agreed not to mention the other in a derogatory manner in any medium, printed or otherwise. This included the combined staff and employees of both publications.

3.   Both parties agreed that upon signing the agreement, all outstanding litigation would be terminated.

4.   Both parties agreed to publish the following statement in their respective publications: "ALL DIFFERENCES BETWEEN TBG AND TNJ HAVE BEEN RESOLVED."

After sending the agreement to Light, I received a reply on November 15, 1975. It was no deal. It seemed Light had consulted his attorney, who advised him not to sign it under any circumstances. Meanwhile, the judicial system moved forward. In early December, the case of *The Nostalgia Journal* v. Alan L. Light moved forward.

Attorney Bradshaw (representing Light) and Attorney Farris (representing *TNJ*) drew up a resolution that was essentially the same document I had devised. I'm sure this was not a coincidence. As a final resolution, the court ordered that the following statement be published in *TBG* and *TNJ*: "ALL DIFFERENCES BETWEEN TBG AND TNJ HAVE BEEN RESOLVED THIS DATE."

I found it odd that Light and *TNJ* were willing to pay several thousand dollars in attorney's fees for work I had done for free. The end result was the same.

Further, the court decreed that the temporary injunction rendered against Blair would become permanent. All court costs were taxed against him. This action came in default. For a second time, Blair did not appear.

These actions brought a temporary peace between the combatants. Light published the court-ordered statement in the next issue. For some reason, *TNJ* took its time. Several issues came and went. This resulted in some verbal jabs exchanged between Light and *TNJ*.

About four months later, the feud was reinstigated by an outsider. I received the following letter, dated April 12, 1976:

RONALD:

We at Syndicate have decided we are against WSA and will blast it in TNJ at every opportunity. Fucking Stan ain't around no more (I hope he's dead), so, podner, you and that organization aren't anything. You're your own ripoff.

Larry Herndon

The letter was postmarked Miami, Florida. For this reason, I knew that Herndon had nothing to do with it. Herndon was confined to a wheelchair and rarely traveled. My first thought was that someone in Florida was trying to provoke a dispute between Herndon and me. At the time, I had no idea about the motive.

The person who wrote the letter was by no means a bumpkin. The bad grammar, the Texas-style euphemisms, were a ruse. The letter does not contain a single misspelling. The punctuation is near-perfect. The writer was not illiterate.

I phoned Herndon the same morning the letter arrived, thinking he might be interested. From Herndon, I learned that my crank letter was only one of many. Each *TNJ* staff member received similar letters, some supposedly written by me. Moreover, each staff member, stockholder, and columnist discovered that their mail had been forwarded to California.

About a week earlier, I received a call from Steve Barrington, who wrote a column for *TNJ*. Barrington discovered his mail was heading west and wanted to know what he should do about it. To say the least, he was not a happy man.

It seems that anyone who was associated in any way with *TNJ* began to receive dozens of unwanted books and records in the mail. Evidently, the same person responsible for the crank letters had submitted unauthorized change of address cards with the post office, along with applications to various book and record clubs.

The tale grew more sordid. Larry Herndon's parents received a letter offering condolences about the recent "death" of their son, Larry. About this same time, an Army recruiter showed up at Herndon's home to speak with him about enlisting. The recruiter discovered he had been made a pawn to a cruel hoax when he discovered Herndon confined to a wheelchair.

The guilty party carefully covered his tracks, making a trace by postal inspectors impossible. Because Light and *TNJ* were still at one another's throats, some of the *TNJ* staff suspected him of being naughty. As a result, a postal inspector paid Light a visit. Light, who had nothing to do with any of it, voluntarily submitted samples of his handwriting and typewriters.

In a telephone conversation with Light, I suggested that he take precautions to protect himself, as he or I could well be the next target. In my mind, we were dealing with a maniac.

The only thing unusual that happened to me in this time frame was receiving a half-dozen phone calls from military recruiters. Someone set them on

No, it's not Fred McMurray wearing long underwear. It's the "Big Red Cheese" doing a guest appearance on the cover of *TBG* #26, December 1972. Of course, Captain Marvel is a copyrighted character of DC Comics, Inc. They might get upset if I failed to mention that.

my trail. One fellow, from the Navy, seemed particularly anxious to drag me into uniform. I thought I would never get rid of him.

Unfortunately, the villain of this drama never revealed himself. At one point, I entertained notions that someone on the *TNJ* staff might have orchestrated the incident to cast suspicion on Light. Some of them hated him that much. But it became obvious that the harassment was too widespread (and painful) to have been self-inflicted.

For some years now, I've had a suspicion about the true identity of the guilty party. This person is still very active in fandom. Unfortunately, I have no physical evidence to substantiate an allegation. For this reason, I'll keep the thought to myself. However, I will say this person had much to gain . . . and did.

In May 1976, the feud picked up where it had left off. On May 4, Light distributed a flyer to the advertisers of *TNJ* #24. After checking *TNJ*'s third-class mailing receipts, Light discovered that 2,612 copies of #22, 1,754 copies of #23, and 1,115 copies of #24 had been mailed. Light suggested that each advertiser demand a refund in view of the misrepresented circulation. It came as no surprise when *TNJ* countered the allegation with an undated flyer of its own.

Once again, advertisers of both publications read about staggered mailings and copies distributed at conventions. Both parties accused the other of every imaginable sin while proclaiming themselves innocent of any wrongdoing. After a while, everyone became tired of hearing about it. Most fans didn't care much one way or the other. It seemed only another date before the judge would put an end to the squabbling.

While these events were going on, several WSA members inquired about WSA's position on the matter. Unfounded rumors began to circulate in fandom that WSA had taken one side or the other. To help clear the air, I wrote the following editorial published in *WE* #106:

> A number of WSA members have written or called to ask about the raging battle of words presently taking place between two of fandom's premier publishers. I am not going to identify them here, as I'm certain you know who they are. The only comment I will make regarding this vendetta is neither side has disclosed all the facts, and both have tended to exaggerate their side of the story. It is not my place to criticize these individuals as this is their affair.
>
> I do believe, however, that the pages of their publications is not the place to bring out their petty squabbles. Disputes of this nature should be brought out in their proper time and place—that being a court of law. It is my advice at this time that you do not concern yourself with this matter. As I stated previously—this is THEIR affair—WE will have no part of it.

Suddenly, the feud came to an end. On June 14, 1976, Light wrote to Gordon Bailey and said, "I'm willing to cut the crap and grow up." Light admitted he had been childish about the feud and that some of his actions were probably unforgivable. Light asked for Bailey's forgiveness, expressing a hope that they might one day be friends. Bailey did not respond, which was probably just as well.

By June of 1976, *TNJ* had run out of steam. The stress of operating at a loss took its toll on the owners' enthusiasm. The conflict with Light did not help. The last few issues were late. As publishing deadlines deteriorated, so did paid advertising. Several *TNJ* stockholders sold their shares to associates.

A new development occurred on June 29, 1976. Light wrote to inform me that Gary Groth of Rockville, Maryland, would become editor of *TNJ* with issue #27. Groth planned to publish an exposé of Light's activities in fandom. Groth announced his intentions by contacting several *TBG* columnists, asking for information about Light.

Through sources of my own, I learned that Groth had purchased *The Nostalgia Journal* for one dollar. Groth and Light had been partners once upon a time, producing a periodical called *Fantastic Fanzine*. After publishing several issues, Groth and Light had a falling out and dissolved their partnership. Not all the facts are available, but it is known that the pair parted ways on the worst possible terms.

A short time later, Groth started an adzine of his own called *Fantastic Adzine*. It lasted about as long as a short beer at a German food festival. The failure of *Fantastic Adzine* contributed to Groth's intense dislike for Light, prompting the exposé.

Groth's exposé contained opinion, rumor, innuendo, and a smattering of fact. As far as I know, Light made no effort to refute the allegations. Instead, he published a lengthy article about himself in *TBG* that pertained to his history in fandom, childhood (with photos), and a brief commentary about his endearing personal qualities.

To most outsiders, Light's article concluded the debacle. This was not the case. Considerable vexation continued between Light and Groth, most of which was unknown to fandom at large. As a courtesy to all, most of it was kept between themselves.

Groth and Light crossed trails at the 1976 New York and San Diego conventions. Groth made a nuisance of himself on both occasions. In New York, Groth and his entourage went out of their way to annoy Light and his assistant, Murray Bishoff. There, Groth conducted his facetious "Interview with Alan Light," published in *TNJ* #27. Light grew weary of the heckling and asked Phil Seuling, the convention chairman, to persuade Groth to desist.

The next month in San Diego, Groth made certain copies of *TNJ* #27 were widely distributed. Again, Groth followed Light and Bishoff everywhere they went, casting insults. Light was forced to ask the convention chairman (this time, Shel Dorf) to put an end to the nonsense.

A few months later, Groth submitted a two-page advertisement to Light, promoting *TNJ*. Light, who was still upset over the aggravation he received in New York and San Diego, cashed Groth's check and rejected the ad. This action was certainly not justifiable, but anger has been known to prompt less than honorable behavior. This action merely angered Groth, who then went out of his way to even the score, according to Light.

Using the telephone as an instrument of revenge, Groth made collect calls to Light in the middle of the night. Light says he then changed his phone number, forcing Groth to resort to new tactics. During regular office hours, Groth made collect calls, pretending to be someone else. When the operator asked if Light would accept a collect call from Jack Kirby or Will Eisner, Light did. Each time he discovered Groth snickering on the other end of the line.

Finally, Light wised up. He refused collect calls from anyone and complained to the telephone company. They must have done something appropriate because the calls suddenly stopped.

On September 7, 1976, I received a letter from WSA Trustee Avery Klein, informing me that he and Bill Cole had begun to correspond with Groth. In an overture of friendship, Groth offered to bury the hatchet about the long-standing WSA vs. *TNJ* feud. Groth wanted *TNJ* to become the exclusive source for all WSA articles and columns. Groth asked Klein to provide him with a copy of the WSA mailing list so that he might send each member a complimentary copy.

Klein favored fraternizing with Groth. Personally, I had mixed feelings. I did not think much of *TNJ #27*. There was something about Groth that rubbed me the wrong way. Shakespeare might have said it best when he wrote, "Beware of Greeks bearing gifts."

Klein and I had several discussions on the subject. He felt Groth was being unfairly penalized. There was some truth to that. Klein insisted that we rescind Blair's directive prohibiting WSA members from advertising in *TNJ*. Furthermore, since Groth was such a good fellow, WSA should endorse him.

Before making a decision I discussed the matter with Blair. At the mere mention of Groth's name, Blair flew into a rage. There had been some past confrontation between them that Blair refused to discuss. It seemed to me that it did not matter if Groth wasn't a boy scout. In my mind WSA had no right to interfere with his business. Blair did not agree. In the end, however, he encouraged me to do what I felt best.

Thus, on November 27, 1976, I rescinded Blair's directive at the WSA Board of Directors meeting in New York. I published a notice to this effect in *WE #110*, February 1977.

A few days after the issue was mailed, I received an irate phone call from

This picture of Gary Groth is from August 1972. It was taken at a convention in Baltimore. Somehow, the bathroom door in the hotel got locked and Groth kicked it in. Hence, the photo. The hotel management must have loved that.
    —*from the collection of Richard Garrison*

Blair. He voiced strong disapproval over my rescinding his directive, and questioned my authority to do so. Blair felt the directive would have died a natural death if left alone. In any event, the deed had been done. There was nothing I could do to change it. My only regret is that it ended our friendship. Blair felt I had betrayed him. Nothing I could say seemed to make any difference. I felt badly about it. However, there are times when a person has to stand on principle. Although my actions cost me a friendship, I felt I had done the right thing.

In December 1976, Bill Cole became a partner with Groth by investing money in *TNJ*. For a short time, Cole and Groth were the best of pals. Since the publication was about to be renamed *The Comics Journal*, Cole asked if I would be willing to write a monthly WSA column. Cole promised a full tabloid page of space and that the column would be published without editorial control.

As a favor to Cole, I agreed to write a column entitled "WSA Hotline." As part of the first installment, I wanted to reprint the transcript from the WSA Board of Directors meeting as it previously had been read by only a few hundred WSA members. I thought that it would serve nicely as an introduction to a new audience. When the column was published in *TCJ* #33, the transcript had been cut.

I phoned Gary Groth to ask why. I ended up discussing the matter with Groth's associate, Mike Catron. I was told by Catron that he deleted the transcript because "he" felt *TCJ*'s readers would not be interested. Catron let me know that he would delete portions of any future column that he didn't like.

Trying to talk sense to Catron was like lying on your back and playing badminton with hailstones. He never stopped talking. I couldn't get in a word edgewise. So for the moment I let the matter drop.

A short time later, I received a postcard from Catron saying that it was important that I contact him soon as possible. I obliged by calling. The ensuing conversation with Groth and Catron proved to be enlightening. It would seem they had just seen my latest column in *TBG* and didn't like it. Catron (who did most of the talking) wanted to know why I was still writing for *TBG*. He told me that I could not work both sides of the street. In essence, he would force me to choose between *TBG* and *TCJ* for column space.

It was simple enough to point out that I was not writing WSA columns for my own gratification. The column in *TBG* was a means of communicating with our membership. As it was, WSA was not lacking for exposure. More members read the column in *TBG* than subscribed to our own publication, *WE*.

Anyone who followed my columns in *TBG* knew they appeared erratically. Often, I had difficulty pounding out fifteen hundred words of prose to fill a column. I wrote out of necessity or when I had the time.

In closing, I reminded Groth and Catron that I had agreed to write a second column only as a favor to Cole. There was nothing in it for me except a lot of work. If they wanted to cancel "WSA Hotline," that was fine. I didn't give a damn one way or the other. At that point, I was tired of wasting my time (and money) and ended the conversation.

An evening or two later, I received a call from Cole. I was brokenhearted to learn that Groth had complained about my attitude. Cole was a little embarrassed. He apologized, and assured me that he would straighten matters out with Groth and Catron. His word was good enough for me. I agreed to continue writing the column.

About this time, Cole requested Harry Hopkins to provide him with a copy of the WSA mailing list. Cole wanted to send every WSA member a copy of the next issue of *TCJ* containing "WSA Hotline." Hopkins told Cole that he needed to clear it with me first. I did not want to do it. While this was going on, Cole talked to Avery Klein, who instructed Harry Hopkins to provide Cole with computerized mailing labels. Cole, in turn, gave the labels to Groth.

Instead of mailing each WSA member a copy of *TCJ*, Groth sent out a flyer soliciting advertising and subscriptions from WSA members. It was a good thing that Groth and I were separated by a thousand miles. Otherwise, I would have been tempted to do him an injury. I had a glorious vision of grabbing his shirt collar and shaking him like a rag doll.

Blair received a copy of the flyer and he was mad as a wet hornet. In a subsequent telephone conversation, Blair said in no uncertain terms that he held me personally responsible for Groth's unauthorized use of the labels. Later, Groth apologized to me. He claimed it was a misunderstanding. Yeah, right. In my mind, Groth saw an opportunity to feather his own nest and took it.

A short time later, Cole and Groth parted ways. Groth used Cole's money to transform *The Comics Journal* into a magazine. At that point, Groth decided that he no longer needed "WSA Hotline." My last column was returned with the explanation that the subject matter was no longer relevant to the scope of the publication. My complimentary subscription was terminated. Groth had gotten what he wanted from WSA and left me with the uneasy feeling that we had been used.

A short time later, Groth stiffed Cole for his investment in *TCJ*. When Groth demonstrated no intention to repay, Cole had no choice but to file suit against Groth. At a later date, the court awarded Cole a default judgment when Groth failed to appear.

Despite his modest claim of being "a highly respected and well known fan publisher," Groth was, in fact, unknown to most of fandom. WSA's endorsement had provided him with instant credibility. The end result was increased advertising and circulation for *The Comics Journal*.

In my mind, only a practicing ingrate would not feel a sense of gratitude. Apparently, Groth did not. His attitude gives credence to Dante's theory that the lowest circle of hell is reserved for those who betray their benefactors. In Groth's case, it's a charming thought.

I had nothing more to do with Groth for almost two years. Then I contacted him to place an advertisement in *The Comics Journal*. Even so, I could not resist the temptation to let him know how I felt. In a letter dated August 28, 1978, Groth replied:

> Well, your subscription wasn't revoked, actually. What happened, I think, was that you were given a complimentary subscription because you were a columnist. After you ceased being a columnist (and it took our circulation director a few issues to make the correction) you were taken off the list. I'm sorry for not writing you of this policy.

During 1986 and 1987, I crossed trails with Groth several times at various conventions around the country. On those occasions, I had little to say to him. My impression was that he hadn't changed much.

WSA Endorses The Comics Journal! Advertising Ban Lifted!

Journal offers discount to WSA members

RIVERDALE MD, April 1977 (TCJ) Ron J. Frantz, Acting Administrator and Chief of Operations of the WSA Program, announced in this month's edition of The Comics Journal that he has "cancelled" Directive Number One of the National Central Bureau. That directive had prevented WSA members from using their WSA Official Logos on their advertising in The Comics Journal (formerly The Nostalgia Journal).

In a personal message to WSA members added to the cancellation announcement, Frantz went on to note that The Comics Journal "has run a very clean and above board operation" since the time it was taken over by Fantagraphics, Inc. in July.

Fantagraphics is wholly owned by Gary Groth and Mike Catron, the editors of The Comics Journal. Frantz concluded his personal remarks by saying "the WSA Program and its affiliates wish to 'endorse' " The Comics Journal.

Groth, a highly respected and well-known fan publisher since his acclaimed Fantastic Fanzine (this eleventh issue was named one of the Top Ten Fanzines of the 1960s by fan historian Doug Fratz), was pleased by the announcement and said, "Mike and I are proud to welcome the WSA into the pages of The Comics Journal. We both attended the first Board of Director's Meeting of the WSA at Riverdale, and were impressed with the sincerity and sense of responsibility

---

OFFICIAL WSA BUSINESS

IN THE MATTER OF: CANCELLATION OF NATIONAL CENTRAL BUREAU DIRECTIVE NUMBER ONE
Issued: Wednesday, November 20th., 1974 PM

TAKE NOTICE ... THAT in the above matter The WSA Program and its affiliates has this date CANCELLED, NULLIFIED or otherwise VOIDED such Directive which "prohibited" the use of its OFFICIAL LOGO of membership in the program either in advertising, related matters, articles, columns, commentary, letters of comment, or other related matter submitted to, and published by the Nostalgia Journal THEN a publication of an entity known as the Syndicate, Inc., a Texas corporation.

WHEREAS; The Nostalgia Journal is NO longer owned, nor published by the Syndicate, Inc., and by bill of sale the Nostalgia Journal is owned and published by FANTAGRAPHICS, INC., Gary G. Groth, Executive Editor, and Micheal Catron, Editor.

TAKE NOTICE ... THAT, henceforth from this time and date, by virtue of the change of ownership, WSA has caused the information as submitted to be entered into the record of the program, and caused such information to be published to the membership of the program in accordance with the rules and regulations as established in precedent by the WSA Program

OFFICIAL NOTICE ...
As authorized by the Chief of Operations
See Directive Number One this POST

/s/ Ron J. Frantz, Chief of Operations
Acting Administrator WSA Program

NOTICE OF CANCELLATION
NCB DIRECTIVE NUMBER ONE

000000000000000000000000000000000000000000000000000000000

PERSONAL MEMORANDUM TO MEMBERS OF WSA: Your comments regarding this matter are welcome. I would like to make further note that it is the personal opinion of both the Chief of Operations and of the Trustee, Avery B. Klein, Esq., that the "New" Nostalgia Journal has run a very clean and above board operation under Gary Groth, its editor and associates. As of this date, the WSA Program and its affiliates wish to "endorse" the New Nostalgia Journal. **

** FORMERLY THE NATIONAL CENTRAL BUREAU **

In April 1977, I quietly announced my plans to resign as WSA Administrator at the end of the year. In the interim, Harry Hopkins and I worked together to assure an orderly transition of the office.

One of the first matters was a complete transfer of the financial records. Here the story takes a bizarre twist. Shortly after Hopkins received the records, I became, without my knowledge, an object of controversy. The following excerpt from a detailed eleven-page report written by Mrs. Stanley R. Blair on April 23, 1980, to the Federal Bureau of Investigation tells the story:

> By February 1977, Mr. Harry Hopkins was receiving and banking all the funds belonging to the WSA Program. During this time, Mr. Hopkins began to mention Ron Frantz' limitations and his suspicions about him to Mr. Stanley Blair over the phone. Then, to finalize these

exhibited by the members in attendance and especially by the Board itself: Avery Klein, Ron Frantz, Bill Cole, and Harry Hopkins."

photo by Harry Hopkins

left to right: Avery Klein, Bill Cole, Ron Frantz, and Gary Groth

accusations, Mr. Hopkins reported that Mr. Frantz had embezzled $502.85 from the funds of the program over the two years he was Administrator. As the program is non-profit and the income very small, this sum was very large. Mr. Blair then asked for Avery B. Klein to ask for Mr. Frantz' resignation.

I did not learn of these allegations until June 1979, when the matter was brought to my attention by Hopkins. At the time Hopkins and Blair had begun to feud. Of course, the allegation had no basis in fact. During the course of my administration, I maintained an accurate record of all funds received for membership dues, subscriptions, advertising, etc. I could account for every dollar.

Furthermore, I contributed over $1,000 to WSA out of my own pocket when revenues failed to meet expenses. This added to the free labor I contributed to WSA made the allegation about on par with accusing a minister of a small church of pinching pennies from the collection plate. The situation is proof of the cynical truism that no good deed will go unpunished.

I was curious why these allegations were not brought to my attention earlier. Hopkins said he kept quiet because he received orders to that effect from Klein. In turn, Klein received instructions from Blair. Supposedly, Blair feared a public scandal and wanted everything kept quiet.

After learning of the situation, I spent a long night with no sleep, with an anger that kept growing. I had done nothing wrong and it made my blood boil to discover I had been vilified in a manner that made Richard Nixon look like a beloved humanitarian.

William Hazlitt once commented about a similar experience from his career in the 1800s, as an essayist and critic:

> If I had sufficient provocation to rail at the public, I think I should do so in good set terms, nearly as follows. There is not a more ungrateful animal than the public. It is a huge monster of ingratitudes. It reads, it admires, it extols only because it is the fashion, not from love of the subject or the man. If you have pleased it, it is jealous of its own involuntary judgment of merit, and seizes the first opportunity, the first shabby pretext, to pick a quarrel with you and be quits once more.

It's remarkable how history seems to repeat itself. Times change, but people tend to remain the same. It is one of those things that gives historians and philosophers lots to argue about.

I phoned Klein a few days later, wanting to hear his side of the story. Klein did not want to talk about it. Before we started, I let him know that I had retained the services of an attorney, and I was ready to file a slander suit. Klein had a choice: He could discuss the matter with me on the phone, or he could testify as a defendant in court. I really didn't care which.

Exercising good sense, Klein chose to talk. He more or less substantiated Hopkins's version of the story. Supposedly, Blair put pressure on Klein to remove me as WSA Administrator during 1977 on the unfounded allegation that I had embezzled money. Klein didn't seem to remember who made the initial allegation. However, since I had already announced my plans to resign at the end of the year, Klein said he was content to sweep the matter under the rug.

I'm not certain it ever occurred to Klein that I might be innocent. It was as if he had forgotten everything he learned in law school about due process. The curious thing is that Klein and I had worked closely together on various WSA matters. I had considered him and me to be friends. Had our roles been reversed, I would have at least asked a few questions before passing judgment. In any event, I told Klein that if a single word appeared in print that I had done so much as spit on the sidewalk, I'd haul his butt into court so fast that he would catch cold from the breeze. I never spoke with Klein again.

My attorney was a former municipal judge named Charles Humbell. As we discussed the possibility of a slander suit, Humbell said it would be an easy case to try. There was nothing he would like better than to have the principals involved explain their actions before an impartial judge and jury.

Initially, I had mixed feelings about Hopkins's role in the debacle. Blair claimed that Hopkins had made the initial accusation about embezzlement. Hopkins pointed his finger at Blair. Klein lurked somewhere in the middle. The only thing I knew is that someone was not telling the truth.

In May of 1977, I had received a letter from Blair offering to sell the WSA Program to Avery Klein, Bill Cole, Harry Hopkins, and me for $5,000. Blair claimed that such a sale would relieve his burden of its wrongful operation. In this way, it would be ours to operate however we saw fit.

I had no personal interest in the offer. The last thing I wanted was to be tied down with WSA. As a matter of courtesy, I agreed to discuss the offer with Klein, Cole, and Hopkins. As it turned out, Klein had no desire to pay for what he already controlled by way of a grant-in-trust. Cole and Hopkins saw it as a poor investment. A short time later, I informed Blair that a sale was not possible.

This rejection angered Blair. He immediately began secret negotiations with Klein to revoke the grant-in-trust, enabling him to resume ownership (and control) of WSA. Blair and Klein reached an oral agreement to this effect on June 17, 1977. The formal papers were not executed until May 3, 1978. For reasons of their own, Blair and Klein kept the matter to themselves.

In February 1977, I began to write this book. About the 15th of March, I announced my intention to publish. Evidently, Blair saw this as a threat to his interests as he intended to write a book of his own.

On March 28, 1978, Blair wrote to Harry Hopkins voicing his displeasure over my writing the book. About this same time, Blair reiterated similar objections to me in a telephone conversation. Blair expressed the preposterous notion that I would violate existing copyright law by writing the book. According to Blair, any knowledge I had about WSA belonged to him. I had no right to make any of it public without his approval.

However, being a generous man, he was willing to offer dispensation. If I were to give him full editorial control (plus a generous percentage of the profits) he would grudgingly allow it to be published. Well, by this time I had had my fill of Blair meddling in my life. I told him that I would publish anything I damned well pleased and if he didn't like it, he should hire an attorney.

Blair ended the conversation by threatening to suspend my WSA membership unless I agreed to his demands. Since I was no longer an active WSA member, my membership held little value. His threat of a lawsuit was absurd.

The die was cast, however. Blair began mobilizing his forces. During the next few months I received about a dozen hostile letters and phone calls. Some were from people I did not know. To hear their comments would make your ears bleed. In the eyes of some people, I had suddenly grown horns and a pointed tail.

If nothing else, Blair was successful in agitating a dispute between Alan Light and myself. It began with a phone call from Light, who grumbled that he had heard I was writing a book that was highly critical, inflammatory, and libelous of him. This was remarkable, considering that Blair had not seen a single word I had written. I replied that it was true that I was writing a book, but nothing in it was libelous. I reminded him that it is not libel to print the truth. In all fairness, I mentioned there were portions that he might not like. Light replied, "That is not what I heard from Stan."

As delicately as I could, I tried to tell Light that Blair needed a good psychiatrist. The butter had slipped off his stack of waffles. For Light, the thought of Blair being anything less than perfect was like believing a patron saint had taken up a career as a child molester. Light could not believe it.

Light ended the conversation by saying, "If there is a problem between you and Stan, I'm sure you're the one at fault! If you print anything in your book about me that I don't like, I will sue you!"

A few days later, a letter from Light arrived in the mail. He apologized for being abrupt and offered to publish *Fandom: Confidential* in *TBG* as a weekly serial. I would be paid at the rate of $25 per installment. However, I would surrender editorial control of the product. Light would have the privilege of deleting any portion he felt unsuitable. No doubt Stan Blair would also have a say.

Now, if I had a nickel's worth of business acumen, I would have smiled, taken Light's money, and gloated all the way to the bank. Yet, for some reason, I felt a peculiar sense of righteous indignation, I told Light to go peddle his papers elsewhere. A short time later, Light wrote again. This time, he politely asked to see the portions of the manuscript that pertained to him. I had no problem with that. Actually, I was curious to see what his reaction might be.

Light did not keep me guessing long. Within a week, I received the following reply: "I was pleasantly surprised with your manuscript. I get my share of hits in it, but you were fair in your reporting. If you decide to publish the book, you won't have any problem with me over it."

About six months after I had resigned as WSA Administrator, Hopkins asked if I would consider returning as a WSA staff member. To say that I wasn't interested would be putting it mildly. Then, John Hemmings resigned as editor of *WE*, leaving Hopkins in a spot. Hopkins didn't have the time or inclination to publish it himself. So, as a favor to Hopkins, I agreed to take over for a short time.

To be honest, the spirit to produce was not there. I managed only a single, belated issue. Somewhere in the process, I acquired the official-sounding title of Chairman, WSA Publications Division. I did not take the title seriously because I didn't plan to be around long.

Blair voiced strong objections to Hopkins over my appointment. He demanded that I be removed from the position. Evidently, fandom was not big enough for both of us. When Hopkins refused to give me my walking papers, it was the beginning of a rift between him and Blair. Personally, I couldn't have cared less one way or the other. I didn't want the job to begin with.

During my brief tenure as editor, I was indirectly drawn into another matter involving a WSA member recently suspended by Harry Hopkins. His name was Horst Schroder, a native of Sweden. Schroder was a collector of Walt Disney material.

Schroder's problems began when he announced the forthcoming publication of an ambitious twelve-volume index entitled *All the Funny Disneys*. With an eye on the international market, the index was to include a listing of Disney dealers that Schroder approved of, and a listing of those he felt were unreliable. Some of the latter were WSA members. In particular, this included Bill Cole.

In October 1977, Schroder had an unsatisfactory transaction with the Book Sail, a firm located in Orange, California. Schroder purchased a rare book entitled *The Mouse Trap* for $750. Schroder felt the item was misgraded, an opinion shared by Disney archivist Dave Smith. Schroder sought to return the item for a refund. The Book Sail refused.

As a result, Schroder filed a fraud complaint against the Book Sail with Scott Tillman, who was then handling WSA mail-fraud investigations. Tillman dispatched the complaint to a second agent, Richard Fifield. The Book Sail responded to Fifield's inquiry by stating they would prefer a lawsuit to making a refund to Schroder.

At that point, Hopkins took a hand. Following a series of letters between Hopkins and the Book Sail to determine the facts of the case, Hopkins decided in favor of the Book Sail. The case became more involved when Schroder complained to the Antiquarian Booksellers Association of America, Inc., an association in which the Book Sail held membership. In its own investigation, the ABAA also found the Book Sail innocent of wrongdoing. Schroder filed complaints against several other WSA members, including Bill Cole. Schroder felt his complaints were falling on deaf ears. Upon the suspension of his WSA membership, his complaints against all parties were summarily dismissed.

Schroder disapproved of Hopkins's resolution of the Book Sail matter and complained to just about anyone who would listen. Alan Light was one of several publishers to whom he voiced objections. The matter came to my attention when Schroder wrote a personal letter to me, protesting his WSA suspension.

After reading a stack of papers an inch thick, it appeared to me that Schroder had been suspended for having the audacity to disagree with Hopkins. In my mind, that hardly seemed fair. When I was running the store, there were several occasions when WSA members disagreed with decisions of mine. However, I tried to avoid thinking like a baseball umpire. I never felt I had the right to throw someone out of the game for arguing with me. It never bothered me to have a little dust kicked on my pants.

In Schroder's case, I felt there had been a misunderstanding. Reading through his file, there appeared to be a language barrier. English was not Schroder's native tongue. I felt that Hopkins may have been hasty in suspending Schroder's WSA membership.

In Schroder's behalf, I wrote to Klein, suggesting he restore Schroder's membership and reopen his fraud cases. This action annoyed Hopkins a little, who felt that I overstepped my bounds by acting without first consulting him. Hopkins said I acted without knowing all the facts, which may very well have been true. Fortunately, we had been friends too long for it to become a serious bone of contention.

Two years earlier, Hopkins and I had discussed the possibility of publishing a WSA Directory. I derived inspiration from a similar directory published by the Oklahoma Alliance of Fans, which listed the name, address, phone number, and a brief profile of each member's collecting interests. After publication, it stimulated a lot of activity within the club. I thought a similar directory might do the same thing for WSA.

Hopkins shared my enthusiasm for the idea. He had considered the same idea himself. Since Hopkins had already completed much of the computer work as WSA Registrar, all we needed was for each member to provide information about his personal collecting habits. Next, I discussed the idea with Klein and Blair. Both felt the idea had merit. Klein provided written authorization for me to begin the project.

My original plans called for a WSA Directory to be published in the summer of 1977. The first public announcement came November 27, 1976, at the WSA Board of Directors meeting in New York.

Afterwards, Blair had a change of heart. He was disturbed by Gary Groth's misuse of the WSA membership labels. Blair feared that if a directory were published, others might exploit it for personal gain. Blair demanded that work on the Directory stop. I ignored him. The project was well beyond the planning stage. I saw no reason to abort simply because Blair had cold feet.

This innocent-looking little periodical caused an unbelievable amount of bitterness and hostility. Friendships of long standing came to an end. Suffering from divided loyalties, many WSA members were compelled to choose sides while Harry Hopkins and Stanley Blair battled over the *Directory*'s ownership. Some were like football fans waving pennants at the Army vs. Navy game. Of course, a few eccentrics managed to mind their own business.

© 1979 by Harry A. Hopkins

Once again, Blair complained to Klein. A short time later, I received written notification from Klein mandating that all work on the the WSA Directory stop immediately. Of course, that decision did not sit well with me. I phoned Klein to voice my objection. I remember saying something to the effect of, "What is this nonsense, Avery? First you give your approval to start the project, now you order me to scrap it. I wish you would make up your damned mind!"

Klein opened the discussion with an admonition over Groth's misuse of the WSA membership labels. However, I cut him off short, reminding him that it was he who authorized Groth to use the labels, not me. I also pointed out that it was he, and Bill Cole, who wanted to play kissy-face with Groth in the first place. All they were concerned about was finding another source to advertise their plastic bags. Sometimes, those damned plastic bags were a nuisance.

But then, I didn't know rumors were circulating that I had embezzled money. To this very day, I have no idea how widespread those rumors really were. Nor did I know that Blair was retaking control of WSA. In any event, Klein said the decision to terminate the WSA Directory was final. Furthermore, if I didn't like it, I should resign.

Believe me, I considering doing just that. As it was, there were a number of matters I wanted to finish before stepping aside. In particular, several mail-fraud cases had evolved beyond the postal system that needed my attention. One case lay at the feet of the Justice Department. A congressman was involved. Thus, all I could do was comply with Klein's ultimatum. For the moment, the WSA Directory was a dead issue.

About a year later, Hopkins convinced Blair of the benefits of a WSA Directory. Blair had a change of mind, when he saw it as a potential source of personal income. Blair and Hopkins became associate editors for the one and only *WSA Directory*, published October 1978.

Its success prompted an expanded version published in February 1979, entitled *The Fandom Directory*. A short time later, Blair and Hopkins engaged in a heated imbroglio deciding its ownership. The rancor between them evolved into a full-scale vendetta, extending far beyond the perimeters of fandom. Before reaching its conclusion, a number of casual witnesses were dragged through a quagmire of governmental scrutiny.

In a letter dated October 2, 1980, to *TBG* publisher Alan Light, Hopkins reminisced over events leading to publication of the first *Fandom Directory*:

Of late, Stan Blair (prodded by Mrs. Blair) has taken up an adversarial stance with several large name fans in organized fandom. Ron Frantz was the first; over three years ago. I felt that Ron was being falsely berated by Blair for alleged improprieties in his handling of the WSA and in his personal life as well. When I wouldn't go along with them and eliminate Ron from all positions of responsibility within the WSA, this marked me as well.

I continued to work toward improving the scope and reputation of the WSA. Since I was Chief of Operations at the time, I wanted WSA to be a success. I even went so far as to give WSA the use of an idea which I had been formulating since 1975; a nationwide computerized directory of fans. WSA needed a steady income and I thought this could provide it. I discussed this with the Blairs' in general terms throughout 1977, intermixed with discussions noting to them how some of the automated concepts could also be used to help the WSA Directory that was also being planned.

I've always been a team player so I saw nothing wrong with outwardly proclaiming the Fandom Directory to be a joint WSA effort, when in actuality doing 95% of the development and publication myself.

The mark I had received from them over our disagreement began to rub them again. I was directed to remove Ron from any position of public attention. I did not agree that a willing, capable, loyal worker should be eliminated from the staff. This coaxed me to protectively assert my ownership of The Fandom Directory. Although I was willing to let the WSA receive the benefits of the Directory, I wanted full recognition of my primacy in its creation. This appalled the Blairs, who were then firmly convinced that it was theirs to do with as they pleased.

In October 1978, Hopkins paid a visit to Oklahoma City on Air Force business. I entertained him one evening in my home. Much of our conversation pertained to the upcoming publication of *The Fandom Directory*. I made one minor contribution by suggesting a professionally illustrated cover. Hopkins had not planned on using one. I mentioned there were several cartoonists of my acquaintance who might provide an illustration for a nominal fee.

While Hopkins waited, I placed a call to former Charlton comics artist Pete Morisi. As a personal favor, Morisi agreed to do the cover. Besides this, my involvement with the first edition did not amount to much. Hopkins, however, was gracious enough to acknowledge my help on the title page, an honor I shared with Chester Cox and John Hemmings.

It irked Blair to see my name associated with the project. It became a major point of contention between Blair and Hopkins. Their friendship ended over the issue. Following publication of the first edition, Hopkins informed Blair that he intended to file copyright registration in his own name.

Blair disputed Hopkins's claim of ownership. He contended that Mrs. Blair had conceived the idea for the directory, a notion that was pure fantasy.

Smelling profit, Blair planned to continue publishing a directory for his personal benefit.

On February 17, 1978, WSA Trustee Avery Klein sent a letter acknowledging Hopkins's ownership of *The Fandom Directory* and the International Fan Location Service. This was one year before the publication of the first edition.

Hopkins filed the copyright registration in his own name. Blair refused to allow this to get by. He immediately wrote to Klein, demanding that Hopkins resign as WSA Administrator. These actions coincided with Blair resuming ownership of WSA on May 3, 1979. Klein remained as a Titular Trustee, meaning he held the title in name only.

In the same time frame, Blair instructed Klein to offer the WSA Program for sale. In a letter dated July 8, 1979, Klein informed Blair he had located a "secret" buyer for the WSA Program. It was a person Klein trusted and for whom he had the highest esteem. Of course, the buyer was Hopkins. Klein should have been ashamed of himself. Such an act of collusion was unbecoming of an officer of the court. It didn't take Blair long to worm the truth out of Klein. Afterwards, Blair considered Klein untrustworthy and appointed his own wife to replace Klein as Trustee.

Such as it was, Blair declined Hopkins's offer of $2,400. It included $1,400 that WSA owed Hopkins, plus $1,000 to be paid in ten installments of $100. The simmering dispute between Blair and Hopkins came to a boil on August 30, 1979.

Blair's wife wrote a letter dismissing Hopkins as WSA Administrator. On November 2, 1979, she suspended Hopkins's WSA membership. On November 8, Hopkins sent a letter to Blair protesting his suspension. Blair did not respond. Instead, Blair announced Hopkins's suspension in a WSA News and Report column in *TBG*. The article hinted that Hopkins had been suspended for various improprieties.

Hopkins considered the article libelous. Hopkins sent a letter to Bill Cole, asking if Cole could recommend an attorney. Cole was represented by the law firm of Watstein and Greece, and he suggested that Hopkins retain their services. Hopkins did just that. As the news of Hopkins's suspension became known to the WSA membership, several members wrote letters of protest. In time, most of these members resigned, including Klein and Cole. Blair considered the letters angry and libelous.

Blair wasted little time reorganizing WSA, appointing new staff. Michael Wahl became the new Administrator. Wahl was a relatively new member. I knew nothing about him. A few members of Hopkins's staff allied themselves with Blair. Joe Stoner returned to assist in some capacity. Blair himself took over the publishing of *WE*. Mrs. Blair began to produce WSA News and Report columns for *TBG*. There was, clearly, blood on the moon. The stage was

It was a sad day for fandom. A once fine and honorable institution had been reduced to its lowest possible common denominator. When this advertisement appeared in October 1979, as part of a WSA News and Report column in *TBG*, it was clearly evident that a cloud of suspicion loomed overhead like the sword of Damocles. Many members had no idea who to believe.

set for a nice little civil war.

About November 15, 1979, I received an unexpected phone call from Blair. We had not spoken for over a year. Judging from his manner, you would have thought we were still the best of friends.

Blair called to announce that he had just fired Hopkins as WSA Administrator. Strangely, he offered the position to me. Blair bent over backwards trying to apologize for his past actions. There was a sincerity in his voice that I could not explain.

Blair claimed that he and I were victims of a nefarious conspiracy instigated by Hopkins, which began when Hopkins accused me of embezzlement. Of course, Blair said he had difficulty believing I was capable of such wickedness.

Blair spoke of asking Hopkins for the financial records in order to see for himself. Blair contended that Hopkins refused to provide them. Only at Blair's continued insistence did Hopkins finally produce the records, three years after the fact. When he finally had the opportunity to audit the books, Blair failed to discover any missing funds. In his own words: "Your records were completely in order. I could not find any evidence that you had taken a penny. Hopkins is a damned liar!"

Perhaps it was all a delusion, but Blair genuinely believed that Hopkins had contrived a sinister plot to seize control of the WSA Program and steal *The Fandom Directory*. Blair apologized over and over for believing Hopkins, pleading with me to come home, clean house, and set everything right with the world. Curiously, Blair offered to give me full ownership of the WSA Program. All I had to do was side with him against Hopkins.

The situation reminded me of a scene from ancient Greek drama: deus ex machina. At a critical moment when no human could resolve a conflict, an actor playing a Greek god would be lifted onto the stage in a contraption to redeem the moment.

Well, I had no desire to redeem anything. I felt sorry for Blair. My feelings of anger and resentment dissolved when I realized that he was not well. However, we ended the conversation on a pleasant note. Although I declined his offer, we wished each other well. I never heard from Blair again.

Then the unthinkable happened. Blair attacked Hopkins where he was most vulnerable, attempting to destroy his military career. On February 28, 1980, Blair wrote a letter to Harold Brown, the United States Secretary of Defense, complaining that Hopkins conspired with others to deprive him of financial benefits associated with the WSA Program. Specifically, this included the theft of money, Blair's "copyrighted book," a computer, and computerized information used to prepare the book.

At the same time, Blair established communication with West Virginia Representative John M. Slack. Slack was instrumental in instigating an investigation by the Federal Bureau of Investigation into the matter.

The commander of the Tactical Air Command requested an investigation of these allegations by the Air Force Office of Special Investigations (OSI). Subsequently, Special Agent Danny Eaton conducted several interviews with Mr. and Mrs. Stanley R. Blair from March 18 through April 9, 1980. In these conversations, Blair outlined the following allegations:

1. *Copyright violations*. In this matter, Hopkins allegedly stole and published information that belonged to and was copyrighted by Blair.

2. *Mail fraud*. Hopkins had allegedly opened mail addressed to Blair and used the United States Postal Service to perpetrate his actions.

3. *Conspiracy*. Blair alleged that Hopkins had the assistance of several other individuals in his actions.

4. *Misuse of an Air Force computer*. Blair alleged that Hopkins diverted and misused USAF computers for personal gain in keeping organizational records and personnel rosters for the WSA Program.

The genuine tragedy of these allegations is that they were pure fiction. With the exception of Hopkins using authorized training time on the Air Force computers to maintain WSA records, there was not a shred of truth to them. Blair contrived the allegations in an attempt to destroy Hopkins's reputation and career. Unbelievably, he came very close to doing it. It was as shameful an act of vengeance as one could conceive.

Hopkins did not learn of the allegations until July 19, 1980. On that date he was first questioned by the OSI. Both the OSI and FBI went to extremes to prevent Hopkins learning of the investigation. The FBI requested that dissemination of information about the investigation be limited, fearing Hopkins might destroy the computer records.

The following OSI memorandum dated April 17, 1980, indicates how serious (and potentially damaging) these allegations were to Hopkins:

BECAUSE OF THE SUBJECT'S SENSITIVE JOB POSITION ON THE TACTICAL AIR COMMAND STAFF, IT IS NECESSARY TO BRIEF HIS COMMANDER OF ALL ALLEGATIONS. IT IS POSSIBLE THAT THE COMMANDER MAY ELECT TO SUSPEND THE SUBJECT FROM HIS MILITARY DUTIES.

One week later, OSI Agent Charles R. Tanner made the following notation on an OSI administrative data form:

THE FBI IS INVESTIGATING THE COPYRIGHT VIOLATIONS, MAIL FRAUD, AND CONSPIRACY UNDER CASE NUMBER 28-460. THEY HAVE STATED IT IS IMPERATIVE THAT SUBJECT NOT BE MADE AWARE THAT HE IS UNDER INVESTIGATION. THIS SHOULD BE STRESSED TO MILITARY PERSONNEL CENTER. SUBJECT PLANS TO SEPARATE FROM THE USAF IN JUNE, 1980.

The Military Personnel Center controls all assignments, promotions, and awards for military personnel. About this time, Hopkins's Meritorious Service Medal for outstanding service on the Inspector General's team was mysteriously canceled. Hopkins had no plans to leave the Air Force.

While the powers that be were conducting a clandestine investigation of an innocent man, Blair showed remarkable impatience. On July 1, 1980, Blair contacted the Detachment Commander of Langley AFB (where Hopkins was stationed) to complain that he was not pleased with the progress of the OSI investigation. Blair threatened to make a personal call to the commanding officer of the base, Col. Forrest Singhoff.

Then, on July 17, Blair telephoned OSI Agent Eaton to inform him that his economic situation was getting worse. He was forced to make a public disclosure of the FBI and OSI investigations to the WSA membership. Three days later, Blair published a "SPECIAL REPORT" distributed to the WSA membership and at various conventions. This report was published one day before Hopkins's initial interrogation by OSI. At that time, Hopkins had no knowledge of the investigation that had been in progress for five months.

The wording in Blair's report smacked of paranoia:

NOW THE TRUTH CAN BE TOLD . . . Surprisingly ONLY A FEW of you were concerned enough about the LIBELOUS reports and SMEAR campaign being made by HARRY A. HOPKINS and HIS FRIENDS to write us and ask. But there were ALSO A FEW who identified themselves as in opposition to the principles and integrity of the WSA Program. They joined the conspirators and began to assist these in trying to bring the program to RUIN!

CHARLES S. RESCHICK and his associate Mr. Callahan, Special Agents of the FEDERAL BUREAU OF INVESTIGATION have been investigating this matter since March 1980. They were provided TWENTY FOLDERS containing HUNDREDS OF DOCUMENTS (letters from Avery B. Klein, Harry A. Hopkins, William Bates, John D. Hemmings, A. Scott Tillman, Kim Wheat, Mariane J. Soroka, Chester D. Cox and all others involved in the conspiracy; which included our answers to these letters over a period of five years).

Also included within those folders were libelous articles published in THE BUYER'S GUIDE, TERRIFIC, CRYPTOC, WOOF and notices of further articles to be published in AFTA, etc. All published libelous statements from former members/former staff members resigning from the program while accusing the founder of HARASSMENT, etc., thereby identifying themselves as co-conspirators with the group who set out to destroy the WSA Program.

Blair added insult to injury by sending a copy of the report to Hopkins's parents. At that point, Hopkins felt that Blair had gone too far. Hopkins persuaded Klein and Cole to join him in a libel suit against Blair. Despite a plea from Blair's attorney that the Massachusetts court (where the suit was filed) had no jurisdiction in the case, the judge enjoined Blair from publishing any further libelous comments about the principals involved.

Prior to the court date, Blair published the first of several issues of *WE* in tabloid newspaper format. Since he had already made enemies of most all of his old friends in fandom, Blair finished the job by attacking *TBG* publisher Alan Light. Light had been Blair's most loyal supporter. For WSA to survive, Blair desperately needed Light's patronage. However, Blair did not have the sense to realize it.

Earlier, Light found himself in the middle of the Blair vs. Hopkins feud. Considering both men friends, his loyalties were divided. Light attempted to remain neutral. This was not possible. After Blair announced that Hopkins was terminated as WSA Administrator, Hopkins wrote an open letter to Light telling his side of the story. Blair insisted that Light not publish the letter, calling it a pack of lies.

Light printed the letter after Hopkins, Klein, and Cole threatened to sue. Blair seemed unable to understand that Light was caught in the middle. After Hopkins's letter was published in *TBG*, Blair added Light to his list of conspirators. They say that a blind man often accuses the world of dwelling in darkness. This was true of Blair. He was convinced the world was dark and everyone was out to get him.

In a personal letter dated March 18, 1984, Light made the following comment:

> I was re-reading my photocopy of your book *FANDOM: Confidential*. It was interesting to note, in retrospect, how right you were in your letters about Stan Blair's mental instability and need to purge all his old friends and associates. I did not know it at the time I got your letter, but he was to do the same to me.

While these events were unfolding, I casually observed the conflict from a distance. I did not participate because I wanted to stay out of it. I had enough problems of my own. Among other things, I was a new father. That, in itself, is enough to keep a man from getting bored. There are few things in life more fun than changing dirty diapers.

I remember having a brief telephone conversation with Michael Wahl about this time. Wahl called to inquire about the status of *FANDOM: Confidential*. I'm not sure what Wahl was trying to accomplish. In a clumsy manner, he tried to cross-examine me over where I stood in the Blair vs. Hopkins feud. I told Wahl that it was none of his business. If Blair had any questions, he needed to call me himself. Following this conversation, I decided I had no reason to remain a WSA member.

About March 15, 1980, I wrote to Blair to inform him of my decision. I kept the letter friendly, telling him that I was no longer interested in what was going on. I had no hard feelings. In closing the letter, I offered my sincere best wishes. I hoped he would not consider my resignation a personal insult.

I should have known better. With Blair, it was always a matter of "either you are for me or against me." There was no middle ground. I later discovered that Blair added my name to his list of conspirators, mentioning me in various documents distributed to the FBI and OSI.

Later, I had reason to suspect that my telephone may have been bugged. Evidently the FBI had nothing better to do. If this be the case, I certainly hope they got an earful. The worst thing they probably heard was my wife complaining to her mother about my smoking cigars while reading in bed.

Considering that my only conceivable guilt was resigning from WSA membership without prejudice, I felt irked to be implicated in this. I have no idea how much my rights of privacy were violated. I was never contacted for questioning by the FBI or OSI.

In the end, the FBI and OSI found Hopkins innocent of any wrongdoing. All charges against him were dropped. Hopkins received an unofficial reprimand from his commanding officer for consorting with a troublemaker. In the future, he advised Hopkins to choose his associates with more care.

Blair was livid. He accused the United States government of some sort of a bizarre inner-service conspiracy. Blair based his allegation on the fact that many of the former WSA members with whom he had feuded were serving in the military, among them:

Harry A. Hopkins, Captain/USAF
William M. Cole, Major/U.S. Army Reserves
Chester L. Cox, Airman/USAF
Mariane Soroka, Lt./ Navy
Kim Wheat, Navyman/Navy

It was a matter of coincidence, but Blair suspected sinister motives where none existed. Evidently, no one in a position of authority took Blair's allegation seriously.

During 1981, Blair and Hopkins continued to struggle over *The Fandom Directory*. It spread to the United States Department of Commerce, specifically the Patent and Trademark Office. Both men filed applications for a trademark on the name at about the same time. By 1981, Hopkins had produced three editions. Blair had produced nothing. It came as no surprise when Hopkins emerged the winner. For the better part of two decades, Hopkins has continued yearly publication of *The Fandom Directory*.

By some miracle, the WSA Program continued to exist for several years. In the aftermath of the Blair vs. Hopkins feud, its prestige diminished to nothing. The 1984 edition of *The Comic Book Price Guide* contained an advertisement for the WSA Program. Sometime after that, WSA ceased to exist. Michael Wahl remained as Administrator to the end. Strangely, of the four men who occupied the post, his tenure was the longest. I daresay it was the least meaningful.

D espite all the unpleasantness associated with WSA during its final years, WSA did a lot of good work. Many fans and collectors benefited by its existence. It is my estimate that, over a period of fifteen years, more than $100,000 was collected and returned to mail-fraud victims.

Chester Cox, who had been very close to the situation, recalled certain events in a letter dated December 25, 1997:

> Some of the memories are a little easier to deal with after the passing of time. I remember being interviewed about the Blair accusations and learning about it before Harry Hopkins. At the time, I was in the middle of cross-training into the OSI and was undergoing a very thorough security check. I remember being sworn to secrecy (under strong coercion) not to reveal that an investigation into Hopkins life was happening—but feeling confident that nothing would come of it. The actual accusation, they told me, was that Harry had driven to Stan's house and tried to kill him. Fortunately, at the time period involved, Harry was on Inspector General deployment and his every moment was well-documented.

A few years ago, I visited with Harry Hopkins by phone. It was interesting to compare recollections about past events. Sadly, Hopkins still felt great anger and resentment toward Blair. Under the circumstances, his feelings were quite understandable. Unresolved anger can be a terrible thing. Somehow, Hopkins had not found it in his heart to forgive.

This charming picture was taken in 1981 at the home of Chester Cox. It was an informal gathering of friends who had fallen from grace in the eyes of Stanley Blair. It explains the gag T-shirts, which were a gift from Harry Hopkins. I still have mine, but I can't fit into it anymore. Kind of like trying to stuff a watermelon into an old sock.
Top row, left to right: Bill Bates, Kathy Bates, Mariane Soroka Hopkins, Harry Hopkins. Bottom row: Chester Cox, Jay Frantz (age 3), Ron Frantz.

As for myself, it was a learning experience. There were times when I wondered how I could have been so wrong about Blair. Upon reflection, I realized what a tragic error it is to worship a fallen idol; to believe for one moment that the light that shines within him is brighter than our own. Perhaps it all boils down to a basic understanding of human nature: that there is so much good in the worst of people and so much evil in the best.

I like to remember the good times, when Blair was in a healthy state of mind. I have fond memories of his compassion, his gentle good humor. Blair was a man who cared about the welfare of others. When he was emotionally stable, I think Blair would have genuinely despised the twisted caricature of himself that he later became.

For almost five years, an uneasy truce existed between *The Buyer's Guide* and *The Comics Journal.* There were few open hostilities beyond a few private insults or an occasional jab on the printed page.

However, the armistice ended in May 1983. In issue #81 of *The Comics Journal,* Groth attacked Light in an editorial, following Light's sale of his periodical to Krause Publications of Iola, Wisconsin, for the reported sum of $500,000. The new owner instantly changed the name to *The Comics Buyer's Guide.* The editorial read:

> We don't have Alan Light to kick around any more. . . . Light's major achievement, aside from making himself rich, was that of being fandom's first real business predator. His career of hustling is a monument to selfish opportunism and spiritual squalor, the kind of overnight success revered by the envious and defied by moneyed barbarians. His business practices may have been execrable, his journalistic standards and critical thought were equally appalling, running the gamut from indifference to downright swinishness.

On February 29, 1984, Light filed a libel suit against Groth in the Fourteenth Judicial Court of Rock Island County, Illinois, asking one million dollars in actual damages and one million dollars in punitive damages. A news story about the lawsuit went out over the wire services. When asked for a comment on the lawsuit, Groth replied:

> I think it's a frivolous pursuit without any merit. Filing such lawsuits is emblematic of the arrogance that kind of money breeds. Light just decided to take some money out of petty cash and harass me.

Unfortunately, existing federal statutes pertaining to libel make it difficult for a victim to receive justice through the courts. Publishers hide behind a distorted view of the freedom of the press. The situation has been compounded by recent Supreme Court decisions making public persons fair game, without recourse. A public person who tries to defend himself against libel must prove malice. Scores of recent court decisions prove this to be a virtual impossibility.

In my opinion, Light had a legitimate grievance. He was, however, deprived of recourse through the courts. After a protracted legal battle, his suit

In case you are wondering, this dapper-looking young man is none other than Alan Light, former publisher of *The Buyer's Guide for Comic Fandom.* This picture was taken about the time that Light and *Comics Journal* publisher Gary Groth locked horns in federal court. I guess a million dollars is worth fighting over. A person can buy a lot of comic books with that kind of money.

against Groth was dismissed by a federal judge. At this point, the last of the great fan feuds ended with a whimper instead of a bang.

I t has taken many years for me to sort out the implications of these matters in my own mind. It is difficult to understand why so many people behaved so foolishly.

I have since come to believe that the practice of fan feuding is a personification of what Augustine called the seven deadly sins of mankind. Most secular discussions on the subject of sin focus on a lack of self-discipline. Some philosophers, however, feel that sins are not evil acts, but universal compulsions. Two hundred years ago, James Madison observed (under somewhat different circumstances) that it is man's nature to squabble and form factions:

> So strong is the propensity of mankind to fall into mutual animosities that the most frivolous and fanciful distinctions have been sufficient to kindle unfriendly passions and excite violent conflicts. This zeal for different opinions has rendered these factions much more disposed to vex and oppress one another than to cooperate for the common good.

It is my personal belief that many people forget why they became fans and collectors. Activity that begins as a means of recreation and pleasure is prone to change when avocation becomes vocation. For some reason, it has an unfortunate tendency to bring out the worst is some people. The problem is not a new one. William Wister Comfort addressed the issue admirably, in a speech to the 1919 graduating class of Guilford College:

> Among the false aphorisms which will not be put down is this: all men are equal. There is a grain of truth in the remark. It is true that we all come into the world in the same way. In the race of life, we are even at the start; but we are never abreast again until by a great mystery, we are all neck and neck as we cross the tape. In the interval of inevitable inequality, which covers the whole period of life, what is to distinguish educated people? I shall claim that one object of an education is to provide us with a by-product . . . a hobby.
>
> It is important to insist upon the development of what we call a hobby as an essential aim of our educational methods. So long as we train men and women merely to earn a living by manual or intellectual skill, we are performing a useful service for them personally. But we are missing the larger conception of education in relation to society, precisely because the disinterested motive, the unselfish considerations which lead to service are lacking.

We love our hobbies because they are of our own choice. No man has foisted them upon us, as he may have imposed the law or a business career. Our hobbies are of our own begetting, and we love them as our own offspring. They represent our inmost selves. We lavish upon them our most unselfish efforts. We guard them from the observation of a cold and unsympathetic world. From them we draw strength and inspiration to continue the struggle of life. They are the truest indication of personality.

Tell me what a man's hobby is, and I have the best criterion of his character and tastes. Show me a man in his leisure hours, and I can estimate the depth of his inner life better than can be done when he is in court, in the stock exchange, or the classroom. A worthy hobby is a sure sign of advanced intelligence in its possessor. Our hobbies then, are essentially personal. They may be the very breath of our nostrils, the very joy of our life. They are in any case invaluable in offering repose, recreation, enthusiasm.

Before considering some of the mental and physical occupations, let me point out one feature of a hobby which is invariable: a hobby has nothing to do with the so-called practical conduct of life. A man should not make his living by it. Upon some hobbies it is possible to spend money; but strictly speaking, if you try to make money out of your hobby, you are taking from it its very life and charm. You are besmirching its character.

A hobby stands for the individual's refusal to sell all of himself for lucre. It represents the one little sacred enclosure of individuality in defense of which the owner is prepared to defy the entire world with its battering rams of criticism, convention, and mockery. The benefits to be derived from a hobby are altogether subjective in the first instance. Selfish, then, if you will; but selfish in the best sense. For the hobby restores the man to himself, renews his vitality every evening, prepares him for the rough and tumble fight in the world to maintain his place and secure the triumph of his ideals.

All work and no play, even in the intellectual domain, makes us dull indeed. The hobbies upon which a man may indulge his taste are legion. The joy of collecting is the same whether you collect diamonds or marbles. He may collect anything under the canopy of heaven. It makes no difference what he does, if it does him or others no harm, and if it daily refreshes his soul with interest and enthusiasm.

I can't help but wonder what Comfort might have thought about this thing we call fandom. No doubt he would have said something profound. Lacking his wisdom, the best I can offer is a realization that life is far too short to waste on matters of minor consequence. There is nothing to be gained from harboring ill feelings that can last a lifetime. Having been there, I know. Trust me on that one.

Fandom Glossary

Many of the following esoteric words were devised in the 1930s by science fiction fans. You won't find many of them in Webster's Dictionary. *Terms about grading and pricing date back even earlier, to coin and stamp collectors. Most of the other words have contemporary origins, conceived by comic book, film, and* Star Trek *fans.*

Actifan: The career fan. One who collects, corresponds, publishes, organizes, and spends most of his time on fan activities.

Adzine: A fan periodical specializing in the publishing of advertising.

Animated cartoon: The art of taking still images, projecting one after the other, producing an illusion of motion. Animated cartoons began as black-and-white, silent films in the early 1920s. Sound and color came later. They remain a favorite of kiddies young and old.

Animation cel: The original art painted on a sheet of clear plastic used in the production of an animated cartoon.

Annish: The anniversary issue of a fanzine.

APA: Amateur Press Association. A special interest group devoted to a particular subject. Individual members prepare information, sending it to a central mailer, who collates the material and distributes it to all members. Donald Wollheim introduced the concept in the late 1930s by founding *The Fantasy Amateur Press Association (FAPA)*. For over thirty years, it chugged along, inspiring imitation. For all I know, it may still be around. In this day of computerized technology, hardly anyone does it anymore.

Apan: A member of an APA.

Argosy: The first recognized pulp magazine, begins in 1882 as *The Golden Argosy*, a boy's weekly paper. Becomes a pulp magazine in 1888. Endures in that format for more than a half century with only minor changes. Becomes a nonfiction, slick magazine in the 1950s.

Arkham House: A book publisher specializing in the publication of limited edition science fiction and fantasy books. Books by this publisher are prized by collectors due to their quality and rarity. H. P. Lovecraft was published in Arkham editions decades before he was discovered by *Time* magazine.

Artzine: A fanzine specializing in the publication of illustrations, cartoons, or other art.

Baker Street Irregulars: A club composed of serious fans of Sherlock Holmes. To be considered for membership, a person must first write a scholarly thesis on the subject. It is a tough group to join. It might be easier to marry into the British Royal Family.

Barsoomian: Anything pertaining to the work of Edgar Rice Burroughs.

BAYOR: "Buy at your own risk."

BEM: Bug-eyed monster. A common theme used on the cover of science fiction pulp magazines.

Blackhawk Films: During the 1950s, this company offered a line of 8 mm films previously unavailable to the public. This included silent Charlie Chaplin and Laurel & Hardy shorts. In the halcyon days before videotape, they were an expensive novelty.

BLB: Big Little Book. A genuine publishing oddity. BLBs were squarebound 3" x 4" books, containing text and illustrations. Whitman was the premier publisher of this genre for children.

BNF: Big Name Fan. A fan of considerable reknown, if there really is such a thing. The way some fans act, you would swear that they were heads of state.

Bondage: A theme depicting voluptuous women, bound and often gagged, facing imminent peril. It was frequently used in the 1940s on comic book and pulp magazine covers. Obviously, such magazines were not kid stuff.

Boys' books: As the name implies, they are books written for boys. Dates range from the early 1900s to the late 1960s. Many were published in a series format. For example, three generations of boys marveled at the scientific adventures of Tom Swift. Victor Appleton milked the gimmick for all it was worth.

Cereal premiums: Toys and trinkets given away in boxes of cereal. In the early 1940s, many of the brands (Ralston, Pep, Cheerios, Wheaties) sponsored radio programs. Thus, the giveaways often have a radio tie-in.

Cinematic memorabilia: All artifacts produced by motion picture companies to advertise movies fall into this category. It includes press books, one-sheets, three-sheets, lobby cards, midget cards, and stills.

COA: Change of address.

Comic book: A magazine of comic strips, narrating a story with panels and dialogued captions.

Comics Code Authority: An organized body, independent from comic book publishers. Founded in 1954, it regulates the subject matter published in comic books. Publishers voluntarily subscribe.

Comix: Underground comics.

Con: Slang for convention.

Convention: A gathering of people, joined by a common interest.

Cover proof: A black-and-white stat of the original art, reduced to actual size and colored for reproduction.

Critic: Someone who gets paid to make critical observations of another person's work. They came in all varieties: art, music, food, literature, theater, and comic books. For some reason, they tend to have a nasty disposition. May the bird of paradise eat their Don Rickles handbooks.

Crud: Worthless material, usually found in fanzines of poor quality.

Crudzine: A fanzine of poor quality. In recent years, the format has resurfaced in the form of black-and-white comic books.

In the aftermath of the Comics Code Authority, comic books were essentially kiddie fare. This unpublished cover, circa 1957, is a fine example. The art is by Dan De Carlo. Curiously, De Carlo is often admired for his pretty-girl cartoons published in various men's magazines during the 1950s and '60s.

Cult: A following of people sharing an overzealous interest in a specific subject. The *Star Trek* phenomenon is one example.

Deadwood: A member of an APA who publishes only the minimum contributions to maintain membership.

Defect: A noticeable flaw in any collectible. Rips, tears, stains, mold, rust, brittleness, and missing pieces are obvious defects. Some dealers have been known to include a disclaimer in their advertising that tape is not considered a defect. Like hell! The more tape, the worse the defect.

Digest: A 5½" x 8½" magazine.

Dime novel: A now extinct publishing medium, the predecessor of pulp magazines and comic books. Dates range from 1860 to 1920. Dime novels featured original fiction for children.

Ditto: A reproduction method using a spirit master and fluid. Many of the early comic book and science fiction fanzines were published by this process. The ink is usually a faded purple color. The damned things are almost impossible to read.

DNQ: Do not quote. This is a postscript added to a letter of comment, indicating that the writer does not wish to be quoted.

Duck art: A term describing the work of Carl Barks, on the *Donald Duck/ Uncle Scrooge* series. In some literary circles, Barks is considered the comic book equivalent of Charles Dickens. It's high praise, indeed.

Duper: A duplicating machine. It can refer to any duplicator or copier: ditto, mimeograph, xerox, etc.

Egoboo: Good words written about oneself in a fanzine. Perish the thought.

English Penny Books: Sometimes called penny papers. Genre begins about 1840, selling on the streets of London for a penny. The penny book format evolved into the British pulp magazines, notably *The Strand*.

ERB: Novelist Edgar Rice Burroughs. Creator of Tarzan, John Carter of Mars, etc.

Fanzines come in all shapes and sizes. They are published on a wide variety of topics. Seems like every whim somehow finds a publisher. Although it looks like something one might find on the cover of a dime novel, this unique specimen was published in 1964 by Edgar Rice Burroughs aficionado John E. Stockman. It was printed on an old-fashioned mimeograph machine, which explains the poor reproduction. If nothing else, call it quaint.

Escapist literature: The classification of fiction in all forms: science fiction, mystery, western, war, romance, humor, etc.

Fair: A grading term.   Definitions vary depending upon the type of collectible.   Shows obvious signs of wear.   A grade above Poor and a notch below Good.   When it involves condition, collectors have a penchant for splitting hairs.

Fan: A follower, admirer, or devotee of any genre.

Fanac: A general classification of fan activity.

Fan club: An organized group of fans sharing a common interest.

Fandom: A loosely knit following of fans, collectors, and dealers.

Fanned: A fanzine editor.

Fannish: Referring to a characteristic of fandom or fans.

Fantasy: A style of fiction devoted to the imaginary.

Fanzine: A periodical published by fans, for fans.

Femmefan: A female fan. Term has fallen out of favor in recent years. It is no longer considered "politically correct." Oh, pooh!

Fen: Plural of fan.

FIAWOL: A slogan meaning "fandom is a way of life."

Film Collector's Registry: The first periodical devoted to film collecting, starting in 1961.

Films: The entertainment medium recorded on 8 mm, 16 mm, 35 mm, or 70 mm celluloid film, shown on a projector and cast on a screen.

Fine: Another grading classification. It is a notch above Good and a notch below Mint. It can be defined as an almost perfect copy. The difference between fine and mint is almost imperceptible to the human eye. A lot depends on whether you are buying or selling.

Flange: A slang term for any object you can't remember the name of.

Four color: A printing process by which many comic books have been printed. Defined as four process colors (cyan, yellow, magenta, and black) that when combined on a printing press produce the illusion of full color.

FUBAR: Fouled up beyond all recognition. The Clinton administration is a marvelous example.

Funk: A colloquial term relating to an esoteric outlook on life. It can refer to the proverbial "jumping on the bandwagon" in changing trends of popular culture.

Gafiate: Getting away from it all. Leaving fandom behind.

Genzine: A fanzine of general interest.

GOH: Guest of honor.

Golden Age of comics: A period of comic book history beginning with the first appearance of Superman in *Action* #1 (1938), ending with World War II (1945). The definition changes all the time. The experts never can seem to agree.

Golden age of music: A frequent subject of argument among record collectors. Every style has its own golden age. For the Big Band sound, it's 1933–42. For rock-and-roll aficionados, its begins with Bill Haley rocking around the clock and ends with the British invasion of the Beatles. Fans of bluegrass celebrate 1929, when Gid Tanner and His Skillet Lickers recorded "It Ain't Gonna Rain No Mo."

Golden age of radio: Generally accepted as 1939–59, when radio reached its zenith as an entertainment medium. Then television came along. You know what has happened to the world since then.

Golden Books: A delightful series of children's books (beginning in the early 1950s) featuring established cartoon characters from Disney, Warner Bros., etc.

Good: An average condition copy of anything. Shows some signs of wear, but is of an acceptable condition to most collectors. Who cares what the rest of those snobs think.

Almost any pulp collector would give his eyeteeth to own this June 1934 issue of *Dime Detective Magazine.* It features an early bondage cover. Some collectors adore this kind of thing. Of course, the Erle Stanley Gardner story is nice, too.

Good girl art: An expression coined in recent years. It refers to comic books or pulp magazines featuring scantily attired women. Bondage themes are often used.

Grading: A system for rating the condition of collectibles, using mutually accepted standards. The most commonly used codes are: Mint, Near Mint, Very Fine, Fine, Very Good, Good, Fair, and Poor.

Gum cards: A marketing device conceived in 1940s. Gum cards were an offshoot of cigarette cards, first distributed in the 1870s. Baseball cards are the most popular. However, other varieties are collected.

Hack: A designation given to an untalented artist or writer by fans. It can also apply to work that is hurried or unrefined, not up to the usual standards of the professional.

Huckster: A person who peddles collectibles for a living. Socially, they fit in somewhere between a banker and a bootlegger. Spiritually, they stand beside Donald Trump. They know how to make a buck.

Hugo Awards: The annual awards presented at the World Science Fiction Convention for best novel, short story, film, fanzine, etc.

IFICC: The International Fandom Inflation Control Club (1974–79).

Illo: An illustration in a fanzine.

The Immortal Storm: An obscure (and highly sought after) book by Sam Moskowitz about the fussing and fighting among science fiction fans in the 1930s. I've seen one copy in the last twenty-five years and the owner refused to let it out of his sight.

Ish: Issue of a fanzine.

Lettercol: Abbreviation for letter column.

Letterhack: A person who contributes many letters to fanzines or magazines.

Lobby card: An 11" x 14" movie poster, used primarily in theater lobbies. It usually depicts a specific scene from a movie.

LOC: Letter of comment.

LNF: Little name fan. A fan of minor reknown.

Mail fraud: The act of using the mails to commit theft of money or merchandise. Such dishonesty is enough to make a man see red. In a civilized society, scoundrels committing such an atrocity would be tarred and feathered, then run out of town on a rail.

Mainstream comics: Comic books published by professional companies, circulated by newsstand distributors. In recent years, Marvel, DC, Harvey, and Archie have been the most successful.

Marvelite: A fan of Marvel comics.

Midget cards: An unusual form of cinematic memorabilia, best described as a miniature one-sheet. They were often displayed in a show case, with candy or cigars.

Mil: The standard for measuring thickness. A unit of measure equivalent to $1/1000$ of an inch. If not for plastic bags, it would be a matter of complete indifference to most collectors.

Mimeograph: A duplication method using stencils and ink. For years, Gestetner was the Cadillac of mimeograph machines. They cost a fortune and were well worth it.

Minicon: A small convention that usually lasts one day.

Mint: A perfect copy. It looks brand new. Advertise a collectible as Mint (asking top dollar) and be prepared for an argument. Collectors are persnickety. Some are known to examine items with a magnifying glass, looking for microscopic flaws or signs of restoration.

Movie material: See Cinematic memorabilia.

Mundane: The world outside of fandom.

Mylar: A special type of plastic preferred by collectors for long-term storage. It is the only plastic known to be inert. It is also expensive. Du Pont is making a killing on this stuff. Like Sears and Roebuck, they are not known for their lavish generosity.

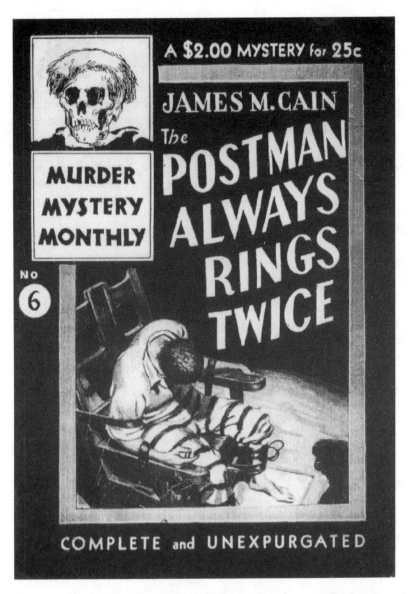

The mere thought of this beautiful 1942 Avon paperback book selling for a measley quarter is enough to make a grown man cry. *The Postman Always Rings Twice* is a classic suspense story. As usual, Hollywood didn't do the book justice. If you haven't read it, shame on you.

Nebula Awards: Honorary awards presented at the annual banquet of the Science Fiction and Fantasy Writers of America for best novel, short story, novelette, etc.

Neo-fan: The lowest rung in the fan order. A person new to the hobby.

Newspaper Sunday pages: Sometimes they are called Sunday funnies. They are usually in color. Dates range from early 1900s to the present. The full-page strips are most desirable for collecting purposes.

NFFF: The National Fantasy Fan Federation. A science fiction organization in existence since 1941.

OAF: The Oklahoma Alliance of Fans (1967–83).

One sheet: A designation given to a 28" x 41" movie poster.

One shot: Any publication discontinued after the first issue.

Original art: The original illustrations prepared by an artist for publication. Originals are always one of a kind.

Overgraded: Any item that is in an inferior condition than what is specified by the seller. Of course, this never happens in nostalgia collecting. Everyone is as honest as the day is long.

OTR: Old-time radio. In its most esoteric form, it involves collecting the original transcription disks produced on a 16" record. The disks were distributed to various radio stations for broadcast. Old-time radio programs are more commonly collected on cassette tape.

Panel discussion: An event at conventions. A panel is composed of guest speakers, professionals, or celebrities to discuss a subject or theme. In particular, science fiction fans adore them. A few years ago at a convention in Kansas City, panelists passed a bottle of booze back and forth. Before long, the discussion degenerated into a dialogue about sex and ended in a brawl. Oh, well. To each his own.

Panelologist: A student or historian of comic art. It sounds a lot more dignified than "comic book fan."

Paperback books: Inexpensive softbound books that became popular in the early 1940s. Sometimes known as pocket books.

Pep pin: A small, round pin given away in the 1940s in boxes of Kellog's Pep cereal. Most feature popular comic strip characters of the period.

Plastic bags: Specially manufactured bags, made of polyethylene or mylar, used to protect collectibles.

Poor: The worst possible grade for a collectible. It is the next thing to not having a copy at all.

Pre-Code: A term used to describe comic books published before the advent of the Comics Code Authority in 1954.

Pressbooks: A magazine of sorts, distributed by motion picture companies to promote their films. Often, they are used by theater managers to order movie posters. They usually contain layouts for newspaper advertising.

Pricey: A term referring to a highly sought after collectible. A "pricey" item will command a stiff price.

Profiteering: The making of excessive profit. Taking advantage of a shortage by charging inflated prices. May those guilty of the practice be cursed by frogs.

Proof: A pricing term used almost exclusively by coin collectors. A proof coin is uncirculated, housed in an airtight container, supposedly untouched by human hands. It is absolutely without flaw.

Prozine: It sounds like a prescription drug. Actually, it is a fanzine published by professionals. The term is also used for professional magazines (as opposed to fanzines).

Pulp magazines: A now extinct publishing genre. The magazines were called "pulps" because they were printed on the cheapest pulp newsprint. Dates range from the turn of the century to about 1955.

Radio premiums: Rings, badges, whistles, and other toys given away by radio sponsors to stimulate interest in a program: *Lone Ranger, The Shadow, Jack Armstrong, Superman,* etc.

Rare: Any collectible of which 20 copies (or fewer) are known to exist. Most people making this claim are full of sheep dip. Who can say for certain how many copies of anything exist? It's a big world. Thousands of collectibles are buried in private collections. It is probably safe to assume that most items auctioned on eBay are not really rare. Don't believe a word those liars tell you.

RBCC: *The Rocket's Blast-Comicollector.* One of the first regularly published comic fanzines (1965-76).

Records: An almost extinct entertainment medium. Dates run from 1900 to the present. Several speeds are common: 16 rpm, 33 rpm, 45 rpm, and 78 rpm. Edison was the first commercially produced record, a quarter-inch-thick monstrosity that must be played on an Edison turntable.

Restoration: Any attempt (either amateur or professional) to enhance the appearance of a collectible. In most areas of collecting, the practice is controversial. Like walking barefoot on hot coals, restoration should be approached with caution.

Reuben Awards: The annual awards presented by the National Cartoonists Society, named in honor of cartoonist Rube Goldberg.

SASE: A self-addressed stamped envelope.

Scarce: Any collectible of which 100 copies (or fewer) are known to exist. It is usually a more accurate classification than Rare. Due to their age, it is probably safe to assume that all dime novels and most pulp magazines are scarce.

Science fiction: Highly imaginative stories about the future, time travel, space exploration, and other fantastic possibilities.

Sci-fi: Slang abbreviation for science fiction, pronounced "skiffy." Most serious science fiction fans despise the term. Good for them.

***Seduction of the Innocent*:**   The famous book written by Dr. Fredric Wertham. It stimulated a nationwide crusade by parents and teachers to ban comic books in the early 1950s.

Serials: A now extinct film genre. Serials originated in the 1930s to entice customers to return weekly. Most serials ran twelve or fifteen chapters. They

This *Rocket's Blast–Comicollector* cover is from the late 1960s. If I had to choose a particular favorite out of the hundreds of fanzine covers I have seen in the last thirty-five years, it might well be this one. It has a lot of sentimental value. Wallace Wood was at the top of his form. As a matter of formality, please note that Daredevil is a copyrighted character of Marvel Comics.

were often based on a popular radio or comic book character. At the end of each chapter, the hero appears to meet his doom. You came back the following week to see if he survives. Of course, he always does.

SFFWA: Science Fiction and Fantasy Writers of America.

Sherlock Holmes: The most famous of all fictional detectives. The stories were first published (in serial form) about the turn of the century in *The Strand* magazine. Fans of the character are often a bit snobbish. Some of them profess to read no other mystery stories. It sounds dull to me, but what do I know?

Silver Age of comics: The period of comics history beginning with *Showcase* #4 (1956) and ending in 1969.

Silver print: Also known as PMT or velox. A space-saving device used by comic book publishers. The original art is usually discarded. The art is saved (in the published size) as black-and-white prints on photographic paper.

Speculation: Obtaining items in hope of making a future profit, based on changing trends of supply and demand. Since no one can predict the future, speculation is a lot like hunting bears with a peashooter. Most of time the bear gets you. Just ask the Hunt brothers.

Spicey pulps: The 1930s equivalent of mens' magazines. They featured risque subject matter and highly suggestive covers. Because of this, they were usually sold under the counter.

Spirit pages: A comic book–style newspaper supplement of the late 1940s and '50s, featuring Will Eisner's popular character, the Spirit.

Sports memorabilia: Almost any collectible pertaining to the wide world of sports. Pete Rose could probably sell his toenail clippings. I once saw a baseball from the 1949 World Series, autographed by an umpire, sell for $250. And they say comic book collectors are crazy!

Spot illo: A spot illustration designed to provide graphics to an article of text.

***Stan's Weekly Express*:**   Fandom's first weekly published adzine (1969–72). Later known as *WE*.

If you can recognize the actors in this publicity still, you probably spend too much time watching television. Linda Day George resists the advances of Tom Bosley on a 1975 episode of *Ellery Queen*. Bosley plays a wicked comic book editor who, of course, manages to get himself murdered.

*Star Trek***:**   The famous science fiction television series beginning in 1967. Later, it spawned a cult following and all sorts of strange behavior. For example, translating the works of Shakespeare into "Klingon."

Still: An 8" x 10" photograph, used by television and motion picture companies for advertising. Stills usually feature a star actor or a specific scene.

*TBG***:**   *The Buyer's Guide for Comic Fandom.*

Television shows: I'll not bore you with a definition. Some of the more beloved examples down memory lane include *I Love Lucy* and *Gunsmoke.* The original 16 mm prints are prized by collectors.

Thish: A contraction for "this issue."

Three sheet: A very large movie poster, ordinarily three times the size of a one sheet.

*TNJ***:**   *The Nostalgia Journal.* Later became *The Comics Journal.*

Toys: A rather diversified field of collecting. Dates range from 1800s to the present. Technically, a toy is any artifact manufactured as a children's plaything. It includes everything from model trains to Barbie dolls.

Trailer: A very short film, usually a minute or less. Motion picture studios used trailers as a promotional device to attract viewers. Enticing scenes from a movie are shown to generate interest.

Trekkie: A fan of *Star Trek.* There is no accounting for taste. Some of the more persnickety fans prefer the term "trekker."

Trufan: The complete fan. One who embraces himself to a particular genre and overlooks nothing.

Typo: Typographical error.

Undergraded: Opposite of overgraded. An item that is in a superior condition than advertised by the seller. It is not a routine occurrence. The last time I heard about it happening, nickel cigars and bathtub gin were fashionable.

Underground comics: Comic style magazines produced by semiprofessional companies. They are noted for a lack of editorial control and questionable

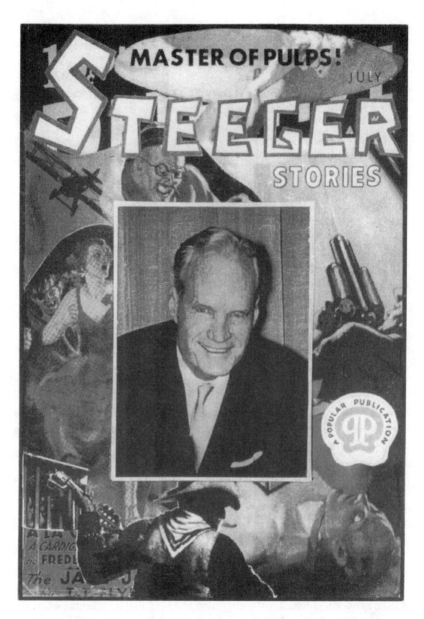

The much admired *Xenophile,* Vol. 3, No. 9, July 1977. Published by Nils Hardin who, for half a decade, served as a conscience for hundreds of pulp magazine collectors. This issue featured a profile of legendary pulp editor and publisher Harry Steeger.

subject matter. Many contain explicit sex and excessive violence. They often illustrate the use of narcotics. Besides that, most underground comics are as wholesome as a bowl of branflakes.

Vitafilm: A foul-smelling chemical used to clean and preserve collectors' films.

WAHF: We also heard from. This is an expression used by fanzine editors to indicate receiving letters of comment.

Warries: Fans of *Star Wars* movies.

Welcommittee: The *Star Trek* welcoming committee. God bless them, every one.

WSA Program: We Seal of Approval (1970–84). Founded by Stanley R. Blair. Known as fandom's protective organization, it promoted fair play in the hobby and suggested professional methods of doing business by mail.

Xenophile: The first regularly published periodical devoted to pulp collecting (1974–79).

Zine: A slang term for a fanzine.

WSA Membership Roster 1970–79

This listing of WSA members is not complete. Some of the records were destroyed by fire in 1974. In other instances, members resigned or were suspended and their names were deleted from the official records. Membership records from 1980–84 were not available at the time of publication and may no longer exist.

Members with names highlighted in bold served as officers within the organization. Names in italics are members well known as publishers, writers, artists, dealers, collectors, or historians. Members noted by asterisk are deceased. The state or country of residence listed is, in most instances, where the member lived at the time of joining the organization.

Many former WSA members are still active in fandom. In the years that have followed, some became retailers, distributors, or professionals in the direct sales industry, or achieved other distinctions. Other members seem to have, more or less, disappeared. Perhaps the publication of this book may draw some of them out of the shadows. For the sake of posterity, I am hopeful that a complete membership listing might be compiled at some later date.

0001	**Blair, Stanley R.***	Ohio		0016	**Klein, Avery**	Ohio
0002	**Blair, Elaine***	Ohio		0017	Conine, Wilt	Oklahoma
0003	McGinnis, Don	Ohio		0018	Evans, Wilfred	California
0005	Schroeder, William	California		0019	*Carlson, K. Martin*	Minnesota
0006	*Ivey, Jim*	Florida		0020	Maule, John	New York
0007	*Sampson, Robert**	Alabama		0021	*Paskow, Abe**	New York
0008	*Frierson, Meade*	Alabama		0022	Misenhimer, Ron	California
0009	Alexander, David	California		0023	Horak, Carl	Canada
0010	Gambaro, Hugh	New Jersey		0024	*Rypel, Ted*	Ohio
0011	Payne, Jim	Colorado		0025	*Schiff, Stuart David*	Maryland
0012	Booksinger	New York		0026	Ritenour, Richard	Virginia
0013	Schwartz, George	Wisconsin		0027	*Slobodian, Calvin*	Canada
0014	Severs, Lawrence	Canada		0028	White, Donald	New York
0015	Bowman, Barry	Ohio		0029	Whitaker, George	N. Carolina

0030	Puff, Donald	New York
0031	Vegetis, Leon	Wisconsin
0033	Lewis, Steve	Connecticut
0034	*McGeehan, John**	California
0035	*McGeehan, Tom*	California
0036	Cauley, John	California
0037	Uditsky, Michael	Pennsylvania
0038	Winfree, R.E.	Virginia
0039	**Stoner, Joe**	Virginia
0040	Myers, Robert	Illinois
0041	Seguin, Manuel*	Texas
0042	Kousek, Gene	Illinois
0047	Wolf, John	Oregon
0050	Cordes, Jack	Illinois
0051	Runfalo, Anthony	Texas
0054	*Durell, Richard**	California
0055	Dobrey, Alan	Canada
0060	Lewis, Glen	Tennessee
0061	Haynes, Randy	Florida
0062	Bednarek, Mitchell	Ohio
0063	Wilke, George	Illinois
0072	Miller, Stephen	Pennsylvania
0077	Woloszyn, Gary	Ohio
0083	**Barrington, Steve**	Alabama
0100	*Bails, Jerry*	Michigan
0101	Bails, Jean	Michigan
0102	Brenholt, Paul	Wisconsin
0106	Askuvich, Jerry	Missouri
0111	Ellioff, Alexander	California
0115	Dang, Lucas	California
0116	Cooper, Arthur	Canada
0119	Langer, Robert	New York
0120	Kelly, Chris	Wisconsin
0121	Hogue, Rose	
0125	*Mosso, Richard*	Maine
0133	Lovece, Frank	W. Virginia
0139	Titchenal, Stephen	Ohio
0150	*Carr, Wooda Nick*	Arizona
0160	Pagan, Kevin	New York
0175	Lameron, H. Mitchell	New York

Note: The following members are listed in alphabetical order because their actual numbers are unknown. Based on the best available information, they became members from 1970–73 and fall somewhere in the previous numerical sequence.

0000	*Ackerman, Forrest*	California
0000	*Ed Aprill, Jr.**	Michigan
0000	*Beahm, George*	Virginia
0000	Beerbhom, Bob	Nebraska
0000	Bishop, Hardy	Texas
0000	Bramble, Wayne	Maryland
0000	Cawley, John	California
0000	Cooper, Robert	Pennsylvania
0000	Crais, Bobby	Louisiana
0000	Crawley, Evan	Illinois
0000	Davidson, Sol	Iowa
0000	*Garrison, Richard*	New York
0000	Grossman, A.	California
0000	Harris, Mark	Illinois
0000	*Hamilton, Bruce*	Arizona
0000	Hasbrouck, Harold	California
0000	Hauser, Rich	Illinois
0000	Henderson, Craig	Maryland
0000	Johnson, Steve	Nebraska
0000	Kasdin, Mark	New Jersey
0000	Kessell, Ed	Missouri
0000	Lee, David	New Mexico
0000	Lichina, Mike	California
0000	Lowery, Bob	Washington
0000	Luttrell, Hank	Missouri
0000	Mayfield, Joel	Arizona
0000	McClannen, Roger	Illinois
0000	McCullough, Donald	Texas
0000	Nemeth, J.W.	Ohio
0000	Newman, Dean	Oregon
0000	Nussell, Frank*	Illinois
0000	Peill, Floyd	Canada
0000	*Plant, Bud*	California
0000	Reguera, Jose Gomez	Mexico
0000	Ricker, Gary	Illinois
0000	Riley, Steve	Massachusetts
0000	*Rozanski, Charles*	Colorado
0000	Sanguino, Anthony	New York
0000	Sauer, George	Illinois
0000	Saunders, Ken	Utah
0000	Stephen, Juan	Louisiana
0000	Stoelting, Wally	Vermont
0000	Snider, Joan	Missouri

0000	Tricarci, Joe	Ohio
0000	*Weinberg, Robert*	Illinois
0000	Wheeler, Rod	California
0000	Wilke, Geroge	Illinois
0200	*Kowtuik, Paul*	Canada
0222	*Siegel, Howard*	New York
0224	Silverman, Jospeh	New York
0233	Campbell, Colin	California
0240	Hartig, Herbert	New York
0250	Sells, Jim	Tennessee
0253	*Pierce, Ken*	Illinois
0268	Rosenthal, Lana	New York
0275	*Austin, Alan*	England
0283	**Miller, Art**	Michigan
0297	*Light, Alan*	Illinois
0298	Light, Lavon	Illinois
0300	Levine, Alan	New Jersey
0303	*Held, Claude*	New York
0305	*Hancer, Kevin*	Minnesota
0306	Wawro, Terrance	California
0307	Knueven, Robert	Illinois
0308	Buck, Jack	New Jersey
0310	Altshulen, Thomas	Minnesota
0312	Pennington, Patricia	
0314	Iavarone, John	New York
0315	Robins, Douglas	Oregon
0320	*Hardin, Nils*	Missouri
0322	Hunt, Jack	New York
0324	Haas, Merlin	Illinois
0325	Riggs, Schultz	Mississippi
0326	Lofaro, Ronald	New York
0327	Hawk, Charles	Wisconsin
0328	Krolik, Joseph	Canada
0329	Kent, John	California
0330	Laurence, Charles	N. Carolina
0331	Hill, Roger	Kansas
0332	Carlson, S.W.	California
0333	Boyd, Melville	Arizona
0334	**Frantz, Ron**	Oklahoma
0335	Cliff Jones	Michigan
0336	Kapustar, Albert	Michigan
0337	King, David	Washington
0338	Roberts, William	Florida
0339	Walent, Daniel	Florida

0340	*Overstreet, Bob*	Tennessee
0341	Thompson, Sue	Missouri
0342	Behymer, Gary	Washington
0343	Ligon, Peggy	Ohio
0344	Page, James	S. Dakota
0345	Byrne, Noel	New Jersey
0346	Harroff, William	Indiana
0347	*Frutti, Tony*	Canada
0348	Sullo, Louis	New York
0349	Coleman, William	Connecticut
0350	Chin, Jack	Illinois
0351	Patton, Jeff	Ohio
0352	Rudolph, Jeffrey	Connecticut
0353	McLean, David	New York
0354	Kokich, James	New York
0355	*Inge, M. Thomas*	Virginia
0356	Johnson, Stephen	Michigan
0357	Goto, Bruce	California
0358	Rainbolt, Russell	Louisiana
0359	**Hopkins, Harry**	California
0360	Hissong, David	Ohio
0361	Wilcutt, Dennis	Kentucky
0362	Quackenbush, Russell	Pennsylvania
0363	Patterson, Bruce	California
0364	Kristansen, Ralph	Massachusetts
0365	Best, Dwayne	New York
0366	Coye, Daniel	New York
0367	Gordon, Stephen	California
0368	*Bell, Robert*	New York
0369	Pennington, Steve	Alabama
0370	McGeary, Mitchell	Washington
0371	Walowina, John	Canada
0372	Green, Glen	California
0373	Bevans, John	Maryland
0374	Lindsay, Jerry	Texas
0375	Kendig, Douglas	Canada
0376	Baker, Jerry	Ohio
0377	Glasser, Fred	New York
0378	Johnson, N.J.	Oregon
0379	Zuras, George	Virginia
0380	Peters, Craig	New York
0381	Ward, Murray	Canada
0382	Nance, Lyle	Kentucky
0383	Lamb, Richard	New Jersey
0384	Stenerson, Dennis	Illinois

0385	Harden, Carl	California		0430	Coxe, J. Michael	S. Carolina
0386	Seiler, Gary	Canada		0431	Klasek, Terry	Missouri
0387	Bender, Fred	Wisconsin		0432	Kuldau, Joseph	Ohio
0388	Daniels, Mark	Connecticut		0433	Poling, Rudolph	Ohio
0389	Barson, Michael	Massachusetts		0434	Ching, Richard	Hawaii
0390	Wakabayashi, Dennis	Colorado		0435	Condello, Russell	New York
0391	Allen, Steven*	Colorado		0436	Trombley, Richard	New York
0392	Gibson, Jim	Canada		0437	Richey, Mark	Washington
0393	Conway, Robert	Colorado		0438	Evangelista, Mark	Maryland
0394	Larson, Dennis	Minnesota		0439	*Hamilton, Frank*	Massachusetts
0395	Duncan, David	Tennessee		0440	Lane, Ed	Florida
0396	Clark, David	Oregon		0441	Karesky, Edward	California
0397	Scheibe, Jeffrey	Wisconsin		0442	Alvarado, Paul	Illinois
0398	Brooks, Barry	Massachusetts		0443	Kautz, Allan	Illinois
0399	Pilarz, John	New York		0444	Grunne, Gerhard	New York
0400	Groves, Eric	Oklahoma		0445	Thomas, Ross	Canada
0401	Du Garm, H. Keating	N. Dakota		0446	Mickelson, Scott	Iowa
0402	Sperling, Mack	New York		0447	Lynch, Edward	Florida
0403	Lovinger, Michael	Michigan		0448	Derderian, Stephen	Michigan
0404	Natalie, Mark	Illinois		0449	Moore, J.P.	Indiana
0405	Yangis, Nicholas	New York		0450	Risdall, John	Minnesota
0406	Braun, Alan	New York		0451	Goyette, Chad	California
0407	Petilli, Dennis	New York		0452	Purcell, C. Anderson	Tennessee
0408	Simmons, Rusty	New Jersey		0453	Irwin, Grant	Arkansas
0409	Lisa, David	New Jersey		0454	Medoff, Randy	New York
0410	Gold, Neil	Florida		0455	*Gold, Stan*	Texas
0411	Soltz, Arthur	Minnesota		0456	Brakefield, Monte	Alabama
0412	Slupczynski, Stanley	Michigan		0457	Guay, George	Massachusetts
0413	Rudin, Dorian	Ohio		0458	Kuhn, Frederic	New York
0414	Lankford, Larry	Texas		0459	Chambers, Leonard	Washington
0415	Miller, Thomas	Pennsylvania		0460	DiStefano, A.	Connecticut
0416	Winters, Richard	Oklahoma		0461	Chrislip, Bruce	Ohio
0417	Crawford, James	Ohio		0462	Thornton, Shiela	New York
0418	*Hill, Melville*	California		0463	Melchert, Chris	California
0419	DeSimone, Robert	Rhode Island		0464	Scott, Steven	Texas
0420	Shetter, Peter	Illinois		0465	Taeusch, David E.	Michigan
0421	*Bacon, Jonathan*	Iowa		0466	Clark, Richard	Alabama
0422	Bird, Robert	Mississippi		0467	Thomas, Ken	Missouri
0423	Schisler, Mark	Canada		0468	Ferris, Gilbert	Virginia
0424	Lozada, Rene	New York		0469	Akselsen, Kent	Florida
0425	Jessup, Andrew	N. Dakota		0470	Ziesing, Michael	Connecticut
0426	Wyles, William	New York		0471	Tanguay, David	Tennessee
0427	Yee, Alan	Canada		0472	Boire, Martin	N. Hampshire
0428	Epstein, Charles	Massachusetts		0473	Petrulis, Leonard	Illinois
0429	Johnson, Steven	Colorado		0474	Embry, Jerry	Kentucky

0475	Clifford, James	Florida
0476	Foreman, Ronald	New York
0477	Hoencke, Gerald	California
0478	Smith, Wayne	Georgia
0479	*Jennings, Robert*	Massachusetts
0480	Hauser, John	Washington
0481	Goldberg, Todd	New Jersey
0482	Nelson, Gunnar	Maryland
0483	Todd, Joseph	Georgia
0484	Hoffman, Douglas	Pennsylvania
0485	Gulliksen, David	Connecticut
0486	**Robertson, Mike**	Washington
0487	Oja, Matthew	New York
0488	Bagby, Howard	Illinois
0489	Meine, Fred	Colorado
0490	Montgomery, Robert	New York
0491	Johnson, Herbert	Massachusetts
0492	Heath, David	California
0493	DeRousse, Roy	Missouri
0494	Walker, Bruce	Florida
0495	Brown, Dale	California
0496	Ehresman, Herbert	Ohio
0497	Sage, Stephen	Kentucky
0498	Trombatta, Robert	New York
0499	Yates, William	Texas
0500	Walker, Alan	Hawaii
0501	Highsmith, Douglas	Illinois
0502	Hayes, Brian	Illinois
0503	Blake, Benjamin	Connecticut
0504	*Morrissey, Richard*	Massachusetts
0505	Hoover, Michael	California
0506	Hecker, David	New York
0507	Kane, Scott	New York
0508	Wooten, Woody	N. Carolina
0509	Hanneman, Paul	Texas
0510	Bezdikian, Jerry	New York
0511	Julian, Tony	California
0512	Way, Fred	New York
0513	Davis, Arthur	Pennsylvania
0514	Nash, Spencer	Michigan
0515	Cohen, Avery	Illinois
0516	Harvey, Robert	Illinois
0517	Steadman, Randy	S. Carolina
0518	Miller, Harry	Florida
0519	Peed, Allie C.	New York
0520	*DeMarco, Anthony*	New Jersey
0521	Detitta, Stephen	New Jersey
0522	Kenton, Larry	Maryland
0523	Spath, James	Missouri
0524	Heath, Guy	California
0525	Ortego, Joseph	Louisiana
0526	Ryder, Michael	Michigan
0527	Youhouse, Robert	Pennsylvania
0528	Jason, Ben	Ohio
0529	**Hennings, John**	New Jersey
0530	Hartman, David	Illinois
0531	Shipp, Wilbur	Virginia
0532	Bousuaros, Athos	New York
0533	Heuberger, Robert	New York
0534	Hurst, James	Maryland
0535	Randolph, Mike	California
0536	Selover, William	Florida
0537	Lewis, Stephen	Virginia
0538	Peters, Hal	Maryland
0539	Zack, Paul	Pennsylvania
0540	Grabek, Jan	Illinois
0541	Jones, Michael	Illinois
0542	Klug, Martin	Missouri
0543	Bienstock, Terry	New York
0544	Siewert, Brent	Washington
0545	Stransky, Thomas	Minnesota
0546	Harris, F. Woodrow	Virginia
0547	Shea, David	Virginia
0548	Yee, Donald	California
0549	McAardle, John	Indiana
0550	McFee, Alex	California
0551	Pearce, Kathy	Oklahoma
0552	*Dellinges, Alex*	California
0553	Fleischman, Arthur	Connecticut
0554	Frazier, Rich	Massachusetts
0555	Eggeling, John	England
0556	Wong, Harvey	California
0557	Salituri, James	Canada
0558	Hegeman, Thomas	New York
0559	Salzo, Michael	Connecticut
0560	Kramer, Jerry	New York
0561	Larkin, Alan	New Jersey
0562	Staley, David	Washington
0563	Warren, Sean	California
0564	Iacampo, Michael	Pennsylvania

0565	Vincent, Eric	Louisiana		0610	Arnold, Mark	Ohio
0566	Wagner, Charles	Indiana		0611	Rosen, Nathan	Maryland
0567	Born, William	Arizona		0612	Catchings, William	New Jersey
0568	Miller, Mark	Ohio		0613	Pulsipher, James	Michigan
0569	Wielgus, David	Wisconsin		0614	Watson, Dale	Michigan
0570	Dewsnap, Terrence	New York		0615	Munjak, Martin	Illinois
0571	Dricks, Howard	New York		0616	Keppler, Joseph	New York
0572	Dricks, Victor	New York		0617	Ziesing, Mark	Connecticut
0573	Molyneux, Guy	New York		0618	Grossman, Alan	California
0574	Schiel, Michael	New York		0619	Rauth, Jerold	Wisconsin
0575	Grossman, Stuart	New York		0620	Kaltz, Robert	New Jersey
0576	Dugar, Jimmy	Louisiana		0621	Schlegelmilch, Gary	Alabama
0577	Hoose, Dale	Ohio		0622	Kernes, Mark	Pennsylvania
0578	Leucht, David	Wyoming		0623	Wallison, Joseph	Pennsylvania
0579	Padilla, Delphin	New Mexico		0624	*Myers, Clyde*	Missouri
0580	Conner, Steven	Kentucky		0625	Whetzel, Garth	Pennsylvania
0581	Yeo, M. Mountfort	Canada		0626	Rodgers, Walter	New Jersey
0582	Smith, Harold	W. Virginia		0627	Klobucar, Henry	Montana
0583	Mazel, Harvey	New York		0628	Vruggink, Gary	Michigan
0584	Lyons, Mark	Nebraska		0629	Henley, David	Canada
0585	Canuel, Michael	New York		0630	Smith, James	California
0586	Ray, Joseph	Missouri		0631	Gleisser, Sheldon	Ohio
0587	Boyce, Alan	New York		0632	Watson, Daniel	Illinois
0588	Hamm, William	New York		0633	Smith, Scott	Missouri
0589	Gronquist, Richard	Oregon		0634	Meyer, Gem	Iowa
0590	Saffel, Stephen	W. Virginia		0635	Keil, Leo	Delaware
0591	Weed, Greg	Oregon		0637	Jensen, Eric	New York
0592	Grimes, Darrell	Oregon		0638	Garcia, Thomas	New York
0593	Davis, Mark	Wisconsin		0639	Lebar, John	Pennsylvania
0594	Antos, Brian	New York		0640	Pluskwa, Edward	New York
0595	Schendt, Larry	Nebraska		0641	Rann, E. Richard	Illinois
0596	Olivieri, Raymond	New York		0642	Guss, Jonathan	Washington
0597	Padilla, Ken	Nebraska		0643	Mason, Thomas	Virginia
0598	Taylor, Phillip	Pennsylvania		0644	Yamaguchi, Russell	California
0599	Boozer, Daniel	S. Carolina		0645	Burnett, Christopher	Colorado
0600	Koutrouboussis, P.	England		0646	Laks, William	New York
0601	Kessler, Raymond	New York		0647	Christie, Gene	Georgia
0602	Teders, David	Indiana		0648	Bennett, John	New York
0603	**Tillman, Scott**	N. Carolina		0649	Hastings, James	Deleware
0604	Bartett, Steve	Philipines		0650	Adamic, Jerry	Ohio
0605	Mangiacopra, Gary	Connecticut		0651	Ashpole, Jeffrey	Minnesota
0606	Cervon, Bruce	California		0652	Hanley, Richard	Massachusetts
0607	Allen, William	N. Carolina		0653	Cuatt, David	New York
0608	Crocker, James	S. Carolina		0654	Robbins, Charles	Mississippi
0609	Grannis, David	Canada		0655	Sherman, Scott	Massachusetts

0656	Horton, Dan	Michigan
0657	Banulis, Jonathan	Virginia
0658	Rocks, Brenton	Oregon
0659	Pecchio, Carmen	Ohio
0660	Scheibner, Steven	New York
0661	Jagodzinski, Edward	Kentucky
0662	*Gleason, Don*	Virginia
0663	Johnson, Tom	Iowa
0664	Myszka, David	Michigan
0665	Gumbus, Arthur	Connecticut
0666	Wise, Ronnie	Mississippi
0667	Brown, Wendell	Connecticut
0668	Zlomek, Joseph	New York
0669	Rogers, Paul	Kentucky
0670	Lyman, Rickie	Idaho
0671	*Wang, Walter*	New York
0672	Kaminisky, Richard	Michigan
0673	Lecuyer, Albert	New Jersey
0674	Ishikawa, Terry	Ohio
0675	Mayes, Steve	Tennessee
0676	Sipos, Dennis	Texas
0677	Kaminski, John	New York
0678	Walker, Gary	Tennessee
0679	Rowe, Kelly	California
0680	Lomelino, Chris	Illinois
0681	*Sulipa, Doug*	Canada
0682	Harris, David	Michigan
0683	Johnson, Leroy	California
0684	Esselman, Michael	Texas
0685	Bender, Hyman	New York
0686	MacIntosh, William	Pennsylvania
0687	Barton, Daniel	Oregon
0688	Anderson, David	Virginia
0689	Selwyn, Chris	California
0690	Nichols, John	Virginia
0691	James, Ronnie	Missouri
0692	Helfrich, Gary	Indiana
0693	Blaikie, Neal	Florida
0694	Burton, Joan	Michigan
0695	Saavedea, David	California
0696	Collins, John	New York
0697	Kudlick. Edward	Illinois
0698	Missal, James	Illinois
0699	Suda, Paul	New York
0700	Flanagan, Donald	New Jersey

0701	King, Dennis	California
0702	Kittinger, Earl	Canada
0703	Houston, Tim	Michigan
0704	Cotic, Victor	Wisconsin
0705	Klein, David	Pennsylvania
0706	Schultz, Marc	Illinois
0707	Cavanaugh, James	Kentucky
0708	Glassman, Lawrence	New York
0709	Evans, Terry	Wyoming
0710	Stephens, Steve	Texas
0711	Albert, Christopher	New York
0712	Reynolds, Mark	California
0713	Oliver, Dale	Michigan
0714	Sobolak, Ed	Pennsylvania
0715	Orr, Alan	Canada
0716	*Sands, Jim*	Oklahoma
0717	Oser, Ronny	Pennsylvania
0718	Rose, Robert	Pennsylvania
0719	Young, C. Alan	New York
0720	Swirynsky, Vladimir	Ohio
0721	Herrick, Darryl	Massachusetts
0722	Preston, Alan	Puerto Rico
0723	Phillips, Douglas	Michigan
0724	O'Conner, Michael	California
0725	Fabrizio, Daniel	Pennsylvania
0726	Ray, Richard	Pennsylvania
0727	Handy, Robb	Arizona
0728	**Wilson, Robert**	N. Carolina
0729	Stellmach, Robb	Iowa
0730	**Cole, Bill**	Massachusetts
0731	Hartman, Harry	W. Virginia
0732	Poole, David	Texas
0733	Goetke, Jeffrey	S. Carolina
0734	Dmowski, Michael	Minnesota
0735	Mays, Stephen	California
0736	Wilkerson, Norman	California
0737	Barber, Wayne	California
0738	Mootrey, James	Massachusetts
0739	Lendley, Richard	Hawaii
0740	Lendley, Patricia	Hawaii
0741	Brownout, Dean	New York
0742	Roberts, Gerald	Kentucky
0743	Elsey, Jim*	Oklahoma
0744	Owens, Joseph	Maryland
0745	Morrison, Melvin	Maine

0746	Coufal, Jefferson	Illinois		0792	Burton, Michael	Alabama
0747	Rankin, William	California		0793	Roth, Peter	New York
0748	Short, Barry	California		0794	Cohen, Sherry	New York
0749	Peppers, Richard	Missouri		0795	Pearson, Brian	Texas
0750	Heap, Robert	Pennsylvania		0796	Valerio, Michael	Massachusetts
0751	Meyer, John	Tennessee		0798	*Landau, Jan*	New York
0752	Sniderman, Daniel	Illinois		0799	Williams, Bruce	Illinois
0753	MacLean, David	Indiana		0800	Granstrom, Karl	California
0754	Smothers, John	New Jersey		0801	Higgins, Terrence	Pennsylvania
0755	Sexton, Kevin	New York		0802	Grogan, Mark	California
0756	Knight, John	Maryland		0803	*Marcinko, Bill*	New Jersey
0757	Esso, Gabe	California		0804	Moynihan, Raymond	California
0758	Bailey, Bill	California		0805	Morgan, David	Virginia
0759	*Bindig, Robert*	New York		0806	Darvin, Leonard	New York
0760	Davidson, Ira	New York		0807	Kilmer, David	New York
0761	Browne, George	New York		0808	Dugan, Charles	Pennsylvania
0762	Long, Jeffrey	Illinois		0809	Freiberge, William	New York
0763	Burgess, Richard	Wisconsin		0810	Davis, Arnold	Connecticut
0764	Smith, Gideon	Ohio		0811	McPherson, James	Rhode Island
0765	Fox, Robert	Pennsylvania		0812	McCoy, Terrence	Illinois
0766	Kuhn, James	Maryland		0813	Tesher, David	New York
0767	**Gray, Brian**	Oklahoma		0814	Tao, Helen	California
0768	Keitz, Eric	New York		0815	Brown, Darrell	Tennessee
0769	Holtzman, Robert	New York		0816	Cracelli, Rusty	
0771	Jones, Sammy	Mississippi		0817	Gray, Timothy	New York
0772	Draper, Robert	California		0818	Thomas, Daryl	Kansas
0773	Schwartz, Robert	New York		0820	Christie, Brian	California
0774	Boyle, Thomas	Illinois		0821	Schumacher, Hans	Illinois
0775	Swan, Gregory	Arizona		0822	Lockett, Thomas	
0776	Wall, Jai	Nebraska		0823	Kott, Michael	Florida
0777	Adamczwk, Robert	Illinois		0824	Ward, John	Massachusetts
0778	Hill, Howard	Canada		0825	Coover, Roland	Pennsylvania
0779	**Turner, William**	New York		0826	Okura, Mike	California
0780	Miller, Daniel	Illinois		0827	DaPrato, John	Massachusetts
0781	Rasmussen, Joel	Minnesota		0828	**Piepel, Gregory**	Washington
0782	Stribling, Ken	Mississippi		0829	Hackenburg, Gary	New Jersey
0783	Mutschler, William	Pennsylvania		0830	DeVette, Glenn	Michigan
0784	Pippin, Edward	Virginia		0831	Erichsen, Kurt	Oregon
0785	*Dingwell, Bruce*	Canada		0832	Allan, Louis	Arizona
0786	Dingwell, Carol	Canada		0833	Satar, Muzam	
0787	Muramato, Glen	Washington		0834	Morris, John	Wisconsin
0788	*Wilson, Bill*	Pennsylvania		0835	Kochman, Michael	New York
0789	McArthur, Robert	California		0836	Timens, Elmer	New Jersey
0790	Thomas, Gary	Pennsylvania		0837	Chojnacki, Michael	California
0791	Zak, Mark	New York		0838	Bermel, Seth	New York

0839	Rudowski, Evan	New York		0886	Helms, Harry	Minnesota
0840	Kapachi, George	New York		0887	Downs, James	Massachusetts
0841	Jurena, Lous	Virginia		0888	Andelman, Bob	New Jersey
0842	Rivera, Wigberto	Illinois		0889	Albacete, Doug	California
0843	Valvo, Vincent	Massachusetts		0890	Langietti, Richard	
0844	French, Tom	California		0891	Fairfax, Gary	Michigan
0845	Gelbstein, Richard	Florida		0892	Byrd, Ronald	Maryland
0846	Bagby, Jim	Nevada		0893	Bryd, Sharon	Maryland
0847	Deutsch, Alan	New York		0894	Martersteck, Chris	Illinois
0848	Orbanc, Carl	New York		0895	Bernard, Barry	Oregon
0849	Matthews, William	Canada		0896	Newman, Mark	New York
0851	Armetta, S. Rosse			0897	Tarbous, Ken	New Jersey
0852	Armetta, Deborah			0898	Von Seydewitz, Pat	
0853	Campbell, Daniel	New Jersey		0899	Barrios, Elen	California
0854	*Margolin, William*	Massachusetts		0900	Thorne, Megan	California
0855	Margolin, Rosalie	Massachusetts		0901	Eckert, Jake	Maryland
0856	MacAvoy, Daniel	Illinois		0902	Eckert, Rowean	Maryland
0857	Mayer, Glenn	New Jersey		0903	**Soroka, Mariane**	Louisiana
0858	Dice, Michael	Washington		0904	Loibl, Frank	New Jersey
0859	O'Leary, Robert	New York		0905	Yascavage, William	Pennsylvania
0860	Atnip, David	Michigan		0906	Schmitz, Kenneth	Wisconsin
0861	Nabutovsky, Ira	Florida		0907	Destreich, Alan	Missouri
0862	Leiphart, Clark	Pennsylvania		0909	Grigsby, Russell	Delaware
0863	Maley, Michael	Missouri		0910	Walter, Mark	Wyoming
0865	Sweet, Daniel	Ohio		0911	Stola, Alfred	Pennsylvania
0866	Smith, Stuart	Louisiana		0912	Kocmarek, Ivan	Canada
0867	Pineros, Richard	California		0913	Boes, Jeffrey	Wisconsin
0868	Mengeling, Marvin	Wisconsin		0914	Butterworth, Jack	Massachusetts
0869	Gore, Kurt	Illinois		0915	Arnott, Chris	Massachusetts
0870	Veripapa, Frank	New York		0916	Duffin, Michael	Illinois
0871	Feimster, Daniel			0917	**Johnson, Raymond**	Michigan
0872	Cignatta, Andrew	Connecticut		0918	Stahl, Diana	Ohio
0873	Horn, Stephen	Delaware		0919	Geden, Robert	New Jersey
0874	Ruscitti, David	Massachusetts		0920	Ballisteri, Martin	Maryland
0875	Ditto, William			0921	Haveles, David	Connecticut
0876	Niznik, Thomas	Pennsylvania		0922	Nardelli, Fred	New York
0877	Pixley, David	California		0923	Scott, Clinton	Maryland
0878	Ziminski, George	Connecticut		0924	Kendrick, Gary	California
0879	Beasley, Alan	Ohio		0926	Smith, James	
0880	Williams, Myron			0927	White, Kevin	Texas
0881	Brink, Bruce	California		0928	Paces, Mildslay	
0882	Satchell, Thomas	Oregon		0929	Plumb, Ralph	Florida
0883	Strobino, Richard	California		0930	Kapitzke, Robert	Connecticut
0884	Freidman, Lawrence	New York		0931	Hahn, Mark	Ohio
0885	Barbaruolo, Tom			0932	Edwards, Chris	Florida

0933	Yosemite, Sam	California		0979	Gall, Anthony	Ohio
0934	Jaeamillo, Alex	California		0980	Stein, Clifford	New York
0935	Miller, David	Missouri		0981	Moro, John	Illinois
0936	Sakai, Kenneth	Hawaii		0982	McDonagh, Thomas	New York
0938	Hay, Marty	Arizona		0983	Sireci, Fiore	New York
0939	Lamprecht, Bill	New York		0984	Smith, Michael	Arkansas
0940	Hof, Thomas	Missouri		0985	Goldman, Thomas	New York
0941	Hager, Stanton	Florida		0986	Jaffe, Allan E.	New York
0942	Haisch, Klaus	Indiana		0987	Greenberg, Michael	New York
0943	Webb, Joseph	New York		0988	Greenberg, John	New York
0944	Smith, Wesley	Michigan		0989	Noble, Harry	New Jersey
0945	Barbarulo, Perry	New York		0990	Ikuta, Gregory	California
0946	Zucker, Harvey	New York		0991	Kohen, Alexander	New Jersey
0947	Flanagan, Robert	N. Hampshire		0992	Tiernan, Lawrence	N. Ireland
0948	Wells, William	Illinois		0993	Schock, Taylor	Pennsylvania
0949	Jones, Frederick	New York		0994	Bailey, Curtis	S. Dakota
0950	Bryer, Stu	Connecticut		0995	Madajewski, Joseph	Pennsylvania
0951	Harper, John A.	Maryland		0996	Scialis, Tony	Connecticut
0952	Collier, Wade	Oregon		0997	Maxim, Michael	Minnesota
0953	Willis, Verle	Minnesota		0998	Schein, Harvey	Illinois
0954	**Latzoni, Patricia**	New Jersey		0999	Polson, Ray	California
0955	Clark, Kevin	Maine		1000	Olasso, Brian	S. Carolina
0956	Ayer, Bryan	Florida		1001	Payne, Eldon*	Oklahoma
0957	Fetterman, John	Pennsylvania		1002	Keatley, David	S. Carolina
0958	Lippincott, William	Maine		1003	Capolupo, Tony	Pennsylvania
0959	Furst, Roger	New York		1004	Cote, Mark	Maine
0960	Matthews, William	W. Virginia		1005	Manos, Greg	Idaho
0961	Woods, Jimmy			1006	France, Mike	Florida
0962	Peters, Alec	New York		1007	Buckalew, David	Indiana
0963	Wade, H. Mark	Maryland		1008	Metz, Curt	California
0964	Shelton, Charles	Connecticut		1009	Crawford, Tom	New York
0965	Preiser, Howard	New York		1010	Blankenship, M.	Illinois
0966	Kolter, Herman	Georgia		1011	Greene, Stanley	California
0967	Beshears, William			1012	Nichols, John	Virginia
0968	Michaelson, Michael	Illinois		1013	Burnham, Robert	Michigan
0969	McNamar, Max	Oregon		1014	Bullough, Bryon	Michigan
0970	Jackson, William	N. Carolina		1015	**Schultz, Mandi**	Michigan
0971	Drum, H. Shelton	N. Carolina		1016	*Barger, Robert*	Tennessee
0972	Kilmer, Robert	New York		1017	Neufer, Ruth	Pennsylvania
0973	Cohen, Evan	California		1018	Schrage, Allan	Pennsylvania
0974	Haines, Douglas	Michigan		1019	Aschbacher, James	California
0975	Soards, John	Kentucky		1020	Johnson, Randy	Oklahoma
0976	Kokol, A.F.	New York		1021	Harper, James	Oklahoma
0977	Friedlander, David	Pennsylvania		1022	Nicholas, Certo	New York
0978	Sharp, Larry	Texas		1023	Slewinski, Rich	Ohio

1024	Phillips, Douglas	
1025	Dillett, Fred	Wisconsin
1026	De Domencio, Paul	Hawaii
1027	Simmons, Chris	California
1028	Hicks, Clay	W. Virginia
1029	Bush, Bart	Oklahoma
1030	Dane, Robert	Connecticut
1031	Krueger, Kenneth	Illinois
1032	Lessley, Louis	Florida
1033	Libraro, Phillip	Maryland
1034	Ehara, Tadashi	California
1035	Cifra, Gary	
1036	Kreidler, Scott	Washington
1037	Ross, Susan	Indiana
1038	Spearman, William	Washington
1039	Faranda, Brian	New York
1040	Roule, Norman	Pennsylvania
1041	Schmidt, Walter	New York
1042	Bufogle, Quentin	New York
1043	Loera, Armando	California
1044	Bernhardt, Jonathan	New York
1045	McLaughlin, Rod	Michigan
1046	Miller, Ken	
1047	Pennington, Mark	Washington
1048	Harding, Phil	Indiana
1049	Costello, Robert	New York
1050	Burkhart, Fred	New York
1051	Olson, Richard	Louisiana
1052	Pugh, Patrick	Maryland
1053	Viramontez, Vaughn	Ohio
1054	Ryan, David	
1055	Rosenburg, Scott	California
1056	Payne, Alexander	Nebraska
1057	*Frazier, Samuel*	New York
1058	Lustig, John	Washington
1059	Barney, Brett	
1060	Salome, Thomas	Florida
1061	Weiglein, James	Ohio
1062	Sturgeon, Claude	
1063	Goodelle, Rodney	New York
1064	Hofmann, Jerry	Ohio
1065	Cafara, Gary	New Jersey
1066	**Cox, Chester**	Missouri
1067	Terrell, Norma*	Oklahoma
1068	Peel, David	Hawaii
1069	Glazebrook, Glen	Alabama
1070	Bates, Bill	Oklahoma
1071	Gummer, Richard	California
1072	Priore, Frank	New York
1073	McEwin, Mike	Arizona
1074	Conroy, Michael	England
1075	Aw, Arthur	
1076	Braunstein, David	New Jersey
1077	Stewart, Fred	Texas
1078	Eisenberg, James	Illinois
1079	Smyth, Roger	New York
1080	Funk, Kevin	California
1081	Gerber, Ian	Illinois
1082	Tipton, Tim	Michigan
1083	O'Brien, Anthony	California
1084	*Chalfin, Ellis*	New Jersey
1085	Chinn, Nicholas	California
1086	Johnston, Jeff	Ohio
1087	Mosora, Emil	Indiana
1088	Choi, Patrick	Texas
1089	Bryan, Robert	New Jersey
1090	Halvorsen, Larry	Washington
1091	Miller, Kevin	Massachusetts
1092	Rudd, William	Pennsylvania
1093	Alexander, James	S. Carolina
1094	Bray, John	Florida
1095	Kluge, Jean	Missouri
1096	Owen, Dixie	Louisiana
1097	Cappel, Linda	New Jersey
1098	Sissala, Gary	Minnesota
1099	**Finn, Richard**	Oregon
1100	Lampen, Stephen	California
1101	Aquila, Nicklas	California
1102	Poling, Albert	Missouri
1103	Broadwater, Maxine	New York
1104	Sawyer, Michael	Ohio
1105	Best, Germaine	New York
1106	Carleton, Lori	Michigan
1107	Bergeman, Vivian	New Jersey
1108	Obertas, Kris	Canada
1109	Hammond, Ward	S. Carolina
1110	*Seeley, Maxwell*	Canada
1111	Roberts, Leonard	Virginia
1112	Bushman, Mary	Arizona
1113	Brittendale, William	Kansas

1114	Pittaway, Gail	Maryland		1160	Hall, Michael	California
1115	Flynn, Mary	Massachusetts		1161	Dehn, Michael	Illinois
1116	Doane, David	New York		1162	Koo, James	New York
1117	**Wahl, Michael**	Michigan		1163	Haerle, Christian	California
1118	Warren, Jon	Indiana		1164	Thomas, John	Pennsylvania
1119	Beam, John	New York		1165	Mittermann, Francis	Illinois
1120	Hylton, Mark	Indiana		1166	Cox, Cherie	Missouri
1121	Worthen, Mark	California		1167	Schroder, Horst	Sweden
1122	Rivera, Alexander	Illinois		1168	Burbridge, Paul	Canada
1123	Reid, Thomas	New Jersey		1169	Swendrowski, Leszek	Canada
1124	Jessup, Robert	Illinois		1170	Bernstein, James	California
1125	Hugfey, Harmond	Tennessee		1171	**Robins, Sean**	Pennsylvania
1126	Kerns, Johnny	Indiana		1172	*Rowe, Steven*	S. Carolina
1127	Semowich, Richard	New York		1173	Gelfman, Michael	New York
1128	Leonardini, Lloyd	California		1174	Yannetti, David	Massachusetts
1129	*Saunders, Buddy*	Texas		1175	Puzzanghera, James	Massachusetts
1130	Player, I.J.	S. Carolina		1176	Fitton, John	England
1131	McKenzie, Alan	England		1177	Gianino, Tom	New Jersey
1133	Jusipowich, Robert	New Jersey		1178	Chmiel, Ron	New York
1134	Smart, Robert	England		1179	Lopez, Jesus	Texas
1135	Urso, Tony	Illinois		1180	Fioranvanti, Joseph	New York
1136	McAuliffe, Robert	Connecticut		1181	Hydro, Douglas	New Jersey
1137	Simpson, Ron	Indiana		1182	Michaelson, James	Iowa
1138	Simpson, Don	Indiana		1183	Feldman, Ricky	New York
1139	**Hall, Richard**	Connecticut		1184	Jackson, John	California
1140	Bauermeister, Garold	Indiana		1185	Trever, James	N. Carolina
1141	Catalino, Samuel	Pennsylvania		1186	Dalton, Henry	Massachusetts
1142	Stockslader, Joseph	New York		1187	Bisble, William	Massachusetts
1143	Snow, Allan	New Jersey		1188	Kennedy, James	Illinois
1144	Wolf, Steven	Massachusetts		1189	Mitchell, Flint	Missouri
1145	Ross, James	New York		1190	Scholz, Steven	New York
1146	Brunelle, Ed	Massachusetts		1191	Stoeckig, Mike	Montana
1147	Grim, Steve	Texas		1192	Stern, Michael	California
1148	Galando, John	New Jersey		1193	Tomlinson, John	Maryland
1149	Laidlaw, William	California		1194	Benton, Mike	Texas
1150	Golden Matthew	New York		1195	**Fifield, Richard**	California
1151	Lechelt, David	Minnesota		1196	Mc Elrath, Jay	Virginia
1152	*Heimanson, Richard*	California		1197	Noland, Richard	Virginia
1153	Johnson, Alisa	N. Carolina		1198	Dram, Dale	Canada
1154	Dolan, Jeffrey	Pennsylvania		1199	Kemple, Clifford	Utah
1155	Curci, John	New York		1200	Sherry, Denver	Tennessee
1156	Wynn, Charles	Minnesota		1201	Fleet, Jani	Canada
1157	Rowane, Mike	Pennsylvania		1202	Walsh, Steve	England
1158	Sutton, James	California		1203	Dram, Daniel	Canada
1159	Lum, Darryl	Canada		1204	Brown, Merlynn	Colorado

1205	Gilman, William	Massachusetts
1206	Gonzalez, Robert	New York
1207	*Reisbord, Stu*	Pennsylvania
1208	McVeigh, Joseph	Pennsylvania
1209	Cregg, James	Ohio
1210	Wilson, James	Illinois
1211	Poulin, James	New York
1212	Deullda, Joe	California
1213	Campello, Lenny	Washington
1214	Rector, Robert	Virginia
1215	Archual, Michael	Ohio
1216	Earle, Dennis	Wisconsin
1217	Contarino, Keith	Georgia
1218	Flores, Paul	Georgia
1219	Smith, Keith	England
1220	Newman, Billy	Texas
1221	Sturdivant, Reed	Tennessee
1222	Cushman, David	New Jersey
1223	Friedrich, Peter	Illinois
1224	Goolsby, James	Arizona
1225	Lum, Glenn	Hawaii
1226	Black, Jarrett	Florida
1227	Krakowski, Robert	Maine
1228	Perkins, John	Missouri
1229	Wiedeman, David	New Jersey
1230	Rowell, Gary	Oregon
1231	Byco, Stan	Oklahoma
1232	Cain, John	California
1233	Elfman, Merrick	Massachusetts
1234	Hedges, David	Oklahoma
1235	Smith, Susan	Illinois
1236	Tabaris, Kelvin	Illinois
1237	Hartman, George	New York
1238	Flynn, Brian	Ohio
1239	Lumsden, Ray	Minnesota
1240	Somers, Fred	Massachusetts
1241	Sobieck, William	Ohio
1242	Ward, James	Pennsylvania
1243	Plenge, William	New York
1244	Kowalkowski, Bill	Wisconsin
1245	Georgison, Ken	Canada
1246	Chin, Linda	New York
1247	Harness, Roy	Arkansas
1248	Peppers, Willie	Kentucky
1249	Regular, Raymond	Canada
1250	McCauslin, Pat	New Jersey
1251	Whitaker, Ernest	Florida
1252	Marquettte, Robert	Arkansas
1253	Nassaney, Perry	New Jersey
1254	Howe, Darwin	Minnesota
1255	McFarland, Thomas	California
1256	Stokes, Jeff	Kentucky
1257	Taylor, Crystal Ann	Illinois
1258	Lanser, Clairre	Ohio
1259	Hirschman, Jack	New York
1260	Group, Clifford	Missouri
1261	Somers, Ralph	California
1262	Pussell, Ronald	California
1263	Mullins, Paul	Kentucky
1264	Huie, Henry	Texas
1265	Brunotts, Bob	Ohio
1266	Weaver, David	Virginia
1267	Wilder, Jeremy	New Jersey
1268	Irizarry, Michael	Maryland
1269	Chan, David	Maine
1270	Vento, Donald	Illinois
1271	Wierdsma, Bob	Canada
1272	Eastwood, Dave	Texas
1273	Mangiaracina, Dave	Indiana
1274	Brubaker, Gil	Ohio
1275	Blevins, Harold	Ohio
1276	Ferrero, Michael	Pennsylvania
1277	Marcus, Frederick	New Jersey
1278	Baber, Robert	Connecticut
1279	Feinberg, Steve	Colorado
1280	Sager, Louis	Florida
1281	Miller, Gene	Iowa
1282	Shippee. Bob	New York
1283	Berlin, Craig	Texas
1284	Schwab, Daniel	New York
1285	Beck, Dan	Utah
1286	Di Pasquale, Robert	Arkansas
1287	Register, Richard	California
1288	Coy, Mary	New York
1289	Nale, Richard	Arkansas
1290	Kinney, Carl	Michigan
1291	*Mullaney, Dean*	Pennsylvania
1292	Mullaney, Jan	New York
1293	Albert, Perry	New York
1294	Dole, Peter	Australia

1295	Sutton, Mark	Michigan	1318	Sprouse, William	S. Carolina
1296	Mamrack, David	Pennsylvania	1319	Wrenn, Charles	N. Carolina
1297	Colella, Mark	California	1320	Saunders, Billy	N. Carolina
1298	Berhent, Donald	Ohio	1321	Chin, Doon	New York
1299	Pine, Nathaniel	New York	1322	McLaughlin, Paul	Virginia
1300	Gibson, James	Kentucky	1323	Flowers, Joseph	Florida
1301	Jabldnksy, Stephen	Ohio	1324	Foss, Chris	N. Carolina
1302	Hicks, Charles	California	1325	Gorman, Ken	Canada
1303	Simmons, Neil	Pennsylvania	1326	Muchin, Richard	New York
1304	Edmunds, Paul	Virginia	1327	Armstrong, David	Connecticut
1305	Gore, Matthew	S. Carolina	1328	Roberts, Jeff	Indiana
1306	Sidelinger, John	N. Hampshire	1329	Ruffner, John	Illinois
1307	Frazer, Bart	Kentucky	1330	Kosinski, David	Illinois
1308	Harding, Ralph	Indiana	1331	Yuen, Bill	California
1309	McDonald, Edward	Florida	1332	Facciola, Jay	New York
1310	McDonald, John	Texas	1333	Scapito, Joseph	New York
1311	Johnson, Ralph	Texas	1334	Moore, Susan	Kentucky
1312	Wojtowicz, John	Ohio	1335	Coy, Richard	Florida
1313	Howley, Paul	Ohio	1336	Cocking, Peter	Canada
1314	Maybruck, Jay	Ohio	1337	Mascia, John	Virginia
1315	Sharpe, Harvey	Georgia	1338	Greenberg, Frederic	New Jersey
1316	Lindenboom, Ronald	S. Carolina	1339	Rosen, Neil	New Jersey
1317	Sick, Jefferey	New York	1440	Sommerkamp, Bob	Florida

About the Author

Ron Frantz was born in Oklahoma City in 1953. He graduated high school in Bethany, Oklahoma, and attended Oklahoma City Southwestern Junior College. He served as Administrator of the WSA Program from 1975–77 before entering a career in retail management.

A lifelong collector of nostalgia, Frantz has been active in various kinds of avocational activities, including the promotion of nostalgia conventions. He has appeared on numerous television and radio talk shows and has lectured about nostalgia at libraries and universities.

Frantz has been a columnist for *The Buyer's Guide for Comics Fandom* (1975–77) and *The Comics Journal* (1977), and has published articles in *The Fandom Directory, Compass, The Journal,* the *IFICC Newsletter,* and numerous other fan publications. Other writing credits include newspaper advertising copy, television commercials, and gag material for a newspaper comic strip. A recent article about Steve Ditko appears at Blake Bell's *Ditko Looked Up* Web site (http://www.interlog.com/ ~ ditko37/ditko/prskyfra.html).

Frantz was Editor and Publisher of *WE*, Official Publication of the WSA Program (1975–77). Later, he was Editor and Publisher of ACE Comics (1986–87), producing such comics as *What Is the FACE, Return of the Skyman, The Adventures of Spencer Spook, Robin Red and the Lutins,* and *The Cosmic Book*, with work by Steve Ditko, Pat Boyette, Alex Toth, Joe Gill, Frank McLaughlin, and many others.

Currently, Frantz resides in the scenic Ouachita Mountains area, near Mena, Arkansas. New books in the works include a biography of former collegiate and professional wrestling legend Dan Hodge and a retrospective study entitled *The Many Faces of Ellery Queen.*

James Warren
145 East 32nd Street
New York, New York 10016
—
Telephone 212-683-6050

November 28, 1978

M.L.F. Enterprises
P.O. Box 830
Yukon, Okla. 73099

Gentlemen:

I have enclosed my personal check #3037
in the amount of $4.75, for a copy of Fandom
Confidential which I would appreciate you
forwarding to the above address, marked 7th
floor.

Thank you.

Sincerely,

James Warren

Harry Truman once said with remarkable candor that no matter what you do, there is always going to be someone who doesn't like it. Literally as this book was on the press, a minor controversy surfaced regarding the title *FANDOM: Confidential.* It would seem that someone else had once used the title for a fanzine comic strip. A few people have taken issue over my publishing the book with the original title I devised in 1978, saying that it might be confused with that strip. I think this is highly unlikely.

For anyone who might be interested, I am hopeful the above letter from Jim Warren will put the matter of authenticity to rest.